The Monster City

The Monster City
Defoe's London, 1688–1730

Jack Lindsay

St. Martin's Press, New York

Contents

	Preface	vii
1.	London the Monster City	1
2.	Tour of London and its People	37
3.	The Mob	73
4.	Journalism and the New Reading Public	86
5.	Women, Fashions, Assemblies	107
6.	The Landed Gentry and the Labourers	121
7.	Marriages and Elections	142
8.	Projectors and Quakers	157
9.	Merchants and Slaves	173
10.	Land and Trade	190
	Notes	201
	Bibliography	207
	Index	213

To Bernard and Josephine Miles

The pantomimic transformations
occur three times a day
in every whistling street.
This world is changing fast
and the people on their way
don't know in what roles they're cast
but hope for the best and treat
the whole thing as a bad joke
with extravagant improvisations,
delighted and aghast
at each improbable stroke.

The murderer's round the corner,
the mountebank on the pavement
makes grandiloquent faces
at beggar and lousy lord.
Before the sudden bereavement
a new round of drinks is poured
and the harlot promptly unlaces
her rouged unruly breasts
for the sanctimonious mourner,
the hanged thief swings on his cord,
angels snore in well-lined nests.

In this crafty impromptu space
each man looks to the stage and its masks
to assess what is happening here
under his quivering nose.
Defoe knows it all inside out;
but when he looks Moll in the face,
for a different truth he asks.
In a flash the whole thing he knows:
the unknown in what all think is clear,
the known in what's hidden in doubt ...
but the vision, too strenuous, goes.

And he's back in the crafty space
the world changing, a mad race,
where only money, it seems,
can measure man and his dreams.

Jack Lindsay

Preface

The period with which this book deals is that between 1688 and 1730: from the Glorious Revolution to the early years of Walpole's domination. It is also the period of Daniel Defoe's active life. He was admitted a Liveryman of the City of London on 26 January 1688, and his first satire in verse, *A New Discovery of an Old Intreague* (on city politics), appeared in 1691. After many years of pamphleteering and journalism came his novels: *Robinson Crusoe* in 1719; *Captain Singleton* in 1720; *Moll Flanders*, *Colonel Jack* and *Journal of the Plague Year* in 1722; *Roxana* in 1724; *Captain Carlton* in 1728. *A New Voyage Round the World* and the first volume of his *Tour thro' the whole Island of Great Britain* appeared in 1724; the second volume of the *Tour* in 1725. He was still busy in his last years. In 1727 he published *The Compleat English Tradesman*, 1728 saw *A Plan of the English Commerce*, and he was at work on *The Compleat English Gentleman* almost up to his death in April 1731.

No writer more fully chronicled and discussed his City and his Time. He lived through a period of extreme change, the significance of which, because of its pivotal nature as the first stage of the modern world, was largely hidden from the men who confusedly brought it about. London at the turn of the century was the largest city of the world. Its population of about half a million was constantly swollen by migration from the countryside. Every year some eight thousand moved to his 'Greatest Emporium of Trade in the World', which spread from Limehouse to Tothill Street and from Southwark to Shoreditch.

I should like to express my debt in particular to the works of J. H. Plumb, especially his book, *The Growth of Political Stability 1675–1725*. A useful work is also *Britain after the Glorious Revolution 1688–1714*, edited by Geoffrey Holmes, in particular the contributions by Holmes himself and W. A. Speck, as well as *The Divided Society* edited by these two scholars.

While on the one hand I have tried to establish a firm structure defining the nature of the profound changes going on, I have on the other hand made as much use as possible of the witnesses of the period itself, since it is from them we get the living sense of how men actually felt and responded.

Jack Lindsay

1

London the Monster City

The year 1688 was of crucial importance for Daniel Defoe. First, he was then admitted as a Liveryman of the City of London. He became a 'free citizen' and could confidently feel that he was in a position to widen considerably the scope of his business interests and play out the role of city-merchant which he so deeply admired. If he now set about soberly yet astutely taking full advantage of his privileges, he would have his share of the rich city-banquets among the other highly respected merchants in impressive apartments where the walls were hung with embroidered satins and sculptured with fruit, leaves, armorial bearings; he would even attend now and then entertainments given by nobles in their mansions between the Strand and the Thames. But what most excited him, we can be sure, was the chance he now had to extend his business activities and get his hands on more money for investment in the projects that stirred his imagination. In a world still dominated by mercantilist theory the merchants were the class considered to hold the fate of the nation in their hands. Their task was to invade the markets of the world and defeat their foreign competitors; thus they decisively increased the national wealth. Though the industrial revolution was in its first unnoted stages, the possibilities of increasing that wealth by home production were not understood. Defoe thought that if someone started a manufactory in a town, he could prosper only by knocking out someone else in the same line in another town. 'Can the poor of one town be employed in the business of another town, and not that town, or some other, do the less?'

But 1688 had a more stimulating effect on him than even the most promising step in his own personal advancement could have had. He saw a new world suddenly born, with barriers falling down in all directions. The year was that of the Glorious Revolution, with one epoch ending and another resolutely begun. As usual, we can set out the conditions for the moment of decisive change, the many forces converging to set it off; but the fact of a definite new start is also as undeniable. The immediate causes of the Glorious Revolution of 1688 lay in the actions of James II during his brief reign, which began in 1685. He was determined to lift the disabilities that weighed on his co-religionists, the Roman Catholics. He promoted them to key-positions everywhere. One commanded the fleet, another was Lord Lieutenant of Ireland, yet another was Master of the Ordnance, and there were many Catholic army officers. In 1686 James issued a Declaration of Indulgence, and in the resulting test-case of Hales eleven out of twelve judges found that the king was entitled to exercise the power he claimed to dispense with the laws. His Jesuit adviser was put into the Privy Council, and a Catholic head was forced on an Oxford college. Even his ready tool, the Lord Chief Justice Jeffreys, said cynically later, 'The Virgin Mary was to do all.'

Under the situation exacerbated by James's hasty and ill-considered actions there lay a set of deep antagonisms and un-resolved contradictions bequeathed by the Restoration of 1660 with its many unstable compromises. The Cromwellian period had completed the unification of England. The New Model Army overrode county authorities and a strong centralisation emerged from the years of army rule. The Councils in the North and in Wales were wiped out and there was a final unification of the legal system round the common law. The ending of local franchises was completed by the breaking-down of the castles of the great lords and the walls of towns, in 1662. The House of Lords was abolished from 1649 to 1660; and though it was restored, the privileges derived purely from peerage were steadily limited. Feudal state fell away and the last heralds' visitation took place in 1686.

In 1660 the landed gentry regained old privileges and made big advances after the control of county committees by men of lesser status and the rule of plebeian major-generals. They took complete charge of the militia and of local government in the countryside, with no more supervision and interference from the crown and its organs. One of James's unwisest steps was to attempt to replace half the JPs in England and Wales, with Judge Jeffreys asserting the supreme authority of the royal government; the boroughs were purged of opponents. And while the gentry had thus in the post-1660 period gained a new power and independence, a series of acts and other measures had facilitated the rapid growth of capitalist forms. An act of 1662 limited the legal liability for debts of the shareholders of some big trading companies, and thus stimulated investment. From the 1660s, if not earlier, came a permanent stock-market in London, which quickly expanded with its credit facilities. And so on.

The Revolution of 1688 was the strongest possible statement by the landed and commercial classes that they would not allow the clock to be turned back. On the contrary, the development from 1660 to 1685 was to be speeded up. 1688 saw the completion of the Cromwellian Revolution on the part of the landed gentry and the commercial and financial middle-classes, with the lower classes this time excluded – except in so far as they were permitted to cheer the event.

Not that things were as simple as may have seemed for a moment in the enthusiasms of 1688. The story of our period is that of the first great working-out of the new possibilities in the national situation, but is also that of the acute contradictions and inner conflicts which at once began to show up in the classes that wanted to dominate things. For the moment, however, let us pause and glance at Daniel Defoe, who was in many ways the characteristic man of the new epoch.

Born about 1660 in the parish of St Giles's, Cripplegate, he was the son of a butcher who was the younger son of a farmer of Northamptonshire. His parents were nonconformists and joined the congregation of Samuel Annesley, the ejected minister of Cripplegate. At the age of fourteen he was sent to the dissenting academy at Newington Green, where all the lessons were given in English (unlike the schools of the gentry with their emphasis on Latin). Later, when Swift jeered at him and another journalist, Tutchin, as two 'vapid illiterate scribblers', he replied that he understood Dutch, Spanish, Italian, spoke French fluently, and could read Latin. He was also taught mathematics. On the first day of 1684, when the winter was so severe that a fair was being held on the frozen Thames, he married Mary Tuffley, who was twenty years old, conventionally prim and domestic. Trained for the ministry, he decided in 1685 to turn to business, and in January 1688 became a Liveryman of the City of London. He later denied having been a hosier and seems to have been a hose-factor, middleman between manufacturer and retailer. From the outset he was an ardent defender of the ideas of his dissenting class, and he remained all his life passionately interested in all commercial and industrial developments, both as a practical man of business and as a busily recording journalist.

When Monmouth raised the revolt against James in the West Country, he came out on Monmouth's side, if we are to trust his claim. Some of his fellow students of Newington lost their lives; but, undeterred, when news came of the landing of William of Orange, he rode off to join him. At Windsor he heard that the Irish Dragoons had been defeated by William and that, dispersed over the countryside, they were spreading bloodshed and terror. He made for Maidenhead, but at Slough was told that that town, Reading, and other places were burned down. However, on reaching Maidenhead he found that the tales were untrue. So he rode to Reading, where he was told that Maidenhead was in flames. He then decided to join William's forces at Henley, and arrived in time to see the second line of the army entering the town amid cheers and songs, the streets gay with orange ribbands. He now heard that James had fled from London, so he galloped to Faversham where the king had been stopped. (Taken back to London, James later got away to Rochester, whence he escaped to France.) On 18 December Defoe rode as a trooper in a volunteer regiment of horse which escorted William into London. All the church-bells were ringing and a huge crowd had gathered at St James's Palace despite the stormy weather, every hat and cane decorated with orange;

at nightfall candles were set in all the windows and bonfires blazed in the streets.

Defoe plunged back into business. Between 1688 and 1694 his speculations involved him in eight lawsuits. He was sued in Chancery over the loss of a ship which he had sold, or said he had sold, to a mariner trading with Portugal. Then a London mariner sued him for £1500 in connection with a cargo for the American colonies. A merchant of Lyme brought an action for arrears of payments. These cases seem to have ended inconclusively. Then came a more complicated suit with a York merchant, in which he was accused of converting a bill of exchange to his own use. While the merchant was trying to recover his money, another lawsuit came up about the patent of a Cornish inventor for a diving machine. Next Defoe was entangled in lawsuits with an old partner and with his mother-in-law about a civet-cat farm at Newington where the cats were bred for the secretions used to make perfumes. It seems that he had been using borrowed money, not to buy cats, but to ward off various pressing creditors. He was always lavish with good advice that he himself found it hard to follow: 'All rash adventurers are condemned by the prudent part of mankind; but it is hard to restrain youth in trade as it is in any other thing where the advantage stands in view and the danger out of sight ... For a young tradesman to over-trade himself, is like a young swimmer going out of his depth, when, if help does not come immediately, it is a thousand to one but he sinks and is drowned.' Failing to the extent of £17,000, he had to go into hiding to escape bankruptcy and the horrors of imprisonment for debt. In his *Compleat Tradesman* he describes what must have been his own thoughts at this moment.

I'll try the utmost, I'll never drown while I can swim, I'll never fall while I can stand. Who knows but I may get over it? In a word, the poor man is loth to come to the fatal day; loth to have his name in the *Gazette*, and see his wife and family turned out of doors, and the like. Who can blame him? or who is not, in the like case, apt to take the like measures? for 'tis natural to us all to put the evil day far from us, at least, to put it as far off as we can ... As long as there is life there is hope; but at last the death warrant comes down.

He dodged off to asylum in Whitefriars, where he was safe from arrest for a month. Here was an old monastery which before the Reformation had been considered a sanctuary for criminals and which still somehow had the privilege of protecting debtors. The fugitive lodged in a dirty cellar or garret among insolvents, crooks, beggars, whores, thieves. Finally he slipped away and got off to Bristol, where again he went into hiding, able to walk the streets only on Sundays. Busily he set his agile mind to work out a variety of schemes which he later published in his *Essay upon Projects*. Meanwhile his wife and friends negotiated on his behalf, and his creditors agreed not to press their claims if he promised to meet his debts later in full. Within a dozen years he had reduced his liabilities by £12,000.

Returned to London, he resumed his indefatigable activities as businessman, publicist, journalist, government spy, and, finally, as novelist. We cannot here follow his often devious and crafty career in detail, but he will keep on reappearing in our narrative as we look at his London and the rest of England in these years when profound changes were going on, tearing up the last of the old feudal roots and reorienting people in new ways. With wry honesty he remarks on the difficulty of reconciling his dissenting standards of morality with the actions dictated by a commercial world – though deep down his obstinate religious views and his passionate concern for the advancement of productivity at all costs somehow came together in a single drive. 'Necessity makes an honest man a knave; and if the world was to be the judge, according to the common received notion, there would not be an honest man alive. A rich man is an honest man, no thanks to him, for he would be a double knave to cheat mankind when he had no need of it ... Ambition, pride, or avarice makes rich men knaves, and necessity the poor.'

London, the great city of fashion and politics, of trade and finance, expanding all the while as it was rebuilt after the

Great Fire of 1666, lay at the centre of the new developments. *Angliae Notitia* in 1702 calls it the Epitome of England, the Seat of the British Empire, the Chamber of the King, and the greatest Emporium or Town of Trade in the whole world. (*Notitia, or the Present State of England,* had been published first as a compendious work of reference in 1668 by Edward Chamberlayne, a Gloucestershire man, who was educated at Oxford. His book went through edition after edition, the first twenty written by himself. After his death in 1703 his son John issued later editions. The very existence of such a work, continually revised, brings out the new consciousness of England as a world-power and of the need to understand what was going on.) London, says Chamberlayne, was the fairest and most opulent city in all Europe, perhaps the whole world. The emergence of London as a single entity, comprising the City, Westminster, Southwark and the squares and streets that link such areas and extend beyond them, was still something new and strange. Chamberlayne remarked that as the areas are contiguous, they 'seem to make indeed one City, and accordingly shall be so considered'. He sees this City as 'of a vast Extension from Lime-house, measured to the end of Tothill or Tattle-street, from east to west', and from Blackman Street in Southwark to the end of Shoreditch, embracing some 5000 streets, lanes, or alleys, some of them a mile long.

Defoe, a few years later, has a vision of a yet vaster city. Chelsea, a Town of Palaces, stands south of Kensington, and 'seems to promise itself to be made one time or another a part of London, I mean London in its new extended capacity, which if it should happen, what a Monster must London be', extending some eleven miles from Chelsea to Deptford Bridge. Here for the first time in history we meet the concept of the Monster City.

Various estimates were made of the size of the population. *Notitia* tried to use the excise figures for the beer and ale consumed. Defoe made a wild guess of a million and a half inhabitants. Modern estimates range from 674,000 to 575,000. London had indeed become the largest city in Europe. In 1600 it had some 200,000 people; about double that by 1650; by 1750 it had 675,000 and 900,000 by 1800. Paris had grown during the previous century from about 400,000 to near 500,000, but by 1801 the census was still just under 550,000. In 1650 about two and a half per cent of the French population lived in Paris, and there was little change by 1750; in England London had about seven per cent of the population in 1650 and eleven per cent by 1750. Amsterdam was the only other place with the same high percentage of the national population, but it soon ceased to grow.

In the period 1650–1750 more people died in London than were born there; the gap was filled by steady immigration, at least 8000 a year, from other parts of the country. Mobility at the time was greater before marriage than after; a large group of twenty-year-olds coming into London would represent survivors from at least half as many more persons born else-where. Also, women had taken to marrying later, which usually means a reduction in the birth-rate. So the immigration into London represented a considerable drain on the rest of the country. Many immigrants, however, were Scots, Welsh and Irish, and London as a great international centre had its Dutch, French, and German communities. The troubles of 1719, with their riots against printed calicoes (considered to be ruin-ing the market for native textiles), were partly caused by the influx of weavers from outside. 'How many country weavers come daily to town,' complained *A Further Examination of the Weavers' Pretences*, 'and turn their hands to different kinds of work than they are brought up to.' In 1720 *The Case of the Linen Drapers* wrote of 'the unreasonable and unlimited increase of weavers in London when hands are so much wanted in other handy-craft trades'. It was impossible 'for them to have work all the year round and when they are idle they form themselves into clubs and from thence into riotous and tumultuous assemblies'. *The Just Complaints of the Poor Weavers* (1719) had argued that 'the grand cause of the weavers wanting work is the covetousness of the masters and mistresses in taking so many apprentices for the sake of the money they have with them'. The incoming Irish were especially resented. In 1736 there were riots in Spitalfields against Irish weavers accused of working 'at an under rate'. In 1757 Burrington said that two-thirds of London's adult population came 'from distant parts'.[1]

Probably at this period one adult in every six in England had some direct experience of London life; the manifold contacts must have done much to break down customary ways of thought and behaviour in backward areas. London life was not at all like that of country-towns where the local landed gentry dominated and mostly did their best to keep up old standards. Here family life was very different. Households were often larger than in the counties: not because of more children, but because of such intruders as lodgers, servants, apprentices. Also, there were the close links of the urban country gentry with London, professional men and the like, who were not based on landed estates; they maintained their way of life largely because of the existence of London, its connections and effects. (We must not forget that London's support had ensured the victory of Parliament over Charles I. London was the overwhelmingly dominant factor in national life.)

Notitia boasts of the forest of masts along the Thames and the worldwide trade that made the London merchants surpass some princes in neighbouring nations for their stately city houses, their country houses for summer, their plentiful tables, their 'great estates in money and land'. London, in short, is 'a huge Magazine of men, money, ships, horses and ammunition, of all sorts of commodities necessary or expedient for the use or pleasure of mankind'. It is a 'mighty rendezvous of Nobility, Gentry, Courtiers, Divines, Lawyers, Physicians, Merchants, Seamen, and all kinds of excellent Artificers, of the most refined Wits, and most excellent Beauties'.

There was enough truth in such claims to make men justly aware of the great part that London was playing in national and international history. The largest section of all imports and exports went through its port; and it was also the clearing house of inland trade, since heavy goods were mostly carried by coastal vessels or up navigable rivers. From various parts of England textiles were sent to London to be finished by pressing, dyeing, printing, and so on. Probably a quarter of the London population depended directly on employment in port trades in 1700, and many more were indirectly connected.

A large fleet of colliers moved between London and the Tyne. By 1600 Londoners were turning to coal for domestic fuel, and between 1650 and 1750 the amount of coal brought from the North doubled, reaching about 650,000 tons in the latter year. No other country in Europe saw anything like this scale of coal production. By thus stimulating coal-mining London helped greatly to bring about the industrial revolution; the technology of the steam engine and the railway developed largely out of the needs of coal-mining. Further, to meet the demand for coal there was an expansion of shipping capacity, the designing of ships that could be worked by fewer seamen per ton of cargo, and the training of men to work such ships. Defoe describes the highway from Lumley to Newcastle: 'a view of the inexhaustible store of coals and coal pits, from whence not London only, but all the south part of England is continually supplied; and whereas we are at London and see the prodigious fleets of ships which come constantly in with coals for this encreasing city, we are apt to wonder whence they come, and that they do not bring the whole country away; so, on the contrary, when in this country we see the prodigious heaps, I might say mountains, of coals, which are dug up at every pit, and how many of these pits there are, we are filled with equal wonder to consider where the people should live that can consume them'. Between river and town wall was a spacious area, which, 'being well wharfed up and faced with freestone, makes the longest and largest quay for landing and lading goods that is to be seen in England, except that at Yarmouth in Norfolk, and much longer than that at Bristol'.[2]

The big industries linked with shipping and export trade were centred in London, complicated businesses like brewing, distilling, sugar-refining. London cutlery was thought better than that of Sheffield; its watches and clocks were particularly highly regarded. There was silk-weaving at Spitalfields, cabinet-making, soap-making, and a wide range of luxury items. But though these manufactures helped London's growth, few of them played an important role in the technological advances or the new forms of economic organisation that produced the industrial revolution. Where London did have a leading role was in its stimulus to market-gardening and agricultural specialisations, in encouraging wholesalers to move back up the chain of production and exchange so that they took part directly in food production or put capital into the improvement of productive facilities. By 1681 John Houghton could write in *A Collection of Letters for the Improvement of Husbandry*: 'The bigness and great consumption of London doth not only encourage the breeders of provisions and higglers thirty miles off but even to four score miles. Wherefore I think it will necessarily follow . . . that if London should consume as much again, the country for eighty miles around would have greater employment or else those that are further off would have some of it.' London as a foodmarket brought about an increase in such trades as those of drovers, carters, badgers (who bought corn and other things and carried them for sale elsewhere), brokers, cattle-dealers, corn-chandlers, hostlers, innkeepers, and so on. London had no malting facilities and few corn mills, so that several country-towns found their main work in processing London corn, and their inhabitants had steady jobs. Defoe could write in 1724 of the 'general dependence of the whole country upon London' for 'the consumption of its produce'. Wages tended to be higher in London, which played an important role in bringing about new levels of real wages and new standards of consumption.[3]

London of this period then led the way decisively forward in many key-matters. A single national market for a wide range of goods and services was built up; changes in agricultural methods that advanced productivity were set off; new sources of raw material were opened up; a wider network of commercial and credit facilities was developed; a more efficient and far-spreading system of transport was stimulated; a steady ripple of outgoing influences encouraged enterprising individuals who broke through traditional ways and created new values, new systems. The resultant pattern of social mobility involved more than a repetitive recycling and strengthened new groups who were not merely concerned to play their roles inside established social classes, but developed their own ideas as to the best use of wealth. At the same time more persons could hope to rise in the world; there was a growing desire to imitate the groups or classes above oneself—an attitude that attracted much satirical attention but was an essential aspect of the new social mobility, the new unleashed economic energies. This was the first stage of the emergence of a society of uniform mass-consumption.[4]

After the Great Fire large-scale rebuilding was necessary, and what emerged was a new London that expressed the first phases of the development sketched above. The outstanding figure connected with the changes was Nicholas Barbon, son of Praise-god Barbon or Barebone, a fanatical anti-monarchist. Nicholas took a medical decree at Utrecht, but never practised medicine. He was a masterly and crafty financier and entrepreneur. No doubt men of his character had existed before, but lacked the right setting. Roger North depicts him in detail, and the account deserves to be given at some length; for Barbon fully and subtly incarnated the big businessman of the new era.

His talent lay more in economising ground for advantage and the little contrivances of a family than the more noble aims of architecture, and all his aim was at profit. But he had like to have lost his trade by slight building in Mincing Lane, where all the vaults for want of strength fell in, and houses came down most scandalously. In other places his buildings stood well enough, and at the upper end of Crane Court in Fleet Street he had made himself a capital messuage, where he lived as lord of the manor. He was bred in the practices, as well as the knowledge, of working the people, under his father in the late times, though he was too young to make any figure himself; but that, with his much dealing in building, and consequently transacting with multitudes, he was an exquisite mob master, and knew the arts of leading, winding, or driving mankind in herds as well as any that I ever observed. He judged well of what he undertook, and had an inexpungable pertinacity of pressing it through. He never proposed to tempt men to give way or join but by their interest, laid plainly before them. Supposing that, however averse at first, the humour would spend, and they would come down to profit; all other arguments and wheedles he esteemed ridiculous and vain loss of time. If he could not work upon all together he would allure them singly by some advantage above the rest, and if he could not gain all divide them, for which purpose he had a ready wit, and would throw out questions most dexterously. If anyone was fierce against him he quarrelled, then that man's objections were charged upon the affronts that passed, and not the reason of the thing. And he would endure all manner of affronts and be as tame as a lamb. If it was proper to his end to be so, he would be called rogue, knave, damned Barbon, or anything, without being moved; then some others, seeing him treated so scurvily, would take the man's part, which advantage he failed not to improve.

Merged with his ability to subordinate all his ideas and emotions to the one great aim of profit, there was his inordinate appetite for money, for success.

His fault was that he knowingly overtraded his stock, and that he could not go through with undertakings without great disappointment to the concerned, especially in point of time. This exposed him to great and clamorous debts, and consequently to arrests and suits, wherein he would fence with great dexterity, with dilatories and injunctions. He had good address and could express himself cunningly and being master of (for none is free from) passion, was never forward to speak importunely, and then made his design the centre of all he said or did. He knew that passion and heat wear off, and as he regarded it not when rashly used by others, he never used it himself but as an engine to work with. He never despaired of a design if it were sound at bottom, but would endure repulse after repulse, and still press his point. If a proposition did not relish one way, he would convert it to another, and adapt himself, as well as his designs, to the caprice as well as the interest of those he was to deal with. And to conclude his general character, he was the inventor of this new method of building by casting of ground into streets and small houses, and to augment their number with as little front as possible, and selling the ground to workmen by so much per foot front, and what he could not sell build himself. This has made ground rents high for the sake of mortgaging, and others following his steps have refined and improved upon it, and made a superfoetation of houses about London.[5]

Barbon may not have invented a new method, but he knew how to combine and extend methods used in smaller ways before him, so that in effect a new system of building did emerge. North had come to know him well during the rebuilding of the Temple and was fascinated by a character so unlike his own. He asked Barbon why he undertook too much and entangled himself in endless lawsuits.

He said it was not worth his while to deal little; *that* a bricklayer could do. The gain he expected was out of great undertakings, which would rise lustily in the whole, and because this trade required a greater stock than he had, perhaps £30,000 or £40,000, he must compass his designs either by borrowed money or by credit with those he dealt with, either by fair means or foul. He said his trade would not afford to borrow on such disadvantages as he must, for want of sufficient security, be at, at 10 per cent at least; so he was forced to take the other way of being in debt.

He kept putting men off by fair words, thus gaining from one to three years. Then perhaps they would threaten to arrest him, and at last would do so. 'So he put in bail, for which he always had a bank of credit with a scrivener and goldsmith or two.' The plaintiff's attorney might make mistakes; but if the matter came into court, he defended stoutly if he had any basis for defence; if not, he let the suit go by default, then brought a bill in Chancery and perhaps got an injunction. 'And at the last, when the injunction was dissolved, and judgment affirmed upon a writ of error (which was one delay seldom omitted) and execution ready to come out he sent to the party, and paid the money recovered, and costs, which might amount to three, four, or perhaps five per cent, and seldom more than half the charge of borrowing, and thus he maintained a gang of clerks, attorneys, scriveners, and lawyers, that were his humble servants and slaves to command.'

North asked him how he managed things when, say, a

hundred or more old houses were to be pulled down and it would be expensive to buy the sites outright. Barbon said that he only bought out the most vociferous of those opposing the deal. He arranged a meeting with them:

They would certainly be early at the place, and confirm and hearten one another to stand it out, for the Doctor must come to their terms. So they would walk about and pass their time expecting the Doctor, and inquiring if he were come. At last word was brought that he was come. Then they began to get towards the long table (in a tavern dining-room for the most part) for the Doctor was come! Then he would make his entry, as fine and as richly dressed as a lord of the bedchamber on a birthday. And I must own I have often seen him so dressed, not knowing his design, and thought him a coxcomb for so doing. Then these hard-headed fellows that had prepared to give him all the affronts and opposition that their brutal way suggested, truly seeing such a brave man, pulled off their hats, and knew not what to think of it. And the Doctor also being (forsooth) much of a gentleman then with a mountebank speech to these gentlemen he proposed his terms, which, as I said, were plausible, and terminated in their interest. Perhaps they are, at this, all converted in a moment, or perhaps a sour clown or two did not understand his tricks, or would not trust him, or would take counsel, or some blundering opposition they gave; while the rest gaped and stared, he was all honey, and a real friend; which not doing, he quarrelled, or bought off, as I said, and then at the next meeting some came over, and the rest followed. It mattered not a litigious knave or two, if any such did stand out, for the first thing he did was pull their houses about their ears, and build upon their ground, and stand it out at law till their hearts ached, and at last they would truckle and take any terms for peace and a quiet life.

North added that he had seen his house in a morning like a court, crowded with suitors for money.

And he kept state, coming down at his own time like a magnifico, in *dishabille*, and so discoursed with them. And having very much work, they were loth to break finally, and upon a new job taken they would follow and worship him, like an idol, for then there was fresh money; as I observed upon his undertaking the Temple. And thus he would force them to take houses at his own rates instead of money, and so by contrivance, shifting, and many losses, he kept his wheel turning, lived all the while splendidly, was a mystery in his time, uncertain whether worth anything or not, at last bought a Parliament-man's place, had protection and ease, and had not his cash failed, which made his works often stand still, and so go to ruin, and many other disadvantages grow, in all probability he might have been as rich as any in the nation.

Barbon's activities extended all over London. In one place he built a square, in another a market, elsewhere some streets or chambers for lawyers. A letter of 1697 states that he laid out £200,000 in building. He had grasped the principle of standardisation and mass-production. His houses were all much alike, planned to save money at the expense of appearances. He endlessly repeated his coarse decorations, his panelling designs; all his staircases had twisted balusters with a superficial effect of up-to-date gentility. Among his main projects was the purchase and development of the Essex House estate, south of the Strand. Here he had to speed up his wrecking of the Tudor mansion to prevent the king from taking it over for a favourite; in a few years he had destroyed the charm of the area with a street of brickhouses 'for taverns, alehouses, cookshops and vaulting schools'. In 1684 he began on another of his big schemes, Red Lion Square. In protest the gentlemen of Gray's Inn beat up his workmen, but as usual he overrode opposition, official attempts by Wren, and warrants from the Middlesex JPs. 'Such was the force of private enterprise, at long last freed by liberating itself from the tyranny of Royal Proclamations' (Summerson). Other areas where he built included Mincing Lane, mentioned by North, several streets on the site of York House, including Buckingham and Villiers Streets, Newport Square, in Soho, and Bedford Row.

An Apology for the Builder of 1685, perhaps his work, sought to

break down the strong resistance to urban expansion by demonstrating that suburban building was a healthy and useful
development which drove up the land-values nearer the town
centre, provided new markets, settled the balance between
town and country, created revenues, and furnished military
recruits for the government. These forward-looking views, more
characteristic of the nineteenth century, suggest the hand and
mind of Barbon.

He ended the exploitation of easily available areas; now
builders had to tackle the entailed and trust estates more to the
west, where the owners knew about rising values. This stage
began in 1713 after the Treaty of Utrecht. The typical Georgian
house had now appeared. Builders wanted to pack as many
houses as possible into a street and also to economise on road-
making. So we find the site composed of a long strip of ground
running back from the street, with the house on the front part,
then a garden or courtyard behind, and past that a coach-
house or stable (in the larger kind of house) with a subsidiary
road serving it. The tall narrow houses built one against another
were called terraces. All but the poorest had basements, which
seem to be deep set from the front with its made-up road, but
which were only slightly lower than the ground-level at the
back. The inner system of the house was simple. On each floor
were two rooms with passage and staircase at the side – though
all sorts of variations could be introduced. London thus had a
strong verticality in its houses, which was all its own. The
partition walling had to be of brick, one brick and a half thick,
to stop fires from spreading. The Barbon houses had had
prominent wooden eaves-cornices at the top, but an Act of 1707
forbade such structures. 'No mundillion or cornish of timber
and wood under the eaves shall hereafter be made or offered.'
So the roof was half hidden by a parapet wall with a cornice
of brick or stone (later of stucco) a few feet below the summit.
Then in 1708 the exposed woodwork of the window openings
was forbidden; the frames, no longer nearly in the same plane
as the brickface, were set back four inches. About the same time
there was the change from casement to sash-windows (a Dutch
invention), and the old mullioned casements were almost everywhere transformed.[6]

The building industry had now been steadily changed from a homogeneous body of independent craftsmen 'to a body comprising, at the top, the speculating master-builder, at the bottom the journeyman, and between the two, but on a pedestal of his own, raising him socially above either, the architect. The loss of status of the individual craftsman is obvious' (Summerson). A few astute men of the lower strata might rise in the world, though not on Barbon's scale. Thus William Tufness, who worked as bricklayer to the New River Company and in other jobs, is said to have got together some £30,000 by the time he died in 1733.

For a while the gentlemen liked to design, at least in part, their own houses. Thus North was drawn into architecture through his involvement with Barbon. 'I had the drawing the model of my little chamber, and making patterns for the wainscot, and from thence the practice of working from a scale, all the while exercising the little practical geometry I had learnt before, and in short found the joys of designing and executing known only to such as practise or have practised it.' He got books on architecture such as those by Palladio and Scamozzi. Also, 'I fell into the humour of contriving new instruments, as well as procuring those of ordinary use, and was never satisfied till I had got a plain table, with a border graduated for holding down paper, and a drawer underneath accommodated to receive all variety of instruments. And with these I did entertain myself many hours.' Later he rebuilt his house at Rougham.

Italianising styles, based largely on Palladio, had come in earlier, mainly through Inigo Jones, but had been checked by the Civil War. Under Anne came a reaction against the baroque elements in Wren, Vanbrugh, Hawksmoor, with a return to Palladianism led by the Earl of Burlington and his set. The decisive turn came round 1715 with the first volume of *Vitruvius Britannicus*, an impressive record of the best classical buildings so far raised in England; then came a fine edition of Palladio in instalments. Among the notables who subscribed to the *Vitruvius* we meet the names of some masons, carpenters, and joiners. Then in a few years came the rush of books for craftsmen themselves. The individual elements that had still obtruded in design under Anne gave way to regular, neat, correct systems. Books on design multiplied. William Halfpenny, a Twickenham carpenter, from 1722 published works addressed now to the gentry, now to the trade. Batty Langley, carpenter, surveyor, architect, produced some score of books from 1726 on. Such books kept appearing till about 1760 when the role of the professional architect was at last established and the initiative of the craftsmen eliminated.

During our period sub-contracting was widely used; one tradesman worked for another, largely on a method of barter rather than of cash-payment. Clearly the craft-groups had worked out definite systems of collaboration, though Robert Morris in 1728, in *An Essay in Defence of Ancient Architecture*, argued for the use of surveyors to bring clarity into a situation liable to become confused, to measure and adjust claims between the craft-groups. Notables used an architect; the less rich might deal direct with a master-builder, taking the risk of something going wrong. Most persons bought houses half-built. The master-builder made an agreement with the ground-landlord before he signed a lease (say, of sixty or ninety-nine years), paying only some token rent for the first year or so. He then raised a rough structure and offered it for sale, hoping to find a purchaser before the token-rent period ran out. The buyer could then arrange further details to his liking, pay a lump sum, and sign the lease proper. In this system the master-builder needed to pay out very little cash. So all sorts of bricklayers and carpenters with hardly any capital tried to act as master-builders and became bankrupt.

Numbering of houses took some time to become general. Hatton's *New View of London* in 1708 remarked as an oddity that 'in Prescott Street, Goodman's Fields, instead of signs the houses are distinguished by numbers, as the staircases in the Inns of Court and Chancery'. But the use of signs was still the normal thing. In an essay of April 1711 Addison printed a letter jestingly suggesting that, in view of the 'daily Absurdities hung out upon the Sign-Posts of this City', a Superintendent of such Figures and Devices should be appointed. 'Our streets are filled with blue Boars, black Swans, and red Lions; not to mention flying Pigs, and Hogs in Armour, and many other Creatures

more extraordinary than any in the deserts of Africa.' As a first
reform, incongruous elements should not be coupled, e.g. Dog
and Grid-iron, Bell and Neats-tongue, Fox and Seven Stars,
Three Nuns and a Hare. 'I must however observe to you upon
this subject, that it is usual for a young tradesman, at his first
setting up, to make his own Sign that of the master whom he
served: as the husband, after marriage, gives a place to his
mistress's arms in his own coat.' Next, a shop should have a
sign that owns some relevance to its wares. 'What can be more
inconsistent than to see a Bawd at the Sign of the Angel, or a
Taylor at the Lion? A Cook should not live at the Boot, nor a
Shoemaker at the roasted Pig.' Finally, there should be some
connection between the emblem and the name of the house-
holder. Thus, it was right for Mrs Salmon to use that fish: she
had the Golden Salmon, a Waxworks Exhibition in Fleet
Street, near Temple Bar.[7]

Bricks were largely imported from Holland. Defoe was one
of the businessmen who tried to develop the local industry. He
set up a factory at Tilbury. In the years 1695–9 he acted as
accountant to the Commissioners of the Glass Duty; and in
1695 he had been appointed trustee to manage the state lottery.
In 1698 he became secretary of the Tilbury firm, using the
money from his government jobs to buy shares. He got contracts
for bricks for the new Greenwich Hospital and soon was employing a hundred families with a profit of £600 a year. His
enemies accused him of sweating his workers; he himself complained that as soon as the men had money in their pockets they
downed tools and went to drink. Kilns were set up wherever
clay could be found round London, spoiling the area with
smoke. For outer walls, hard stock-bricks of grey and red were
general; but cheap place-bricks, with much ash in their composition, weakened structures, being used for unseen walls or
partitions. Grey stocks were preferred outside as combining
better with stone and white-painted wood. A crimson 'cutting-
brick' was brought from farther afield for window arches and
decorative dressings. The timber used was mainly Baltic fir
and English oak. Roofs were covered with plain tiles or pantiles
(sometimes glazed). The stone was almost always Portland.
Water was laid by the New River Company or the Chelsea

Water Works, and was available at fixed hours for a small quarterly rate. It flowed into a cistern, and at times a hand-pump raised it to a second roof-cistern. Brick drains under the house led to a public sewer or a garden cesspool. Lead pipes carried rain from the roof to branch drains connected with the main one. A bog-house stood at the back of the house or garden, a bricklined round pit joined to the main drain. At times water was laid on to flush out the pit, but the water-closet came in only late in the century, and then only for the rich.

Defoe tells us that 'there are two great engines for the raising of the Thames water, one at the Bridge, the other near Broken Wharf; these raise so great a quantity of water, that, as they tell us, they are able to supply the whole City in its utmost extent, and to supply every house also, with a running pipe of water up to the uppermost Story'. The New River 'brought by an aqueduct or artificial stream from Ware', supplied most of the city. 'A new head or basin at Islington on a higher ground' was filled 'by a great engine worked formerly with six sails, now by many horses constantly working'. There were also several water-houses, one at Wapping, one in Southwark, one at York Buildings.[8]

The window-glass came mostly from Newcastle, brought in coal-barges, but some was made in East London, at Ratcliff. Defoe describes the landward side of Newcastle as 'exceeding pleasant, and the buildings very close and old, standing on the declivity of two exceeding high hills, which, together with the smoke of the coals, makes it not the pleasantest place in the world to live in; but it is made amends abundantly by the goodness of the river', which 'makes it a place of very great business'. Here were the Glass-Houses and Salt Pans. The smoke ascended so thickly over the hills that Defoe saw it at least sixteen miles away.

The new sash-windows were considered in France an English invention. In *A Journey to Paris* of 1698, a Frenchman shows his big sash-windows, 'how easily they might be lifted up and down, and stood at any height, which contrivance he said he had out of England, by a small model brought on purpose from thence, there being nothing of this poise in windows in

France before'. Weights were concealed in the hollow-box frames, which, with cords running over pulleys, counterbalanced the sash. In fact they could jam, and Swift, in *Directions to Servants*, tells the maid: 'You are sometimes desirous to see a funeral, a quarrel, a man going to be hanged, a bawd carted, or the like: as they pass by in the street, you'll lift up the sash suddenly; there, by misfortune, it sticks; this was no fault of yours: young women are curious by nature: you have no remedy but to cut the cord and lay the fault upon the carpenter, unless nobody saw you, and then you are as innocent as any servant in the house.' But there could be compensations. In Steele's comedy *The Conscious Lovers*, the housemaid Phillis and Tom the footman recall their first meeting.

> *Tom.* I remember I was ordered to get out of the window, one pair of stairs, to rub the sashes clean – the person employed on the inner side was your charming self, whom I had never seen before.
> *Phillis:* I don't think I remember the silly incident. What made you, ye oaf, ready to fall down into the street?
> *Tom:* You know not, I warrant you. You could not guess what surprised me. You took no delight when you immediately grew wanton in your conquest, and put your lips close, and breathed upon the glass, and, when my lips approached, a dirty cloth you rubbed against my face! and when I again drew near, you spit and rubbed, and smiled at my undoing.
> *Phillis:* What silly thoughts you men have.

Fire was a great problem. Many towns still had thatched roofs and wooden chimneys as well as crowded conditions. London with its new brick houses was less vulnerable, but the danger was still acute. Some towns suffered again and again. Tiverton was burned down in 1598, 1612 and 1731; and preparations for market-day, profaning the Sabbath, were blamed for the first two occasions. In 1731 a collection made for the destitute denied that there was any truth in the allegation. London kept on having lesser fires after 1666. In July the very next year Samuel Newton wrote on 25 July, 'Thursday happed about 2 of the clock in the morning a fire in Southwark at a cook's house at the sign of the Shoulder of Mutton on St Margaret's hill, which consumed about 12 houses, I myself being then in London and see the smoke.' Swift on 2 March 1712 states, 'I was waked at three this morning, my man and the people of the house telling me of a great fire in the Haymarket. I slept again, and two hours after my man came in again, and told me it was my poor brother sir William Wyndham's house burnt, and that two maids leaping out of an upper room to avoid the fire, both fell on their heads, one of them upon the iron spikes before the door, and both lay dead in the streets. It is supposed to have been some carelessness of one or both those maids.' That night he learned: 'Wyndham's young child escaped very narrowly; lady Catharine escaped barefoot ... Wyndham has lost above £10,000 by this accident; his lady above a thousand pounds worth of clothes.' On the 25th of the same month he notes: 'We had a terrible Fire last night in Drury Lane, or thereabouts, and three or four people destroyed; one of the maids of honour has the smallpox.' Defoe in his *Tour* comments on the noble stone gate at Newcastle, 'which so lately was a safeguard to the whole bridge, by stopping a terrible fire which otherwise had endangered burning the whole street of houses on the city side of the bridge, as it did those beyond it'.

At times a big fire gave a chance to rebuild a town. Defoe tells us, 'Warwick was ever esteemed a handsome, well-built town, and there were several good houses in it, but the face of it is now quite altered; for having been almost reduced to a heap of rubbish, by a terrible fire two and twenty years ago, it is now rebuilt in so noble and beautiful a manner, that few towns in England make so fine an appearance.' At Alresford, 'by a sudden and surprising fire, the whole town, with both the church and the Market House, was reduced to a heap of rubbish; and except for a few poor huts at the remotest ends of the town, not a house left standing: the town is since that very handsomely rebuilt, and the neighbouring gentlemen contributed largely to the relief of the people, especially by sending in timber towards their building; also their Market-House is handsomely built; but the church not yet, though we hear there is a fund raising likewise for that.' When Penn founded

Philadelphia in America he wanted each house to stand separate and tree-surrounded, so that the place would be 'a green country town, which will never be burnt, and always wholesome'.

But country mansions were no more secure than town houses. At Peterson the Earl of Rochester had built a fine house, splendidly furnished with paintings and with an irreplaceable collection of books and manuscripts. 'Even while this is writing,' says Defoe, 'the place seems to be but smoking with the ruins of a most unhappy disaster, the whole house being a few months ago burnt down to the ground with a fire, so sudden, and so furious, that the family who were all at home, had scarce time to save their lives.'

Candles and open fires caused much of the trouble. Samuel Newton reports under 31 May 1715, 'Tuesday about 2 a clock in the afternoon died Alderman John Frohock at the Bull in Bishopsgate street in London after 5 weeks lying there wounded sick by means of a candle got by chance hold of his neckcloth and clothes burning him in a very sore manner.' Northampton was destroyed in 1675 when a woman left a pot of washing unwatched on the fire. On 9 April 1691 a fire broke out at Whitehall, 'occasioned, (as said) by the carelessness of a maid in burning of a candle from a bunch of candles, and leaving the other lighted', says Luttrell. Evelyn says 'a sudden and terrible fire burnt down all the buildings over the stone gallery at Whitehall to the waterside, beginning at the apartment of the late Duchess of Portsmouth (which had been pulled down and rebuilt no less than three times to please her), and consuming other lodgings of such lewd creatures'. To stop the fire spreading, several buildings were blown up, including the lodgings of the king's favourite, Portland, who lost jewels valued at £6000. Queen Mary was 'heartily frightened; everyone at once thought it a Jacobite plot on her life'. There was another ruinous fire at Whitehall in 1698 when a Dutch washerwoman tried to dry linen quickly at a charcoal fire indoors. Fires were easily caused by candles setting off curtains in a draught or neighbours borrowing a bucket of burning coals rather than deal with a tinderbox. The workshops of dyers, brewers, soapboilers and the like, located among houses, were also a source of danger. Chimneys were cleaned by being set on fire or having a gunpowder charge exploded in them.[9]

Persons with grievances also started fires, and witches were often blamed for them. The dissenter Oliver Haywood at Wakefield in March 1680 records: 'Sitting in the house we heard a very astonishing noise in the street, multitudes of people shouting – we inquired the cause. They said it was a woman whom they were hurrying to the House of Correction on a sledge, who (they said) had threatened to burn the town. Some said she was mad, others drunk, but they abused her body in a prodigious manner, whipping her fearfully, carrying her into a dark place like an entry, or dungeon, where they lay their dung. There she lay all night. In the morning her body rose up in blebs, miserable sore. Oh, horrid cruelty. It was said she came from Halifax.' When Wesley's father was rector at Epworth, Lincolnshire, the family lived in a house 'all of timber and plaster, and covered all with a straw thatch, the whole building being contrived into three stories'. The parishioners, out of resentment at the rector's uncompromising temper, set fire to the place. His wife narrowly escaped, and John, aged six or seven, was saved, just before the roof fell in, by being lifted through an upper window by a man standing on another's shoulders.

For fire-fighting there were leather buckets, ladders, and iron hooks for pulling thatch down. A manual engine by which a gang of men could raise water to a height was patented in 1625, but only in the later part of the century were such machines being popularised. On 29 August 1673 Isham records: 'Carter brought a machine in a cart, which throws up water with great force, and is adapted for extinguishing fire. My father gave him £9 for it.' The leather hosepipe, a Dutch invention, reached England in the 1670s; then the invention of the air chamber enabled men to send out a steady stream instead of a pulsating jet. Under Anne an Act required each London parish to own a large fire-engine, a hand-squirt, a leather pipe, and a socket for attachment to the street water-supply. Some towns tried to ban thatch and order householders to keep water-buckets ready by doors. There were no fire-brigades till the insurance companies began to organise them. As we saw, houses near a burning house were often blown up; and as soon as the flames died down, looting began.

In the last two decades of the century organised fire-insurance came into being. Before this a man might lose everything. A victim could apply only for a church brief allowing him to beg for money in places of public worship. Such begging letters were used for a variety of purposes, and often involved frauds. Barbon was a pioneer in house-insurance. Between 1686 and 1692 he insured 5650 houses, the premiums being based on $2\frac{1}{2}$ per cent for brick houses and 5 per cent for timber. (He also opened a Land Bank and was a defender of the debased coinage on the grounds that money was only an agreed symbol of value.) He had made a very acute study of economics and in his *Discourse of Trade*, 1690, he tried to define the relation between use and value, value and price, as well as the nature of currency, credit, and interest. He stressed the social and economic importance of building and argued that it was 'the chief promoter of trade' because of the large number of trades linked one way or another with it.

Behind the insurance companies and the new kind of reasoning about economics there lay the whole rationalising development of science which culminated in Newton. The expansion of the clock and watch industry, with its ever greater precision, gave men a new sense of time and a new control of it, a new power of organising their lives and their work – and the work of others. Round 1700 much of the national wealth lay in stocks of materials in the hands of merchants, dealers, domestic workers. The longer the time taken in production, the greater the capital cost. So people grew ever more aware of the time taken in jobs and sought ways of quickening them with innovations in bleaching, more effective transport, faster turns of the wheel. After 1688 governments made use of statistics, such as those collected on the balance of trade, on public revenue and expenditure, on the state on the coinage. Charles Davenant, economist, was appointed Inspector-General of Imports and Exports, providing the Treasury and the Board of Trade with statistical information. In our period the whole method of government was revolutionised by the use of such material, and the civil servants who carried out this work were often

Fellows of the Royal Society. The teaching of arithmetic had so much advanced that adults at all social levels now gave up using the abacus.[10]

But fires were only one of many things making life precarious. In the late seventeenth century the expectation of life was even lower than in Elizabethan days. Child mortality was very high. A third of noble babies died before the age of five; of Queen Anne's seventeen children only one survived infancy and he died at the age of eleven. In the period October to September 1707–8 in London there were 21,270 burials and 16,120 baptisms. Things were much worse in 1741–2 with 31,590 burials to 13,760 baptisms. Of the total burials in 1739 slightly more than half were of children under eleven, 38 per cent were of those under three. Some other years show even worse percentages. London must have been the supreme deathtrap, but everywhere young children had a poor hope of life. In the registers of the large towns burials normally outnumber the baptisms. Until the coming of sanitation the death-toll of cities carried heavily on, though as the century continued more children survived. Bills of mortality show burials more common in the early winter months of the year, and they varied with the weather. Severe cold or rain in 1708–10, 1735–9, and 1739–1742, led to a sharp rise in deaths, through cold, fevers, lack of food.

The callousness of the age may be gauged by the way in which parishes treated children in their care. Defoe, in *Parochial Tyranny*, 1727, declared, 'Some vestries are more barefaced and even make a trade of a parish. In mean churchwardens and vestries who lump it with harlots and whore-mongers and take bastards off their hands at so much per head, for which they get a good treat, from two guineas to five according to the circumstances of their chap, which they call saddling the spit, besides a good sum with the bantling, which 'tis to be feared is entirely sunk, all being done by connivance.' Hanway, summing up the situation before the Foundling Hospital was opened in 1739, said that saddling-the-spit did 'not give a day of life' to the infant; the only concern of the officers was to get a 'speedy release from all expense'. So, 'the Officers are defendant, jury and executioner, and they think it to their *interest* that the *prisoner* should die'.

Those who survived their first years had the likelihood of much illness and pain. About one harvest in six seems to have been a failure. Most people suffered from a lack of vitamin A (yellow and green vegetables), hence their sore eyes; or of vitamin D (milk and eggs), hence the widespread rickets. Scorbutic diseases and rheumatic troubles were common: hence the many persons with crooked legs and arms. Hernia from lifting heavy weights was also common; with the advent of newspapers we find the evidence from the advertisements for trusses. The green sickness of young women, given a sexual interpretation, was anaemia through the lack of iron in diet. The upper classes disdained fresh vegetables and were con-stipated from eating too much meat. Infections of the urinary tract often produced stone in the bladder. The poor escaped gout and stone, and probably had better teeth than the rich, but were undernourished, liable to gripes and tuberculosis. Lack of hygiene affected all classes, and even the fastidious Pepys had his head combed every night for lice. There were continual epidemics of influenza, typhus, dysentery (the bloody flux), and smallpox. Dr Richard Mead in his *Short Discourse concerning Pestilential Contagion* (1720) advocated better and more humane ways of isolating the infected, and strongly attacked the dirty condition of streets and houses; but he had little effect. This world was a malodorous one. In dining rooms cupboards held chamber-pots for the finely dressed diners to relieve themselves. It was a matter of wonder that at Windsor Queen Anne sat on 'a seat of easement of marble, with sluices of water to wash all down'. Stinks indeed were thought helpful; a town in Holland was said to have escaped plague through its piggish filth.

Smallpox was a constant hazard. 'You must by no means stop at Swaffham for the man's sake, but rather take warm at Hilborough if need be. The smallpox rages at Swaffham' (Roger North, 17 December 1731). Evelyn tells us: 29 Decem-ber 1694: 'The small pox increased exceedingly, and was very mortal. The Queen died of it on the 28th.' 5 November 1700: 'Came the news of my dear grandson (the only male of my

family now remaining) being fallen ill of the small pox at
Oxford, which after the dire effects of it in my family exceedingly afflicted me, but so it pleased my most merciful God that
being let blood at the first complaint', he recovered. On 8
November 1702 his young kinsman John Evelyn of Nutfield
came on a visit to London and within a fortnight died of smallpox. Swift was very afraid of contagion. On 15 March 1711, he
notes, 'Poor Biddy Floyd has got the smallpox. I called this
morning to see lady Betty Germaine; and when she told me
so I fairly took my leave. I have the luck of it; for about ten
days ago I was to see lord Carteret, and my lady was enter-
taining me with telling me of a young lady a cousin, who was
then ill in the house of the smallpox, and is since dead; it was
near lady Betty's, and I fancy Biddy took the fright by it.' However she recovered. 'But will lose all her beauty; she had them
mighty thick, especially about the nose.'

The adoption of inoculation against the disease was due to
Lady Mary Wortley Montagu, who in 1716 accompanied her
husband to Turkey when he was appointed ambassador to the
Porte. She found that 'the small-pox, so fatal, and so general
amongst us, is here entirely harmless by the invention of
ingrafting, which is the term they give it'. She decided: 'I am
patriot enough to take pains to bring this useful invention into
fashion in England; and I should not fail to write to some of our
doctors very particularly about it, if I knew any one of them
that I thought had virtue enough to destroy such a considerable
branch of their revenue for the good of mankind.' She adds, 'Perhaps, if I live to return, I may, however, have courage to
war with them. Upon this occasion admire the heroism in
the heart of your friend, etc, etc.' It was not, however, till
about 1760 that inoculation began to have widespread results.

Medical theory was still mainly based on the idea that disease
came from an imbalance between the four humours of the body
(blood, phlegm, yellow and black bile). The balance could be
restored, it was thought, by bloodletting, venesection, scarifica-
tion, purges, emetics, the application of leeches; and there was
much use of plasters, ointments, potions, and great interest in
a patient's urine. 'We are all very well here,' wrote North to
his sister on 13 February 1706, 'only the little boy had a violent

access of a cold (I take it) but for fear of worse we resorted to his sheet-anchor, bleeding in the jugular, which once saved his life, and perhaps has done the same, for he is much better after it, but weak, having lost eight ounces.' The famed Dr Radcliffe had as his favourite remedy a Blistering Plaister. When the Queen's son was ill with a 'malignant fever in all its symptoms', he had been given five blisters before Radcliffe arrived; later 'we ordered him in the evening two more blisters which were applied and to continue the method he was in, hoping by the assistance of them and his other medicines he would have a better night, but before the blisters could take place the malignity of the distemper retreating from the skin to the vital parts', he suddenly died. In April 1714 the doctor himself was badly ill, but 'there are hopes that Dr Radcliffe may escape. Charles Bernard has taken an hundred ounces of blood from him.' He died on the first of November.[11]

Thomas Wilson in his account of toothache in June 1732 shows how helpless people were before most pains:

Dined at Corpus Christi Gawdy. A very elegant entertainment. Cost at least £60 (servants 2s). Went home exceedingly pained with the Tooth Ache and lay all night and next day tormented to the last degree. Tried all kinds of medicines but found no relief. Such as Spirit of Turpentine, Sulphur, Harts Horn, Camphire, Laudanum etc. Resolved to send for the famous operator from Wickham.

Saturday 10. Dr Perkins came and with a good deal of reluctance and he assuring me it would spoil both the teeth it touched upon, I suffered him to draw it out (an ugly kind of pain) being one of the worst kind and a part of the Jaw Bone forced away with it, tho' I thank God without much damage and the Tooth Ache quite gone for the present. (Paid him 19s 6d). *Mem*. To be very careful in keeping them clean washing behind the ears and combing the head to divert the Rheum that falls in great quantities upon my gums. In the evening at the Common Room which was very wrong. Catched a bad cold in my mouth.

Amputations or operations for the stone were extremely painful. The surgeons, inferior in status to physicians, dealt also with tumours, ulcers, fractures, venereal disease; they did brain-trepanning, set bones, and incised abcesses. Richard Wiseman's standard *Severall Chirurgicall Treatises*, 1676, was understand-ably nicknamed Wiseman's *Book of Martyrs*. There was a limited number of physicians; the Royal College kept their ranks small for London and a seven-mile radius. But in the country, where church and universities had more licensing power, the number of physicians kept on growing, though Baxter wrote, 'Many a thousand lie sick and die that have not money for physicians.' In 1687 the Royal College ruled that members could advise the poor freely, and soon after set up a short-lived Dispensary where medicines were cold at cost price, infuriating the apothecaries (grocers and druggists). The parishes were expected to pay medical fees for paupers, and a few municipalities appointed town doctors. But only a few utopians like John Bellers in 1714 thought of a state medical service. Bellers considered that half the persons dying in a year could have been cured but were too poor to seek remedies. In 1687 a midwife stated that two-thirds of stillbirths, abortions and childbed-deaths were due to lack of skill and care. (We find midwives licensed by the church.) The way in which parishes objected to poor folk getting sick is shown by an item in the accounts of the constable for Great Staughton, Huntingdon-shire, for 1710: 'Paid, Thomas Hawkins, for whipping 2 persons that had small-pox 8*d*.'

Most people in illness turned to the apothecaries. In 1701 there were said to be a thousand of them in London, with some 1500 apprentices, outnumbering physicians by five to one. They diagnosed and prescribed as well as supplying medicines. The physicians tried to curb them, but in 1704 they won the right to give medical advice if they did not charge for it: a practice long carried out in the provinces. More progressive than the physicians, they were thus able to evolve into general practitioners. The pressure of work and the variety of com-plaints with which they had to deal led them to break through the narrow theory of the physicians and to try out new drugs, many of which came in through the eastern trade. The poorest classes turned to the empiric, the wise woman, the herbalist, who often had genuine folklore of herbs, though others were

quacks. Each housewife had her own collection of customary
remedies, which at least in the country she mostly made herself.

There were indeed many quacks and mountebanks, and the
satirists loved to depict them, while newspaper advertisements
prove how lavish were their claims. Ned Ward in his picture of
London shows how low was the opinion of the physicians and
how ubiquitous the quacks. (Ned, born in 1667, came of a
plebeian family; he visited the West Indies in early life and then
set up as a publican in Moorfields, moving in 1699 to Fullwood's Rents where he kept a punch-shop and tavern next door
to Gray's Inn till his death in 1731. He was a voluminous writer
of squibs and satires attacking the Whigs in particular. In his
London Spy, starting in monthly parts in November 1699 he
gives a vivid picture of low life.) He tells of a visit with a friend
to the Physicians College, built by Wren on the west side of
Warwick Lane. The portico was so lofty and large 'that when
we had entered it we were no more in proportion to the
spacious lanthorn o'er our heads than a cricket to a biscuit-
baker's oven'. His friend declares, 'They lately committed a
more able physician than themselves without bail or main
prize, for malpractice in curing a woman of a dangerous ulcer
in her bladder by the use of a Cantharidid, which they affirm
not fit for internal application, though the patient's life was
saved by taking it; which shews they hold it a greater crime to
cure, out of the common method, than it is to kill in it.' They
walk down Ludgate Hill to Fleet Bridge, 'where nuts, gingerbread, oranges and oysters, lay piled up in movable shops that
run upon wheels, attended by ill-looking fellows, some with but
one eye, and others without noses. Over against these stood a
parcel of trugmoldies in straw hats, and flat-caps, selling socks
and firmity, nightcaps and plum pudding'. Two women start a
brawl and a crowd gathers. So a quack passing on his nag halts
and plucks out 'a packet of universal hodge-podge'. Ned gives
his oration:

> Gentlemen, you that have a mind to be mindful of preserv-
> ing a sound mind in a sound body, that is, as the learned
> physician, Doctor Honorificacabilitudinitatibusque has it,
> *Manus Sanaque in Cobile Sanaquorum*, may here at the

expense of sixpence, furnish himself with a parcel, which
though 'tis but small, yet containeth mighty things of great
use, and wonderful operation in the bodies of mankind,
against all distempers, whether homogeneal or complicated; whether derived from your parents, got by infection, or proceeding from an ill-habit of your own body.
In the first place, gentlemen, I here present you with a little
inconsiderable pill to look at; you see not much bigger than
a corn of pepper. Yet is this diminutive panpharmica so
powerful in its effect, and of such excellent virtues, that if
you have twenty distempers lurking in the mass of blood, it
shall give you just twenty stools, and every time it operates
it carries off a distemper, but if your blood's wholesome,
and your body sound, it will work with you no more than
the same quantity of gingerbread.

He also offers a plaster, a powder, a Venice treacle (a cordial
dispelling poisons). The troubles he guarantees to cure include
wounds, fistulas, ulcers, pains in head, limbs or bowel, con-
tusions, sprains, tumours, and 'that epidemical distemper,
worms, which destroy more bodies than either plague, pestilence
or famine'. The people eagerly buy, untying their purses and
the corners of their handkerchiefs. An advertisement of August
1691 from the *Athenian Mercury* shows how close Ward was to
the sort of claims made by the purveyors of medicine.

In Plow-Yard in Gray's-Inn-Lane lives Dr Thomas Kirleus, a collegiate physician, and sworn physician to Charles
II until his death; who with a drink and pill (hindering
no business) undertakes to cure any ulcers, sores, swellings
in the nose, face or other parts; scabs, itch, scurfs, leprosies,
and venereal disease, expecting nothing until the cure be
finished. Of the last he hath cured many hundreds in this
city; many of them after fluxing, which carries the evil
from the lower parts to the head and so destroys many.
The drink is 3s the quart, the pill 1s a box, with directions,
a better purge than which was never given, for they cleanse
the body of all impurities, which are the causes of dropsies,
gouts, scurvies, stone and gravel, pain in the head and
other parts; with another drink, at 1s 6d a quart, he cures

all fevers and hot distempers without bleeding, except in a
few bodies. He gives his opinion to all that writes or comes
for nothing.

There were only two hospitals in London in 1700: St Bartholomew's with Christ's adjoining, and St Thomas's, which were
meant solely for the poor, as better-off persons were treated at
home. During the next century more and more hospitals were
added till there were some fifty, though in some ways they
were rather centres of infection than of cure. Trade with the
East had brought in a new pharmacology, with a large increase
in drugs, but only a few of the new ones, quinine for malaria
and guiacum for syphilis, gained a lasting use. Apart from
smallpox inoculation there were few innovations that helped
the chances of better and longer life till the nineteenth century,
and, apart from sanitation, no solid advances till the second
quarter of the twentieth. Defoe mentions that St Thomas's had
suffered from several great fires in Southwark.

Christ's, called the Blue-Coat Hospital, took in poor
children. 'Here was lately above a thousand poor children,' says
Notitia of 1702, 'most of 'em orphans, maintained in the house,
and out at nurse, upon the charge of this foundation, and six
or seven score put yearly forth to apprenticeship; the maidens
to good and honest services'. It adds with exaggeration that
some of the cleverest lads reach the universities or even become
Lord Mayor, but it also calls the Bridewell a hospital where
poor, vagrant and idle people are put to work and hopeful lads
are made apprentices. 'Hither likewise sawcy and incorrigible
servants, night-walkers, strumpets, and the like, are sent to
work; and, according to their crimes, receive daily such a
number of stripes as the Governor commands; bread and water
being their best allowance, unless by repentance and industry
they deserve better.' We see that the ideas of hospital and workhouse are still entangled in men's minds; sickness and idleness,
destitution and criminality are felt to be closely related.

In 1725 another hospital was opened, built from the £230,000
left by Thomas Guy. He was born about 1645 in Southwark,
son of a coal-merchant and lighterman. At his father's death
his mother took him to Tamworth, Staffordshire, but in 1660

he returned to London, was apprenticed to a Cheapside bookseller, and set up for himself in 1668. He imported English
Bibles from Holland and joined forces with the university
printers at Oxford (who published Bibles) when the King's
Printers objected and tried to undersell them. He lost his Oxford
contract in 1691 but was already rich. He had endowed an
almshouse for poor women at Tamworth and for twelve years
(till 1707) was MP for that town. Chosen Sheriff, he preferred
to pay a fine than to serve. He made much money through
buying up seamen's tickets (postdated instruments by which the
hard-up navy deferred payment to its ratings) at a considerable discount. He also did well out of the South Sea Bubble,
being shrewd enough to start selling £45,000 worth of the
original stock when it stood at 300; he had sold all his holdings
by the time it reached 500. After reaching 1050, the stock
collapsed to 124, but Guy was safe. He set about establishing his
hospital. Defoe, writing not long after Guy's death, remarked
that the hospital was 'to consist of two great squares of buildings, in which, besides the offices and accommodation for necessary servants and overseers, who must be lodged in the house,
such as stewards, treasurer, masters, matrons, nurses, &c are to
be beds and apartments furnished for four hundred patients,
who are all to be supplied with lodging and attendance, food
and physick'.[12]

In cases of mental illness those considered melancholic were
purged or blood-let, or they were diagnosed as suffering from
hysteria (a condition of the uterus). Indeed the uterine origin
of nervous diseases was not challenged till late in the eighteenth
century when T. Willis set out a theory of cerebral origins and
pioneered the science of neurology. Persons violently disturbed
were locked up by their relatives, kept under guard by parish
officers, or sent to houses of correction. Some inferior practitioners ran private madhouses. Bethlehem Hospital (Bedlam)
took lunatics in for a year; if they were then not cured, they
were discharged. The place was open to sightseers who found
the antics of the mad very amusing. There was still a strong
concept of madness as a form of diabolic possession. *Notitia*
says of Bedlam, 'The building is very magnificent, and beautiful,
in a good air, with great accommodations: It cost £17,000 by

reason which this poor Hospital lies under the disadvantage of
a great debt, and deserves the consideration of those that are
charitably inclined. Here is commonly cured about 40, 50, or
60 in a year.'

2
Tour of London and its People

In this world of obscure and deepgoing change, with many pressures of fear, uncertainty, and anxiety, men felt a great need to escape and forget, and the main recourse was to strong drink. Drinking was an accepted part of almost every social activity, of every public and private ceremony, commercial bargains, craft rituals, personal occasions of grief or joy. Fairs and markets were free from normal licensing restrictions till 1874. The consumption of strong liquor was vast, and the drunken man a common part of the social scene. 'Mr Charnock came, and being well drunk, fell down from the table in the midst of the ladies, so that no one could refrain from laughing' (Isham, December 1672). In 1725 Benjamin Franklin worked in a London printing house near Lincoln's Inn Fields, where nearly fifty men were employed, a large establishment for the period. Himself a water-drinker, he called the others 'great guzzlers of beer'. There was an alehouse boy always in attendance to bring supplies. 'My companion at press drank every day a pint between breakfast and dinner, a pint in the afternoon about 6 o'clock, and another pint when he had done his day's work.' He thought it was necessary 'to drink strong beer that he might be strong to labour'. Despite Franklin's efforts, he drank on 'and had 4s or 5s to pay out of his wages every Saturday night for that muddling liquor'. Thus 'these poor devils keep themselves always under'. However, Franklin managed in the end by argument and example to get several of the men to give up 'their muddling breakfast of beer and bread, and cheese, finding they could with me be supplied from a neighbouring house with a large porringer of hot-water gruel sprinkled with pepper, crumbled with bread, and a bit of butter in it, for the price of a pint of beer, viz., three halfpence'.

In 1702 Defoe remarked that 'an honest drunken fellow is a character in a man's praise'. And he describes the True-born Englishmen:

> Good drunken company is their delight;
> And what they get by day, they spend by night.
> Dull thinking seldom does their heads engage,
> But drink their youth away, and hurry on old age.

Again he says of the worker: 'Ask him in his cups what he intends. He'll tell you honestly, he'll drink so long as it lasts, and then go to work for more.' So it was argued that long hours of work and low wages were necessary to save the workers from idleness and self-destruction. William Temple in *The Case Between Clothiers and Weavers*, 1739, declared that it was imperative to lay the workers 'under the necessity of labouring all the time they can spare from rest and sleep, in order to procure the common necessaries of life'.

Notitia stresses that the English, who 'content themselves with small Ale or Cider, are observed to be much more healthy, and much longer lived than some other of our neighbouring nations'. It adds that in London, as well as imported wines, there are sold 'about twenty sorts of other drinks, as brandy, rattafia, coffee, chocolate, tea, rum, punch, usquebaugh, &c, mum, cider, perry, mead, metheglin, beer, ale, many sorts of ale, Hull, Derby, Northdown, Nottingham, Sandbach, betony, scurvy-grass, sage-ale, sherbet, college-ale, China-ale, butlers ale, &c, a piece of Wantonness, whereof none of our Ancestors were ever guilty'. There were many odd names for beers. Dr King of Christ Church in an account of a journey to London mentioned an ale called Humtie-dumtie. The scholar Bentley, attacking King for other matters, remarked, 'We must not expect from the Doctor that he should know the worth of books: for he is better skilled in the catalogue of ales, his Humtie-Dumtie, his Hugmatee, Three-Threads and the rest of that glorious list.'

In 1684 the duty in England and Wales was on a total of 6,318,000 barrels (4,384,000 of strong ale, the rest of small beer), each barrel holding thirty-six gallons in London, thirty-four in the provinces. By these figures each man, woman, and child consumed near a pint a day; but King in 1688 estimated that they represented only 30 per cent of the real consumption. But even the official figures show a higher consumption *per capita* than anything known in modern times, and we must add the imported wines and spirits that were increasingly drunk. Thirst was stimulated by the amount of salted fish and meat eaten; and the listlessness born of a largely cereal diet may have strengthened the need for fermented liquor. Tea and coffee were still expensive; not until later in the century was tea a working-class drink.

During the wars British geneva and whisky came in as substitutes for French brandy; they cost little to make and were sold at low prices. The landed gentry favoured their popularity since the distillers provided a market for home-grown wheat and barley, and Parliament encouraged the market. For more than a generation the only restraint was a low excise-duty (3d to 6d a gallon), and the retail trade needed no licences. The result was a disastrous spread of heavy drunkenness. In 1736, belatedly, an act tried to control the trade but only drove it underground; in the early 1740s the output of spirits reached its peak, roughly six times as much as round 1700. For a while there were fears of a sort of national suicide, at least in London.

Alehouses were often kept by constables, who broke the law with impunity. Thus in 1712 there was a Middlesex complaint that the keepers applied to the stewards of courts-leet (courts held in hundreds, lordships, manors) to be sworn in as constables 'with the intent to favour and connive with several offenders who keep houses of bawdy, musick-houses, and other disorderly houses, and by that means encourage such offenders and refuse to present them to this or any other court of justice'. In 1736 a report on excessive drinking stated that nearly half the constables were victuallers and dealers, in spirituous liquors. Other trades found ways of being excused; only the drink-sellers were keen to assume the office.[1]

The upper classes set the tipsy example. When in 1689

William and Mary came to London to celebrate Twelfth Night
at Whitehall, they dined at Lord Shrewsbury's. Mary retired
to Kensington to play at cards and gamble with her sister
Anne; the men were left at dinner. 'In the end they all became
so drunk,' reported a Frenchman, 'that there was not a single
one who did not lose consciousness.' Marlborough and Lord
Selkirk staggered back dead-drunk to Whitehall, and Marlborough at once fell asleep in the antechamber of the king's
bedroom and didn't stir as the king swayed past him. William
himself could not stop eating huge meals washed down with
volumes of wine and strong ale. In November 1697 he wrote to
Portland, 'In the evening we went on a debauch – at least those
of us who hadn't celebrated the day's hunting too enthusiastic-
ally.' At times he lost all control of himself. Once, waving a
glass, he hit a companion in the face and spilt the wine over
his clothes. 'He walked away sobbing with regret.' When
Pembroke came one morning to apologise for a show of drunken
temper the previous night, he laughed the matter off. 'No
apologies. Make not yourself uneasy. These accidents over a
bottle are nothing among friends.'

Swift therefore jeered unfairly at Steele for remarking that
Queen Anne was a lady, and unless a prince will now and then
get drunk with his ministers, 'he cannot learn their interests or
their humours'. Steele himself was continually as drunk as any
king could be. We have for instance his scrawled letter to Prue,
who was to be his wife, on Saturday night, 30 August 1707:
'Dear lovely Mrs Scurlock I have been in very good company
where your unknown name, under the character of the woman
I loved best has been often drank, so that I may say I am
dead drunk for your sake, which is more yn I dye for you.
Svt [Servant], R. Steele.' He crossed out 'unknown name' and
wrote 'Health' over it.

Two of Dr Radcliffe's bottle-companions were Lord Craven
and William Nutley, barrister. In 1710 Craven died of excessive
drinking. Radcliffe wrote to the Duke of Bedford with advice
to abstain, saying that Craven 'had it not in his power to
abstain from what was his infelicity, while it was thought to
be his comfort'. The Duke was treated by the doctor success-
fully for smallpox, but in 1714 he died at Badminton. 'After

having heated himself at shooting, he drank a great quantity of small liquor, which made him vomit blood and he died in three days.' Nutley, ill, was nursed by the landlady of the Mitre Tavern; Radcliffe, called in, decided that the prescription needed was relief from heavy debts; he brought a green purse of 200 sovereigns and promised 300 more. But Nutley went on drinking and died in a few days. The great doctor advertised under an engraving of the Lion and the Unicorn with Hygeia: 'Dr Radcliffe's Royal Tincture, or the General Rectifier of the Nerves, Head and Stomach. It corrects all irregularities of the Head and Stomach by hard drinking or otherwise.' He also advertised 'the best purl in the world' (a purl was an infusion of wormwood or other bitter herbs) 'in beer, ale or wine, or purl royal in sack. Merchants and shopkeepers may be supplied with these drops with good allowance to sell again, at Lloyd's Coffee House, Lombard Street, London. Price 1s a bottle'.

In *The London Spy* the satirist Ned Ward takes us on a Night Walk through London. 'Now,' says a friend, 'we'll spend the evening over a cheerful glass. Here's a tavern hard by, where a parcel of pleasant companions of my acquaintance use; we'll see what diversion we can find in their society.' So 'we stepped in, and in the kitchen found half a dozen of my friend's associates, in the height of their jollity, as many as so many Cantabrigians at Stir-bitch Fair, or cobblers at a St Crispin's feast. After a friendly salutation, free from all foppish ceremony, down we sat, and when a glass or two had given fresh motion to our drowsy spirits, and we had abandoned all those careful thoughts which make man's life uneasy, wit begot wit, and wine a thirst appetite to each succeeding glass; then open were our hearts and unconfined our fancies. My friend and I contributed our mites to the treasure of our felicity. Songs and catches crowned the night and each man in his turn elevated his voice to fill our harmony with the more variety.' After many songs, 'the spirits of the reviving juice had rather overpowered than enlivened the noblest of our faculties, and my friend and I thought it high time to take our leave; which after the payment of our clubs we did accordingly, agreeing to give ourselves the pleasure of two or three hours' ramble in the streets. Having spent the time at the tavern till about ten o'clock, with mirth and satisfaction, we were now desirous of prying into the dark intrigues of the Town, to experience what pastime the night accidents, the whims and frolics of staggering bravadoes, and strolling strumpets might afford us.'[2]

Outside, they found it was actually nine o'clock, with the alarm of Bow Bell calling the weary apprentices from their work to unhitch the folded shutters and button up the shops till next morning. The streets were lit with dazzling lights so that 'I could see nothing but ourselves and thus walked amazed. like a wandering soul in its pilgrimage to Heaven when it passed through the spangled regions.' (These streetlights, set at every tenth house, had been brought in by Edward Heming, who got in 1685 the letters patent for the exclusive lighting-up of London. Misson, in his *Travels*, 1697, described them: 'Instead of lanterns they set up in the streets of London lamps which, by means of very thick convex glasses, throw out great rays of light which illuminate the path for people that go on foot, tolerably well. They begin to light up these lamps at Michaelmas, and continue them till Lady Day; they burn from six in the evening till midnight, and from every third day after the full moon to the sixth day after the new moon.')

On every side was 'the music of sundry passing-bells, the rattling of coaches, and the melancholy ditties of *Hot Baked Wardens and Pippins*'. The friend pointed out a shop where sat three or four 'very provoking damsels, with as much velvet on their backs as would have made a burying-pall for a country parish, or a holiday coat for a physician, being glorified at bottom with gold fringes, so that I thought at first they might be parsons' daughters who had borrowed their father's pulpit clothes to use as scarves to go a visiting in. Each had as many patches as are spots in a leopard's skin or freckles in the face of a Scotsman.' They were whores costing about a guinea each, sitting in a head-dresser's shop, which 'is as seldom to be found without a harlot as a bookseller's shop in St Paul's Churchyard without a parson'.

The roamers went up a dark passage and climbed dark stairs

to the Widow's Coffee House. The widow welcomed them and ushered them into a room

> where, at the corner of a long table next her elbow chair, lay a large Bible open, with her spectacles upon one of St Paul's epistles; next to it was a quartern pot, two or three stone bottles, a roll of plaster, and a pipe of tobacco; there was a handful of fire in a rusty grate, with a pint coffee-pot before it, and a green earthen pot in the chimney-corner. Over the mantel-tree were two bastard china dishes, a patch-box, and a syringe. On a little shelf among phials and gally-pots, were half a dozen long bottles of Rosa Solis, with an advertisement of a rare whitewash for the face nailed on one side, and a brief account of the excellencies of Doctor John C——se's *pills for the speedy cure of violent pains without loss of time or hindrance of Business* on the other; a grenadier's bayonet, musket and cartouche-box were behind the door; a head-dresser's block, and a quart pot (as terrible as Death's head and an hour-glass) stood frightfully in the window; also an old-fashioned clock in a crazy case, but as silent as a corpse in a coffin, stood bolt upright like a stiff-necked constable, more for orna-ment than use. Also, an abstract of the Acts of Parliament against drinking, swearing, and all manner of profaneness. The floor was broken like that of an old stable, the windows were mended with brown paper, and the bare walls were full of dust and cobwebs.

Case, who died in 1700, was a famous quack and astrologer, who had inscribed over his door: 'Within this place Lives Doctor Case', a jingle, says Addison, that brought him in more money than Dryden made with all his poems. Round his pill-boxes ran: 'Here's fourteen pills for thirteen pence Enough in any man's own conscience.'

If we read again this account of the room and its contents, we see that it is the first full expression in literature of the new realism that comes to a head in Defoe and Hogarth. The careful detail is used to build up the character of the room's inhabitant and at the same time has an emblematic value. The quart-pot standing 'frightfully in the window' as an emblem of human mortality has the quality with which Hogarth was to imbue his objects.

The house shook and two lads burst in from an upper storey, looking like merchants' sons or 'the apprentices of topping tradesmen', with cropped hair, stone-buckled shoes, broad gold hatbands and no swords. The friend called for a bottle of cock-ale, which Ned disliked for its taste like small beer mixed with treacle. 'Prithee, give me a glass of brandy, or something that will dart like lightning into my spirits.' A pair of whores came down from above, painted to show waxwork complexions. 'Their under petticoats were white dimity, embroidered like a turkey-work chair, or a fool's doublet, with red, green, blue and yellow; their pin-up coats of Scotch plaid, adorned with bugle lace; and their gowns of printed calico. But their heads were dressed up to the best advantage, like a vintner's bar-keeper or a church-warden's daughter upon an Easter Sunday.' The girls tried to captivate the visitors 'with as many whimsical vagaries and diverting pranks as a young monkey with a mouse at his tail'. But the friend, who was a surgeon, asked one of them to pay the arrears for his treatment of her last illness, and she grew furious. They called for more drinks. A sober citizen in cloak and band, who looked about sixty, grovelled in, and the girls took up with him.

The wanderers went out and heard the watchmen croaking the hour of eleven. Tavern-topers were lurching home and there were few harlots in the streets. The pair decided to go on to Billingsgate. On the way, at the door of a shop in Grace-church Street, they found a squalling baby exposed in a basket, with a poem pinned to its breast that ended: 'For all that my mother can say, The Parish must be my father.' They left the basket to the watchmen and went on, but were surrounded by a crowd of 'strange hobgoblins covered with long frieze rugs and blankets, hooped round with leather girdles from their cruppers to their shoulders, and their noddles buttoned up unto caps of martial figure'. One wielded a faggot-bat and the others had odd wooden weapons shaped like clyster-pipes but almost as long as speaking-trumpets. They blew into these instruments and made 'such a fearful yelling, that I thought the world had been dissolving and the terrible sound of the last trumpet to be within an inch of my ears'. The surgeon explained that these were the city-waifs who played on winter nights through the streets.

Next the pair came on a little army of ragamuffin tatter-demalions. The surgeon asked who they were, and was told, 'We are the City Black Guard, marching to our winter quarters. Lord bless you, Masters, give us a penny or a halfpenny, amongst us, and you shall hear any of us, if you please, say the Lord's Prayer backwards; swear the compass round; give a new curse to every step in the Monument; call a harlot as many proper names as a peer has titles.' So Ned gave them a penny. (These were a pack who infested the stables and kitchens of large houses. A Proclamation of 1683 of the Lord Steward's Office denounced them as 'a sort of vicious, idle and master-less boys and rogues, commonly called the Blackguard, with divers lewd and loose fellows', who haunted and followed the court. Those who had intruded into the royal court and stables were charged 'to depart upon pain of imprisonment'.)

At last the pair reached Billingsgate and found a smoky boozing-den in a narrow stinking lane. There round the fire sat 'a tattered assembly of fat motherly flat-caps, with their fish-baskets hanging upon their heads instead of riding hoods, with every one her nipperkin of warm ale and brandy, and as many rings upon their thumbs as belong to a set of bed curtains; every one as slender in the waist as a Dutch skipper in the buttocks, and together, looking like a litter of squab elephants'. They were all talking loudly, 'and every word they spoke was at least in the pitch of a double gamut'. They were abusing the fashionable high head-dresses (commodes) and patches. The roamers took refuge in another room packed with all sorts of rakes. 'One, in a long wig and muff, looked as fretful as a broken gamester, biting his nails as if he were ready to curse aloud, Confound the dice. Another was as full as if his grey mare were the better horse, and had denied him entrance for keeping late hours; the next, as brisk and lively as if he had just come of age and had got his means into his own hands, bought his time of his master and feared no colours, but thinking the day too short for his fortune had resolved the night should make amends in lengthening out his pleasures. In a corner sat a couple of brawny watermen, one eating broiled red herring, and the other bread and cheese and onions.' A drunken sailor blundered in and was led upstairs to bed. Then a spruce blade with a pretended wife asked for the boat to Gravesend. He was told that the next went at 4 am. 'Alas, that will be too long to sit,' he said. 'Can't my wife and I have a bed here?'

'Yes, yes, sir, if you like,' replied the old woman in charge. 'We have several couples above in bed, that wait for the tide as well as you, sir.'

Next came in two seamen with a little crooked fiddler, whom they hung up on a hook in the mantel beam. He wriggled till he broke the string of his breeches and fell into the ashes. The sailors told stories of their voyages in the tropics. Then entered 'a kind of mongrel matchmaker. He made more a-roaring than half a dozen drunken porters, and was as full of freaks as a madman at full of the moon.' He read out a list of the girls and women he was trying to arrange marriages for. Our pair then took thought of the business they had next day, and decided to ask for a bed. 'So, accordingly, we were conducted to a room which stunk as bad as a ship between decks, when the tars are in their hammocks. But the seasonableness of the hour forced us to be content. And so good night to ye.'[3]

Next to drink, tobacco was the most important opiate for males. In 1614–21 some 140,000 pounds were consumed; in 1699–1709, 300,000. Not till 1907 was such a level again reached. Ned Ward tells of a visit to a tobacconist, probably Benjamin Howes at the corner of Shoe Lane. Fleet Street was so thick with coaches that it was some time before he and his friend 'at last ventured to shoot ourselves through a vacancy between two' of them and entered the shop. The place was full of smokers wrapt up in Irish blankets, with meagre jaws and shrivelled looks, and with bodies seeming as dry and light 'as if they had been hard baked in an oven as a sea-biscuit, or cured in a chimney like a flitch of bacon'. They ended each sentence with a puff and spoke in short sentences for fear of losing the pleasure of a whiff. 'Hoy d'ye-do?' *Puff*. 'Thank ye.'

Puff. 'Is the weed good?' *Puff.* 'Excellent.' *Puff.* 'It's fine weather.' *Puff.* 'G–d be thanked.' *Puff.* 'What's a clock?' *Puff,* etc.

Behind the counter was a young fellow serving customers very quickly and expertly. 'He never makes a man wait the tenth part of a minute for his change, but will so readily fling you down all sums without counting from a guinea to three pennyworths of farthings, that you would think he had it for you ready in his hand, before you asked him for it.' Ned and his friend smoked a pipe and filled their boxes, then 'left the society in stinking mist, parching their entrails with the drowsy fumes of the pernicious plant, which being taken so incessantly as it is by these immoderate skeletons, renders them such slaves to a beastly custom, that they make a puff at all business, are led astray by following their noses, burn away their pence, and consume their time in smoke'. Some tobacconists did well. Richard Lapthorne in notes dated November 1688 states, 'Two rich aldermen died, one Alderman Jefferys, Tobacconist, £300,000, no children. Alderman Lacy, very rich, 1 daughter.'

Snuff too was much used. Charles Lillie, the perfumer from whose shop at the corner of Beaufort Buildings, the *Spectator* was first distributed, composed a book of recipes and observations, *The British Perfumer, Snuff Manufacturer, and Colourman's Guide* (not printed till 1822). He says that snuff-taking dated from 1702 when Sir George Rooke raided Cadiz; before that snuff was used only by visiting foreigners and English who had travelled abroad. Rooke's fleet, failing to take Cadiz, went on to cut off the French ships in Vigo Bay; on the way they plundered Port St Mary and places nearby, where, among other merchandise, they captured several thousand barrels and casks, each with four tin canisters of the best snuff. At Vigo huge quantities of coarse snuff were taken, brought from Havana in 'bales, bags, and scrows' (untanned buffalo-hides with the hairy side outwards). The coarse snuff was shared among the sailors, who sold waggonloads of it at Plymouth, Portsmouth, and Chatham, at a mere threepence or fourpence a pound; the main buyers were Spanish Jews, who resold the stuff at a big profit. The fine snuffs were divided among the officers, some of whom sold their share cheaply at once, while others kept their stock and sold at a high price later as the habit of snuff-taking grew patriotically popular.

Snuff was taken with pipes about the size of quills out of small spring boxes. The pipes let out a small amount on to the back of the hand, which was then sniffed up into the nostrils to produce a sneeze. The sneeze, Lillie remarks, 'I need not say forms now no part of the design or rather fashion of snuff-taking.' He defined the different ways of offering snuff to a stranger, a friend, or a mistress, as 'the careless, the scornful, the politic, and the surly pinch', each with its appropriate gesture. Fine ladies took up the fashion, which Addison derided in the *Spectator* in April 1712. 'This silly trick is attended with such a coquet air in some ladies, and such a sedate masculine one in others, that I cannot tell which most to complain of.' Mrs Saunter 'takes it as often as she does salt at meals; and as she affects a wonderful ease and negligence in all her manner, an upper lip mixed with the snuff and the sauce, is what she presents to the observation of all who have the honour to eat with her'. Her niece 'makes up all she wants in a confident air, by a nauseous rattle of the nose, when the snuff is delivered, and the fingers make the stops and closes on the nostrils'. Others play about with the snuff 'to give themselves occasion for a pretty action'. But Flavilla is so 'taken with her behaviour in this kind, that she pulls out her box which is indeed full of good Brazil) in the middle of the sermon; and to shew that she has the audacity of a well-bred woman, she offers it to the men as well as the women who sit near her: but since by this time all the world knows she has a fine hand, I am in hopes she may give her self no further trouble in this matter. On Sunday was sennight, she gave her charity with a very good air, but at the same time asked the church-warden if he would take a pinch.'

The snuff captured by Rooke may have done much to spread the custom, but the stuff was already used earlier as we see from Ward's account of the fashionable Man's Coffee House (behind Charing Cross, near Scotland Yard). Through a dark entry one went up some stairs, into an old-fashioned tenement. There 'a very gaudy crowd of fellows were walking backwards and for-

wards with their hats in their hands, not daring to convert
'em to their intended use, lest it should put the foretops of their
wigs into some disorder'. Hardly anyone was calling for a dish
of Politician's Porridge (coffee); all the men were concerned
only 'to charge and discharge their nostrils, and to keep the
curls of their periwigs in their proper order. The clashing of
their snuff-box lids, in opening and shutting, made more noise
than their tongues, and sounded as terrible in my ears as the
melancholy ticks of so many Death-watches.' He would have
liked to smoke, but at first dared not. Most of these men were
army officers, though 'at the end of the principal room were
other apartments, where, I suppose, the Beau-politicians retired
upon extraordinary occasions to talk nonsense by themselves
about State affairs'. The tables were neat and shone with
rubbing, 'as nut brown in colour as the top of a country
housewife's cupboard', and the floors were clean swept.
However, Ned and his friend at last called for candles and lit
their pipes. The men around grimaced their displeasure and
then withdrew to a large window overlooking the street, 'where
there was such shifting and snuffling that the rest of the company could scarce keep their countenance'. Here then snuff-
taking is shown as the preserve of the aristocrats and army
officers; but in a few years it was to become much more
general.[4]

The tobacconists and snuff-makers were among the tradesmen who helped to break up customary systems by employing
young workers under a skilled foreman instead of journeymen
who had served an apprenticeship. Other such employers were
brewers, distillers, vinegar-makers, soap-boilers, sugar-refiners,
makers of colours, of blue, varnish, glue and printers' ink. The
employers were relatively highly capitalised, and such apprentices as they took paid a large fee, hoping for a partnership
or for a start in business on their own, or at least to become
foremen or bookkeepers. The workers were considered
labourers, but were often paid as well as journeymen in less
profitable trades. Older trades of a similar kind, such as those
of tallow-chandlers, wax-chandlers, tanners and fell-mongers,
employed journeymen who, however, often got labourers'
wages. In the complaints of 1725–6 and 1735–6 about the

growing consumption of gin by the poorer classes, tobacconists were among those said to sell the spirit illegally.

With the heavy reliance on strong drink there were other outlets for the pressures of anxiety and demoralisation, gambling and violent behaviour. North, telling how he strove to escape the burden of drinking, goes on: 'Next to drink I declined cards and all manner of play.'(5) Betting was universal. Wagers were laid on all sorts of events, horses, prize-fights, cockfights, foot-races. Part of the fascination of the brutal baitings of animals was the betting. Already by 1653 Pepys was amazed to see ordinary folk lose ten to twenty pounds on bear-baitings and cockfights. The lower classes betted on their skill in field sports or at skittles or dominoes in taverns. For the man-about-town there were cardgames (ace of hearts, faro, basset, hazard) at the flashy clubs; if nothing else was to hand, he betted on the speed of his footman in Hyde Park. Everyone betted on the turn of coin, the cast of a dice, the sex of an unborn child; and gambling was not unknown in church. Ladies of rank not only wagered or played for money; they even set up gaming houses. Swift describes their passion for cards. 'Supper gobbled up in haste', they ran back to the table. At last came the watchman's knock: 'A frosty morning – past four o'clock.' No chairman could be found. 'Come let us play the other round.' Finally they huddled on hoods and cloaks, and went off, but not before the winner had invited them to come along next morning.

The spread of gambling was linked with the rise of the speculative spirit, the increasing power of the cash-nexus and its alienating effects. John Law in 1694 killed a man in a duel and fled to France; there he won and lost vast sums in gambling, it was said, before embarking on his Mississippi scheme. Tom Brown brings out the link with criminality and a cynical spirit that saw only predatory tricks in all the ways of the world. (Son of a Shropshire farmer, he went to Christ Church, Oxford, in 1678 but left without a degree. Unable to live on his pen, he took to schoolmastering for a while, then returned to pamphlets and jesting verse, being jailed once for a satire on the French king. He lived loosely, spending much time in a tavern in Gower's Row in the Minories and dying in June 1704. He was buried in the cloisters of Westminster Abbey. Addison says he was the first satirist who, dealing with living persons, printed the names with dashes for the vowels. The poet Durfey attacked him as the Mongrel of Parnassus.) Tom remarks that

> in some places they call gaming-houses Academies; but I know not why they should inherit that honourable name, since there's nothing to be learned there, unless it be sleight-of-hand, which is sometimes at the expense of all our money, to get that of other men's by fraud and cunning. The persons that meet are generally men of an infamous character, and are in various shapes, habits, and employments. Sometimes they are squires of the pad [highwaymen], and now and then borrow a little money upon the King's highway, to recruit their losses at the gaming-house; and when a hue-and-cry is out to apprehend them, they are as safe in one of these houses as a priest at the altar, and practise the old trade of cross-biting cullies, assisting the frail square dye with high and low fullums and other napping tricks, in comparison with whom the common bulkers and pickpockets are a very honest society.

Cross-biting and napping were ways of cheating with dice. Hogarth, we may note, has a highwayman among his gamblers in the *Rake's Progress*.

Tom Brown describes the gamblers. 'Some had never a penny left them to bless their heads with. One that had played away even his shirt and cravat, and all his clothes but his breeches, stood shivering in a corner of the room, and another comforting him, and saying, "Damn you, Jack, who ever thought to see thee in a state of innocence? Cheer up, nakedness is the best recipe in the world against a fever." And then fell a ranting, as if hell had broken loose that very moment.' (Again we think of Hogarth's print, with its demented central figure.) At this point a bully, who has heard Tom talking, struts up and tells him, 'Split my windpipe, Sir, you are a fool and don't understand trap [trickery], the whole world's a cheat.' And he goes on to attack the law, poetry, politics, love, surgery, and so on. 'Why should we not recruit by the same methods that have ruined us?'

Men laid wagers on the yield of the hop duties; in the West Indies, on the size of the plantation crops. There was no clear line between gambling and speculation, the dealings in the stock of chartered companies and the various forms of public debt. An act of 1733 tried to curb such stock-dealings as putting: the option of delivering an amount of a given stock or produce at a certain price within a specified time. Partly to evade the usury-laws merchants bought and sold foreign bills, not merely to get payment for goods, but to profit from changes in exchange rates, from the anticipation of the rise or fall of currency values, and to get immediate control of money in return for a promised payment in the future. Insurance too was used, not only to lessen risks, but in gambling forms. The government set the pace with its lotteries from 1694, each linked with a loan or debt-conversion. It tried to gain a monopoly by an act of 1721, though now and then special acts were passed to permit individuals or local authorities to use them for raising funds: for instance, for building Westminster Bridge in 1738.

Steele, always on the look-out for a money-making dodge, inserted in the *Spectator* a notice of 'a new design, of which I am partly author, for getting money'. It was called the Multiplication Table, and anyone buying a half guinea ticket might gain an 'easy fortune' according to numbers drawn at the lottery. But on the very day he set out his scheme the government closed illicit lotteries, and he was threatened with arrest. He advertised that he would attend at the Ship Inn, Bartholomew Lane, to repay all sums advanced; if he had not done so, he would have lost his Commissionership in the Stamp Office. Making the best of a bad job, he wrote to his Prue: 'I cannot come home to dinner. All is safe and well. My disappointment has produced a good, of which you will be glad, to wit, a certainty of keeping my office for resigning so great a prospect. I am, dear thing, yours ever.'

Ned Ward gives us glimpses of gamblers in action. He and his friend visit a raffling-shop, a rendezvous of jilts, harlots, and sharpers. There they, 'like poor spectators, with willing hearts and low pockets, stood in the rear peeping over the shoulders of those that raffled. I observed this ridiculous vanity, that whatever the gentleman won, they presented to the fair lady that stood next, though perfect strangers to one another.' The friend explained, 'You are insensible to the cunning that's used by sharpers, to make this kind of diversion turn to a good account. That pretty sort of woman who receives so many presents, to my knowledge is mistress to him who is now handling the box, who has no other business but to improve such a lucky minute to his maintenance; and he seems, as you, to be utter stranger to that lady he's so kind to, and only makes her mistress of his winnings, purely to draw other gentlemen on to do the like, that what presents they foolishly bestow on her to-night, may serve to furnish his pockets for the hazard table on the morrow.'[6]

They then go up some steep narrow stairs, over which was written in gold THE GROOM-PORTER, in two or three places, 'designed, as I suppose, to make fools think it was the honester for his name being there'. (The Groom-Porter was official in the Royal Household, who saw that the king's apartments were supplied with cards, dice, and other gambling paraphernalia. At Christmas he had the right to keep an open gambling table; he also had the duty of supervising and licensing all gambling houses and of taking action against disorderly ones. But he rarely took such action and the worse disorders often occurred in his own house. His name above the stairs reminds visitors that gambling was royally patronised.) Ned and his friend went at the top into a small room on the left where lawyers' clerks and gentlemen footmen 'were mixed higgle-de-piggle-de, like knaves and fools at an East India House auction, and were wrangling over their sixpences with as much eagerness as so many mumpers at a churchdoor about the true division of a good Christian's charity'. In the next room 'a parcel of old battered bullies, some with carbonadoed faces, and others with squashed noses, were seated close round a great table. Amongst 'em were a few declining tradesmen, who, I suppose, were ready to leave for some foreign plantation, and came hither to acquire the qualifications of a libertine that their portion in this world might be a merry life and a short one. Curses were as profusely scattered as lies among travellers, and as many eyes lifted towards the heavens in confusion of their stars, as there are on board a ship in a storm to implore safety. Money was tossed about as if a useless commodity.'

The noisiest figure was a butcher with cheeks as puffed-out as those of a man playing a trumpet. Making his stake, he cried 'Go again!' – the phrase used to urge dogs on at Hockley in the Hole, Clerkenwell, one of the three bear-gardens. There the bear was chained to an iron ring fixed in a stake, the chain being some fifteen foot long. Butchers and others, keen to exercise their dogs, stood round. At a signal one of the dogs was let loose to worry the bear or be itself mauled and killed. The other bear-gardens were in Marylebone Fields (now Soho Square), and Tothill Fields, Westminster.

Such baitings of animals as well as cockfights were highly popular and much money was bet on the results. Prize-fights were also popular as well as cudgel-fighting. In pugilism no gloves were used and a man hammered his way to fame. Backers of a fighter who was doing badly often forced their way into the ring, which was scarcely raised above ground-level, and did their best with kicks and blows to disable his opponent. Women fought like the men. The *Daily Post* on 7 October 1728, announcing a Boxing Match to be held that day in an amphitheatre in Islington Road, printed the challenge and reply:

Whereas I, Ann Field, of Stoke Newington, ass driver, well known for my abilities in boxing in my own defence ... having been affronted by Mrs Stokes, styled the European championess, do fairly invite her to a trial of her best skill in boxing for £10, fair rise and fall; and question not but to give her such proofs of my judgment that shall oblige her to acknowledge me championess of the stage, to the satisfaction of all my friends.

I Elizabeth Stokes, of the City of London, have not fought in this way since I fought the famous boxing woman of Billingsgate nine minutes, and gained a complete victory, which is six years ago; but as the famous Stoke Newington ass woman dares me to fight her for £10, I do assure her I will not fail meeting her for the said sum, and doubt not that the blows which I shall present her with, will be more difficult for her to digest than any she ever gave her asses.

Such fights at times were a sort of female duel. In June 1722 the *London Journal* printed this challenge:

I Elizabeth Wilkinson, of Clerkenwell, having had some words with Hannah Highfield and requiring satisfaction, do invite her to meet me on the stage and box with me for three guineas, each woman holding half-a-crown in each hand, and the first woman that drops her money to lose the battle.

The idea of holding the coins was that the women would thus be prevented from scratching out each other's eyes and tearing each other's hair. Hannah replied to Elizabeth that she would not fail 'to give her more blows than words, desiring home blows and from her no favour'.

With the breakdown of old systems of living men felt the need to get together in new ways. Hence the rise of the club and the coffee house. Some of these groupings were highly exclusive, like the Kit-Kat Club named after the Quaker pastrycook, Christopher Cat, who served mutton pies in a tavern near Temple Bar, though later moving to a bigger place in the Strand with the sign: 'A Fountain Red with Ever-flowing Wine'. His pies were 'filled in with fine eatable varieties fit for Gods and Poets', and baked in dishes lined with paper that was covered with epigrams, eulogies, squibs about him. The forty-eight club-members included the most intellectual Whig lords and various leading writers, such as Congreve, Addison, Steele, with Kneller (who painted the members' portraits) and the physician Dr Garth. The Hanover Club of 1713 had thirty-one members, each with the privilege of toasting one of the reigning Whig Beauties. They met once a week in Charing Cross to drink to the night's toast, 'very instrumental in keeping up the Whig spirit in London and Westminster'.

Button's Coffee House in Russell Street, Covent Garden, held another literary club, mingling 'merriment with decency and humour with politeness', as was not always the case elsewhere. Here Phillips, attacked in Pope's Pastorals, set up a great

rod which he vowed to try on the poet if he ventured in.
And here Addison presided. He fixed a lion head on the front
door, which served as a box for letters later supposed to serve as
text for essays in the *Guardian*. He asked his readers to diet the
beast, with Aegyptian face compounded out of that of lion and
wizard, on wholesome food, not gorging it with nonsense or
obscenity, and not defiling the mouth with scandal. Nearby
was Tom's where play was said to be carried on till the small
hours of the morning, and where members of the government
did not disdain to have a chat with the frequenters. Here people
were 'too polite to hold a man in discourse by the button'.
Steele in the *Guardian* makes the first reference to button-
holing and distinguishes conversations by the amount of
buttons they cost. 'In the coffee-houses here about the Temple
you may harangue even among our dabblers in politics for
about two buttons a day, and many times for less. I had
yesterday the good fortune to receive very considerable addi-
tions to my knowledge in State affairs, and I find this morning
that it has not stood me in above a button.'[7]

'The Coffee Drink preventeth Drowsiness.' It was puffed as
'an excellent cure for the Spleen, the Dropsy', and other ail-
ments. 'A simple innocent thing to be taken as hot as possibly
can be endured, the which will never fetch the skin off the
mouth or raise any blisters.'

A worried lover wrote to the *Athenian Mercury*, saying that
he thought excessive coffee-drinking was making his beloved
sexually unresponsive. The editor advised him to scare her by
saying that coffee would make her look old and spoil her teeth,
with similar inconveniences. If that failed, 'fall a-drinking
coffee yourself, drink before the lady till you out-top and
conquer her, resolving to drink it as long as she does'. Then,
from pity and fear that intemperate coffee-draughts 'should
injure the frame of your body and incline you to some
paralytical distemper', she might give coffee up herself.

By the early years of the eighteenth century there were more
than five hundred coffee houses in London. For a penny at
the bar, you could take your seat by the fire, smoke a pipe,
join in the talk or listen. Foreigners were astonished at the way
men aired their ideas; Misson commented on 'the universal

liberty of speech among the English' and the way one could see 'the blue ribbons and stars of the nobility sitting familiarly with private gentlemen, as if they had left their quality and degrees of distance at home'. There was much discussion of political events and of news from abroad, undistracted by the need of politeness to ladies, though the barmaids or *dames de comptoir* in frilly caps might invite a man 'by their amorous glances into their smoky territory', receiving 'all day long the adoration of the Youth within such and such districts'. In 1713 Defoe complained that coffee, tea, and chocolate 'are now become capital branches of the nation's commerce'.

Coffee houses served as addresses, as places where one could expect to meet a certain person. John Byrom writes in 1723: 'Jo Clowes is not within; I write from Kent's coffee-house, where they expect him, it being his wonted hour.' Again, 'Prithee, good girl, write to me as oft as thou canst afford; I have stepped into Richard's coffee-house to write this.' In 1735: 'A gentleman of the Temple, one of my latest [pupils], said he could not hear where I lived, that he had enquired in the city, and at last heard of Richard's coffee-house.' Dr Johnson was told before he came to London in 1737, 'A man might live in a garret at eighteenpence a week; few people would enquire where he lodged, and if they did it was easy to say, "Sir, I am to be found at such a place."' Steele, writing to his Prue, describes the scene pressing in on him: 'There is a dirty crowd of busy faces all around me talking of politics and managing stocks –'; he crosses out the last four words and sums them up in one, 'money', adding, 'while all my ambition, all my wealth is love'.

Here one read the newspapers or periodicals. Swift asked Stella on 7 November 1711: 'Do you read the Spectators? I never do; they never come my way; I go to no coffee-houses.' Discussions on all subjects went on. 'They have established a nominal Christianity,' writes Byrom in a letter of 1729, 'and forsaken the practical Christianity – but I cannot talk of Christianity in a coffee-house' – though the *Grub Street Journal* of 21 September 1732 remarked jokingly: 'Just notions of government and religion are best to be acquired in a coffee-house.' Addison, arguing that the different quarters and divisions of

London are 'an Aggregate of various Nations distinguished
from each other by their respective customs, manners and
interests', contrasts the ways in which the same item of news is
treated in the regions of the court and the city. Recently there
was a report of the King of France's death. At St James's
coffee house in the outer room there was 'a buzz of politics.
The speculations were but very indifferent towards the door,
but grew finer as you advanced to the upper end of the room,
and were so very much improved by a knot of theorists, who
sat in the inner room, within the steams of the coffee-pot, that
I there heard the whole Spanish monarchy disposed of, and all
the line of Bourbon provided for in less than a quarter of an
hour.' At Giles's, he found the Whigs certain that the king had
been dead about a week, so they went on 'to the release of their
friends on the gallies, and to their own reestablishment; but
finding they could not agree among themselves, I proceeded
on my intended progress'. Next, at Jenny Man's, an alert
young fellow who had just gone in before him, accosted a
friend: 'Well, Jack, the old Prig is dead at last. Sharp's the
word. Now or never, boy. Up to the walls of Paris directly.'
With several other deep reflections of the same kind.

Nothing much new came up in the coffee houses between
Charing Cross and Covent Garden. At Will's the wits had
passed on to a discussion of poets, regretting that Boileau,
Racine, Corneille were dead and could not write the king's
elegies. At a house near the Temple the argument raged on who
would succeed to the Spanish monarchy. In St Paul's churchyard a learned man was giving an account of the deplorable
state of France during the dead king's minority. In Fish Street
the chief politician, after smoking a pipe and ruminating,
declared, 'If the King of France is certainly dead, we shall have
plenty of mackerell this season; our fishery will not be disturbed
by privateers, as it has been for these ten years past.' Later he
considered how the event would affect pilchards and infused a
general joy into his whole audience.

Finally in an obscure coffee house at the end of a narrow
lane a dissenter was arguing with a lace-maker who was the
main supporter of a neighbouring conventicle, whether the
dead king had been more like Augustus Caesar or Nero. To

escape being drawn into the dispute the investigator hurried off to a coffee house in Cheapside where a man was expressing great grief at the news, not 'from the loss of the monarch, but for his having sold out of the bank about three days before he heard the news'. Then a haberdasher, the place's Oracle, called several persons to witness that he had been confident of the king's death more than a week before. But as he was talking, in came a man from Garraway's, who said that letters had just come in from France with an account of the king's good health and of his riding-out on a hunt. The haberdasher took his hat from its wooden peg and stole out.

Steele describes the different types who dominated at different times of the day. 'I, who am at the coffee-house at six in a morning, know that my friend Beaver the haberdasher has a levy' at that hour. 'Every man has, perhaps, a newspaper in his hand; but none can pretend to guess what step will be taken in any one court of Europe, till Mr Beaver has thrown down his pipe, and declared what measures the Allies must enter into upon this new posture of affairs.' At half past eight, the students from the near Inns came in. Some were dressed ready for Westminster, others 'in their nightgowns to saunter away their time'. Then in turn they gave way to men 'who have business or good sense in their faces, and come to the coffee-house either to transact affairs or enjoy conversation'. Steele liked best those in whose faces you could see that 'they are at home, and in quiet possession of the present instant, as it passes, without designing to quicken it by gratifying any passions, or prosecuting any new design. These are the men formed for society, and those little communities which we express by the word *Neighbourhoods*.'

Steele describes also the correct posture of the listener in a coffee house. It consisted 'in leaning over a table, with the edge of it pressing hard upon your stomach; for the more pain the narration is received with, the more gracious is your bending over: besides that the narrator thinks you forget your pain by the pleasure of hearing him'. He also defines the various kinds of coffee house liars, including the Embellishers and the mere Reciters. He once knew a young fellow 'who used to divert himself by telling a lie at Charing-Cross in the morning

at eight of the clock, and then following it through all parts of
the town till eight at night; at which time he came to a club
of his friends, and diverted them with an account what censure
it had at Will's, how dangerous it was believed to be at Child's,
and what inference they drew from it with relation to stocks at
Jonathan's. I have had the honour to travel with this gentleman in search of one of his falsehoods; and have been present
when they have described the very man they have spoken to, as
him who first reported it, tall or short, black or fair, a gentleman or a raggamuffin, according as they liked the intelligence.'

Steele also describes a young fellow in a coffee house near
the Temple, 'who constantly sings a Voluntary in spite of the
whole company', and has even 'danced up to the glass in the
middle of the room, and practised minuet-steps to his own
humming'.

> Moreover, in the open coffee-house, with one hand
> extended as leading a lady in it, he has danced both French
> and country-dances, and admonished his supposed
> partner by smiles and nods to hold up her head, and fall
> back, according to the respective facings and evolutions of
> the dance. Before this gentleman began this his exercise, he
> was pleased to clear his throat by coughing and spitting a
> full half hour; and as soon as he struck up, he appealed
> to an attorney's clerk in the room, whether he hit as he
> ought *Since you from Death have saved me*? and then asked
> the young fellow (pointing to a cháncery-bill under his
> arm) whether that was an opera-score he carried or not?

Houses frequented by the law students were Squire's, by Gray's
Inn, a roomy red-bricked place by the gate of the Inn, in
Fullwood's Rents, Holborn, then leading to Gray's Inn Walks,
which lay open to the country (Squire died in 1717); Serle's
at the corner of Serle and Portugal Streets; the Rainbow near
the Inner Temple Gate. Budgell, describing the Inns of Court
as nurseries of statesmen and lawgivers, tells of an argument
among the students in a coffee house (October 1711). 'The
management of the late Ministry was attacked and defended
with great vigour; and several preliminaries to the peace were

proposed by some, and rejected by others; the demolishing of Dunkirk was so eagerly insisted on, and so warmly controverted, as had like to have produced a challenge.' So he sets down some rules for controversy; coolness and modesty, lack of dogmatism, control of temper. 'Sometimes to keep your self cool, it may be of service to ask your self fairly, What might have been your opinion, had you all the biasses of education and interest your adversary may possibly have?' This idea of objectivity, taking into consideration both social conditioning and class-interest, shows a new kind of social consciousness.[8]

Ned Ward depicts another of the coffee houses in the Temple area, Nando's, above the Rainbow near the west corner of Inner Temple Lane. He finds the company grave and taciturn, smoking hard, so that he feels 'something extraordinary in 'em, or else that they were a parcel of cunning fools'. However, in comes an old newshound, who asks if any straggling news has turned up. A jolly red-faced toper bursts out in praise of steps being taken in the City against dissenters. At that everyone starts talking 'like a pack of true beagles at full cry, to hunt down the Church's enemies with all imaginable speed'. At a coffee house in Aldergate Street, frequented by physicians, on the contrary all the talk is in praise of the Dutch Republic and the Cromwellian Commonwealth, and against the present state of things 'so much boasted of by the blind lovers of kingly power and episcopacy'.

Auctions, now common, were usually held in a coffee house or at the house of a dead man whose property was being sold. The first regular auction-room was established in 1690 in Covent Garden by Edward Millington; the sales were in winter, at 4 pm, to suit men of fashion who dined at 3. (In the spring auctions were held at Tunbridge Wells.) In 1720 Cock appeared on the scene and soon opened his sales-room under the Great Piazza. At Lloyd's Coffee House was started the custom of selling goods by 'inch of candle'. That is, the last offer before the inch was burned out won the article. Lloyd in 1696 published a newspaper for his patrons, thrice a week, with shipping news of the ports at home and abroad. After six months the government suppressed the paper, but Lloyd followed it up with a news-letter that gave shipping and trading intelligence and was passed from hand to hand or read out from what was called a pulpit. The coffee house became the centre for all kinds of maritime business. In 1726 Lloyd's *List* began to appear, giving the rates of the London Exchange on foreign markets, current prices of stocks and funds, a tide-table, news of the arrival, sailing, or accidents of ships foreign or domestic, and so on. Underwriters made much use of several coffee houses, Hains's, Garraway's, Thomas Good's as well as Lloyd's.[9]

There were drunken brawls in coffee houses as elsewhere, as when the poet Savage and two friends had been drinking late and wandered into such a house. They tried to get beds there, but the beds were all filled. They went 'to ramble about the streets, and divert themselves with such amusements as should offer themselves till morning'; but seeing a light in Robinson's Coffee House near Charing Cross, they went in. There they got into a dispute with some men who were leaving and in a sort of drunken daze Savage killed one of them.

Among the many clubs was the Tory October Club, where, says Swift, 'a set of above a hundred Parliament men of the country, who drink October beer at home, meet every evening to consult affairs, and drive things on to extremes against the Whigs, to call the old Ministry to account, and get off five or six heads'. Under Anne it was mainly concerned with composing satires and lampoons as well as drinking. The Mug-House Club was in Long Acre, where, on Wednesdays, 'a mixture of gentlemen, lawyers, and tradesmen meet in a great room. A grave old gentleman, in his grey hair, and nearly ninety years of age, is the president, and sits in an armed chair some steps higher than the rest. A harp plays all the while at the lower end of the room, and now and then some one of the company rises and entertains the rest with a song (and, by-the-by, some are good masters). Here is nothing drunk but ale, and every gentleman chalks on the table as it is brought in; every one also, as in coffee-houses, retires when he pleases.'

The Scribblers' Club had members like Gay, Parnell, Swift. Will's, we saw, was also a literary club, and Ward, going in, 'shuffled through the moving crowd of philosophical mutes, to the upper end of the room, where three or four wits of the upper classes were rendezvoused at a table, and were disturbing the ashes of the old poets by perverting their sense, and making strange allegories and allusions never dreamt or thought of by the authors'. The Beef-Steak Club met in a tavern of the Old Jewry, under the cheery actor Dick Estcourt; it had a grid-iron for badge. 'Our modern celebrated Clubs', said Addison, 'are founded upon eating and drinking.' He notes: 'We take all occasions and pretences of forming ourselves into those little Nocturnal Assemblies, which are commonly known as Clubs. When a set of men find themselves agree in any particular, tho' never so trivial, they establish themselves into a kind of Fraternity, and meet once or twice a week, upon the account of such a fantastick resemblance. I know a considerable market-town, in which there was a Club of Fat-Men.' Those who could enter the large club-room by the ordinary door were disqualified; only those who needed the pair of folding-doors were admitted. In opposition there sprang up a society of Scare-Crows and Skeletons. In several parts of London there were now Street-Clubs. Lady Mary Wortley Montagu tells us of the Schemers, a club or 'committee of gallantry' who in 1724 met three times a week 'to consult on gallant schemes for the advantage and advancement of that branch of happiness'.

Servants at times imitated their masters. The footmen whose masters were Members of Parliament formed themselves into a club where they debated the same matters as those coming up in the House. Swift, in November 1710, after mentioning the election of the Speaker in the Commons, switches mockingly to the footmen. 'Pompey, colonel Hill's black, designs to stand speaker for the footmen. I am engaged to use my interest for him, and have spoken to Patrick [his own man] to get him some votes.' Pompey, the black servant of the brother of Lady Masham, the Queen's favourite, stood for the court and Tory interest. On 19 December 1711 Swift writes, 'Patrick is gone to the burial of an Irish footman, who was Dr King's servant; he died of consumption, a fit death for a poor starving wit's footman. The Irish servants always club to bury a country-man.' [10]

Ned Ward took us across the night of London. Tom Brown describes a journey across its day. London is a world in itself, he says, and we daily discover new countries in it. Cities before had had their differing quarters and groups; now suddenly the complexity has grown to the point of intersecting unknown dimensions. 'Some carry, others are carried.' A gouty chairman shouts, 'Make way there!' carrying a whore of quality to a morning's exercise with a baby-beau newly launched out of a chocolate house, with his pockets as empty as his brains. 'Make room there!' cries a man with a wheelbarrow of nuts. One man draws, another drives. 'Stand up there, you blind dog!' shouts a carman. 'Will you have the cart squeeze your guts out?' One tinker knocks, another bawls, 'Have you brass-pot, iron-pot, kettle, skillet or frying-pan to mend?' A fishman yells yet louder, 'Two a groat and four for sixpence, mackerel!' and another howls, 'Buy my flounders!' A sooty chimney-sweeper takes the wall of a grave alderman, a broom-man jostles the parson of the parish. A fat greasy porter runs a trunk bang against you, while another comes up with eggs and butter. A bully, with a sword two yards long jarring at his heels, warns the latter, 'Turn out there, you country-putt!' and throws him into the gutter. Next comes a christening-party, with the mid-wife strutting in front, and behind them a vendor, 'Kitchen-stuff ha' you, maids!' with a trumpeter summoning people to see a calf with six legs and a topknot. Over the way is a funeral with the men of rosemary at its rear, licking their lips after the wine they've drunk at the house of mourning, the big bluff sexton leading the party, while a poet scampers off to escape the bailiffs.

Thus Tom Brown conjured up the hurlyburly of the streets. He and his friend moved on through 'a hurry of objects': parsons, lawyers, apothecaries, projectors, excisemen, organists, picture-sellers, fiddlers. They listened awhile to three old fellows who always sit on the same bench by a fire. One asserted his claim to be the most abstemious man in the world. The man in the middle, having nothing inside, emitted nothing and remained a humble auditor. The third man, with an odd hat buttoned behind, held opinions 'contrary to the rest of the world; and he was grown so scabbed with the itch of disputing that for the sake of shewing his parts the worst of persuasions were as orthodox with him as the best. Sometimes he argued on the side of Popery because it tolerated pictures; another time Geneva was a blessed place on account of its inhabitants not regarding 'em, whence he deduced this lucky inference, that a man who sold 'em again might buy 'em cheap there. Whatever the doctrine was, interest was the application.'

They decided to go on via the Exchange. Evading the brawling fishwomen and those selling puddings and pies on Fleet Bridge, they skirted the prison and found themselves in the midst of St Paul's as it was being rebuilt, amazed at 'the multitude of workmen, the bulk of the stones, and the prodigious circumference of the pillars', but not impressed by the service going on under the dome with a roaring preacher and a subdean chanting in a deep voice. They moved on down Cheapside, and watched the booksellers in the churchyard. One, who has done well with the clergy, walked about restlessly, dressed like a parish-clerk; another sat behind his counter amid 'reams of divinity waste-paper', waiting for some clergyman to drink with; a third was angrily working out how much he lost on the last issue of *Dampier's Voyages*. Here too all was 'self-interest, which is accounted the *summum bonum*'.

In Cheapside the tradesmen stood at their doors 'to be taken notice of'. At the conduit were the chimney-sweepers. On the way to Woodstreet Tom saw a linen-draper friend at his shop-door, and thought of getting some shirts and handkerchiefs, but veered off on noting the sign: 'No trust upon retail'. Near the Woodstreet corner he crossed the street to avoid officers at the prison-gates, man-eaters, who were no company for poets. His friend had a vision of London as a vast animal. 'The streets are so many veins, wherein the people circulate. With what hurry and swiftness is the circulation of London performed.' (The image is drawn from Harvey's work on the heart now become general property, and gains its force from the growing movement of money and goods.) Tom replied: 'You behold the circulation that is made in the heart of London, but it moves more briskly in the blood of the citizens; they are always in motion and activity. Their actions succeed one another with so much rapidity that they begin a thousand things before they have finished one, and finish a thousand others before they may properly be said to have begun them. All their study and labour is either about profit or pleasure.' They are trained in the Mystery of Trade. Some call it 'overwitting those they deal with', but others deny the definition, 'for wit was never counted a London commodity unless among their wives and other city-sinners'. Some derive the term *trade* from the Hebrew and call it Over-reaching, but Jews say the name and thing is wholly Christian and cite the case of the alderman who sold a Jew five sets of right-handed gloves, then sold him the left-handed ones at double value. Others call trade Honest Gain and Godliness. But the best definition, said Tom, was drawn from dicing: Trade was the art of 'dropping fools' pence into knaves' pockets, till the sellers were rich and the buyers were bankrupt'.

At last they reach the Exchange, a magnificent building, which about noon buzzed with news and queries. 'What news from Scanderoon and Aleppo?' asks the Turkey merchant. 'What price bear currants at Zante? apes at Tunis? religion at Rome? cutting a throat at Naples? whores at Venice? and the cure of a clap at Padua?' 'What news of such a ship?' asks the insurer. 'Is there any hopes of her being cast away?' asks the adventurer, 'for I have insured more by a thousand pounds than I have in her?' Someone appeals to a broker: 'I have a parcel of excellent logwood, block-tin, spiders' brains, philo-sophers' guts, Don Quixote's windmills, hens' teeth, ell-broad packthread, and the quintessence of the blue of plums.' A sergeant stalks by with his mace, smelling the merchants' back-sides like a hungry dog. Nearby is a public notary tied to an inkhorn to deal with bills of store and charters.

Besides the chaffering in wares there is a market in posts and places. Bribery goes on fast. Among the items sold are 'justice for fat capons, to be delivered before dinner, a reprieve from the whipping-post for a dozen bottles of claret; licences to sell ale for a hogshead of stout to his worship; and leave to keep a coffee-house for a cask of cold tea to his lady. Name what you want, and I'll direct you to the walks where you shall find the merchants that will furnish you. Would you buy the Common Hunt, the Common Crier's, the Bridge-master's, or the Keeper of Newgate's places: Stay till they fall, and a gold chain and great horse will direct you to the proprietors.' But you can also buy articles such as comb-brushes, tweezers, cringes or compliments in the French Walk; old clocks, plain shoes and formal gravity in the Spanish. Further, there are advertisements:

Why first here is a ship to be sold, with all her tackle and lading. There are virtuous maidens that are willing to be transported with William Penn into Maryland, for the propagation of Quakerism. In another is a tutor to be hired, to instruct any gentleman's or merchant's children in their own families; and under that an advertisement for a milch-cow, to be sold at the nightman's in White-chapel. In another column in a gilded frame was a chambermaid that wanted a service; and over her an old bachelor that wanted a housekeeper. On the sides of these were two less papers. Some concerning an advertisement of a redheaded monkey lost from a seedshop in the Strand, with two guineas reward to him or her that shall bring him home again with his tail and collar on. On the other side was a large folio filled with wet and dry nurses; and houses to be let; and parrots, canary-birds, and setting-dogs to be sold.

After the Great Fire the Exchange had been fitted out with rows of shops, each with its own sign.

The wanderers next went to see Bedlam, after which they drifted into a Cripplegate church where the parson, once a non-juror, is perched in the pulpit, with a Bible in his pocket, 'spreading his word very dexterously'. Then they passed through Barbican and Long-lane, where they were scared by a rag-seller who grabbed Tom's arm to ask him what he lacked. 'At first it made me tremble worse than a Quaker in a fit of enthusiasm, imagining it to be an arrest, and I was just asking the customary question, 'At whose suit?' But their rudeness, continuing at every door, relieved me from these pannicked fears.' He pushed the next assailant into the gutter, saying, 'I want nothing out of your shops. Methinks you all want good manners and civility, that are ready to tear a new suit from my back under pretence of selling me a new one.'

They passed through Smithfield, where things were quiet as it was not one of the main market days and Bartholomew Fair was not on. Next came the quarters of the jockeys and the graziers; and walking through Baldwin's Gardens they struck an old acquaintance at the Hole in the Wall. He had taken over the place, so they sat down to a tankard with him. But there was 'such a jargon of contradictions' among the company, 'such a difference of trade and opinions', that they went off while a bookbinder was talking of the adventures he had had with two or three more gentlemen, and made their way through Gray's Inn.(11)

Tours of London were indeed now a popular diversion. Swift noted on 13 December 1710: 'Lady Kerry, Mrs Pratt, Mrs Cadogan, and I, in one coach; Lady Kerry's son and his governor, and two gentlemen, in another; maids and misses, and little master (Lord Shelburne's children) in a third, all hackneys; set out at ten o'clock this morning from Lord Shelburne's house in Piccadilly to the Tower, and saw all the sights, lions, &c; then to Bedlam; then dined at the chophouse behind the Exchange; then to Gresham College (but the keeper was not at home), and concluded the night at the puppet-show, whence we came home safe at night, and I left them.'

As part of the attempt to order things under William, the Common Council in 1695 enacted that 'No person should presume to sell any goods or merchandise, in any street, lane, passage, tavern, inn, ale-house, or other public place within the city or the liberties thereof, other than in open market and fairs, upon the penalty of forty shillings for every such offence.' Any citizen buying from such unauthorised persons was liable to the same fine. At the same time a tax was imposed on pedlars, who were reduced to selling one thing and one only, though shopkeepers had begun to mix up various companies and crafts on the same counter. More, the Council laid down that the markets were not to be used for selling goods obtainable from the shops or warehouses of Freemen of the City; and the prohibition carried on till the nineteenth century. Previously the streets had been thronged by men and women with baskets, carts, barrows, trays, boxes, all yelling their wares. In the country, however, the pedlar continued to carry round in villages and farms the various things in demand for which there were no shops.

As part of the new development wholesalers were ready to

supply retailers on credit. William Stout, who went from Lancaster to London in 1687, found it easy to get goods for his first stock (cheese, soap, ginger, cutlery, copperas for dyeing, sugar, dried fruit, tobacco, brandy, hardware, nails) to the value of £200 and had to pay only half in ready cash 'as was then usual to do by any young man beginning trade'. A carry-over from the old days was the custom of haggling over prices, which Stout as a Quaker disliked. He usually 'set the price at one word, which seemed offensive to many who think they never buy cheap except they get abatement from the first price set upon them'. Haggling indeed was for some time stimulated by the state of the wholesale market, no one seller or buyer knowing the appropriate price at a given time. As the market expanded, price-lists appeared and newspaper advertisements enabled more people to know what the wholesalers were charging; retailers became content to get a fixed percentage of profit on their outlay. (Price-tickets were becoming common by the end of the century.)

Another aspect of the clean-up, which sought to channel the profits of trade into the purses of respectable tradesmen, was the development of the shop proper as distinct from the work-shop where a craftsman sold the things he made. Street-criers had been common from Tudor times. Shops then seem to have been open rooms on the ground floor, with wide windows and at times with projecting and movable stalls. About 1600 the stalls became roofed sheds, and soon they turned into enclosed stalls or shops, with a shutter on the lower part. Tobacconists were particularly common. Barnaby Rich estimated that there were 7000 of them in London, and tobacco was also sold by apothecaries. The Great Fire broke up the old system and dispersed the shops. New streets became shopping districts, and suburban shops also appeared. By the turn of the century specialisation was growing common. A foreigner in 1715 described the mercers' shops as 'perfect gilded theatres' and the mercers as 'the sweetest, fairest, nicest, dished-out creatures' with 'elegant address and soft speeches'. Ushers, 'completely dressed at the door, bowed to all coaches that passed, and handed the ladies out or in'. The visitor pronounced the mercers 'the greatest fops in the kingdom'.

How recent this sort of thing was is brought out by the surprised distrust of Defoe at what seemed to him an expression of degenerate luxury. The shop with glass windows and goods attractively displayed was so different from warehouses stocked with staple English manufactures (e.g. the cloths and kerseys of the drapers) or from the mere stalls, for instance those kept in Westminster Hall by milliners and sellers of pamphlets. (Tom Brown stresses the odd mixture of milliners and lawyers in the Hall. 'In this shop are sold ribbons, gloves, towers and commodes, by word of mouth; in another shop lands and tenements are disposed of by decree. On your left hand you hear a nimble-tongued painted sempstress, with her charming treble, inviting you to buy some of her knick-knacks; and on your right a deep-mouthed crier, commanding impossibilities, viz. silence to be kept among women and lawyers. What a fantastical jargon does this heap of contrarieties amount to?') Only goldsmiths of the more esteemed trades had had laid-out goods, and those usually their lesser products.

What upset Defoe was that so many 'pastry cooks, coffee houses, periwig makers, cane chair men, looking glass shops, tinkers, china and earthenware men, brandy shops and the like, whose places of trade used to be found only in back streets, lanes and allies and are fittest for such places' were now in prominent streets. 'We find the most noble shops in the city taken up with the valuable utensils of the tea table.' He is outraged at the money spent on such shops: 'two thousand pounds reckoned a small stock in copper pots and lackered kettles, and the very fitting up one of these brasen people's shops [shops of braziers who sold the goods] with fine sashes, etc, costs above £500 sterling, which is more than half the best draper's or mercer's shop in London requires. This certainly shows an increase in our trade, brass locks for our doors, chambers and parlours, brass knockers for our doors and the like, add to the lustre of our shops ... and the same sash works and shop windows, only finer and larger, are now used to range your brass and copper, that the goldsmiths had always to set out their less valuable silver and old plate.' He asks: 'How do pastry cooks and periwig drapers, brandy shops and toy [trinket] shops succeed linen drapers, mercers, upholsterers and the like, a hundred pounds rent a house to set up a brandy shop and afterwards not a hundred pound stock to put into it.' In St Paul's Churchyard the shops of trivial luxuries supplant 'eighteen or nineteen topping drapers'.

'It is a modern custom,' he asseverates, something 'wholly unknown to our ancestors, who yet understood trade in proportion to the trade they carried on, as well as we do, to have tradesmen lay out two-thirds of their fortune in fitting up their shops': that is, 'in painting and gilding, fine shelves, shutters, boxes, glass doors, sashes and the like'. He thinks that future ages will not credit that in 1719 £300 was spent in fitting out a pastry-cook's shop, 'which twenty pounds would effectively furnish at a time'. He describes the windows, tiled walls, sash windows with panes of plate glass (twelve inches by sixteen) instead of lattice windows with diamonds or circles of leaded glass. The walls of the front and back shop are lined with galley tiles, and both shops have large looking-glasses. They are expensively lighted with a big branch candlestick or chandelier as well as great glass lanterns (three large and eight small) and twenty-five wall sconces. The back room has a pair of big silver standing candlesticks. The wares are put on silver salvers, 'with twelve large high stands or rings, whereof three silver, to place small dishes for tarts, jellys, etc, at a feast'. The ceiling is painted; there is gilding on the lanterns and windows, and there is carved work – the whole costing at least £55.[12]

The new and old ways of selling goods were long to be seen side by side. Complaints about streets being blocked by sheds went on; also tradesmen trying to catch something of the new elegance pushed out their bay-windows and made narrow streets yet more difficult. Some shopkeepers had links with the bigger country-towns. Thus, in 1717 Greaves fostered the sale of tameys and prunellas, with various figured and flowered stuffs, from Kidderminster. In the country itself the growth of shops proper was much slower. At times the shops were grouped around or under the church or public buildings.

Women spent much time in the new shops. In March 1712 Addison describes a complaining shop-woman:

I am, dear Sir, one of the top china-women about town;

and though I say it, keep as good things, and receive as fine company as any o' this end of the town, let the other be who she will: In short, I am in a fair way to be easy, were it not for a Club of female rakes, who under pretence of taking their innocent rambles, forsooth, and diverting the spleen, seldom fail to plague me twice or thrice a day to cheapen tea, or buy a screen: *What else should they mean?* as they often repeat it. These rakes are your idle ladies of fashion, who having nothing to do, employ themselves in tumbling over my ware. One of these no-customers (for by the way they seldom or never buy any thing) calls for a set of tea-dishes, another for a basin, a third for my best green-tea, and even to the punch-bowl, there's scarce a piece in my shop but must be displaced, and the whole agreeable architecture disordered ... Well, after all this racket and clutter, this is too dear, that is their aversion; another thing is charming, but not wanted: the ladies are cured of the spleen, but I am not a shilling the better for it.

Gay in a *Town Eclogue* makes his Lydia wonder whether she will dress, go out, and take her usual walk 'throughout each Indian shop, through all the Change'.

The development of the shop made it possible for a woman, if she had enough capital or was helped by friends, to set up on her own as a shopkeeper. Hogarth's two sisters, who never married, did so; and at the end of Defoe's *Captain Singleton*, William gets a letter from his sister in London saying 'that she was left a widow with four children, but kept a little shop in the Minories, by which she made shift to maintain her family; and that she had sent him five pound lest he should want money in a strange country, to bring him home'. The bill was made upon an English merchant in Venice; we see how credit facilities had been extended. (The sister was unaware that William was now very rich.)

3

The Mob

The lighting system that Ned Ward described did not work well. In 1716 the City enacted that householders were to hang out lights in the six winter months on 'dark nights' from 6 to 11 pm during eighteen nights of each moon. But again the system did not work well; and in 1736 an act gave the City power to rate the inhabitants in order to hang out lamps throughout the year. Outside the City the first parish to get a Watching and Lighting Act was Christchurch Spitalfields in 1739, to be followed by several more parishes. In 1745 we find the Westminster Sessions trying to get the system carried out, since 'its due execution would greatly contribute to the preventing of murders, burglaries, street robberies, fires, misdemeanors, and debauchery'.[1]

People, feeling uprooted from old ways that had given a sense of security, and exposed to the play of forces that they could not understand, were liable to erupt in violence whenever the chance offered. In many aspects the slogan under which they acted was irrelevant, since they could see no cause worth their devotion, no way out of the dilemmas pressing in on them. They took up the cry of the moment, felt the satisfaction of a violent release, and then returned to everyday life. The term *mob* now comes up out of the Latin *mobile* (movable, excitable, fickle). The *Oxford English Dictionary* cites *mobile* as used for the crowd in 1678, *mob* as appearing in 1688. The dates are significant. In 1688 the important political changes stirred the people without giving them any clear objectives, any cause to which they could cleave. Samuel Newton records events at Cambridge on 13 and 14 November of that year:

> This night and several nights before there were up in arms a great many in this town some nights two or three hundred (many scholars among them) of the rabble called the Mobile who at first under a pretence to seek for papists and such who favoured them and to ransack their houses for arms, at last came to be very insulting and wherever they pleased to enter men's houses and do them much mischief.
>
> Friday at night between 8 and 9 of the clock it was reported by one Turkington that came from or about Huntingdon that five or six thousand of the Irish lately disbanded had burnt Bedford and cut all their throats there and they were coming on for Cambridge to do the like there, whereupon the whole town and all presently up in arms crying out in the streets *arm arm for the Lord's sake*, and it being a rainy and dark night candles alight were set up in all windows and next the streets, and it was said they were coming in at the castle end, others said they were come in and cutting of throats, so that the scare for the present was very great and dismal, many running and riding out of Town to escape the danger till it was considered how improbable such a thing should be.

Some examples will bring out the unruly conditions over these years. On 3 March 1691, a newsletter states, 'Yesterday two persons of the number of those who assaulted the Earl of Danby, stood in the pillory, but received no affront, by reason of the Press masters, who at the same time pressed sixty young fellows and carried them aboard.' In October 1693, at Nottingham, poor folk seized sacks of wheat from carts of local corn-dealers and sold them at what was judged a fair price. On 10 June 1695, birthday of James Stuart, son of James II, a crowd of Jacobites gathered in a tavern off Drury Lane, where they drank the Prince's health; then they rushed into the street with flags and drums, and insisted on everyone drinking the same toast.

So the people poured out, armed, and attacked the Jacobites. They routed them, took one prisoner, and sacked the tavern. Later in the year, when William was in France, a man rode through the streets, shouting that he was dead. On his return there was a plot to murder him while hunting in Richmond Park; the trained bands were called out. On 4 July 1691 Richard Lapthorne noted, 'Fray between the Alsateans and gentlemen of the Temple. A fight: one of the sheriff's posse killed; several wounded. 70 Alsateans sent to the various prisons.' Alsatia was a part of the Savoy where a writ could not be served; there were several such sanctuaries, and their rights were not abolished till 1697. On 22 August 1691 Lapthorne tells us: 'A grenadier shot in Hyde Park for mutiny. Murders nearly every day. Dr Clench sent for to a patient – strangled in coach.' [2]

In 1710 came the trial of Dr Sacheverell who preached against the 1688 Revolution as a crime and who advocated passive obedience to the Lord's anointed. He attacked dissenters violently as 'vipers in our bosom', 'clamorous, insatiable and Church-devouring malignants', 'miscreants begot in rebellions, born in sedition, and nursed up on faction', threatening the ruin of both Church and State. His sermon had been preached on Guy Fawkes' Day in St Paul's before the city-fathers, a day sacred to the Whigs for its deliverance of England from the curse of Popery; and the court of aldermen laid an explicit ban on its publication. The Doctor published and was prosecuted. The result was rioting in places as far apart as Gainsborough, Wrexham, Barnstaple; in cathedral cities, clothing boroughs, and market-towns such as Oxford, Exeter, Hereford, Frome, Cirencester, Sherborne. When in the summer the Doctor went on a progress, there were fresh outbursts along his route and elsewhere. In the autumn Sacheverell mobs roared around many hustings in the most tumultuous general election of the century. But all these events were mild beside the great uprising in London on the night of 1 March. True, there were only two deaths and some fifty rioters wounded; but this was partly due to the small but capable detachments of troops from three crack guard units which were called out. The militia were summoned only after the situation was well under control. The Riot Act had not yet been passed and soldiers had to be careful or they might be charged with murder.

Many recent events had disturbed the Tories and the landed interest, and had enabled them to agitate effectively against the monied interest. The Whig government was accused of making no effort to end the war of the Spanish succession, which suited the financiers. Among the latter in the City were many of foreign extraction: Spanish Jews, Walloons, Huguenots, Dutchmen – some whose families had settled in England two or three generations back, but many of whom were more recent immigrants. The Bank of England, which symbolised the financial revolution and the rise of war-profiteering, had nearly thirty of these immigrants among its leading stockholders in 1709; and most of such men did not belong to the established church. Moreover, only a few months before the Doctor's sermon the General Naturalisation Act had been strongly opposed by Tories and High Church clergy; and some ten thousand refugees from the Palatinate had arrived at the government's invitation and been temporarily settled for the most part in the London area. About four-fifths of the parish-clergy in the land were sure that the Whigs would sell out to dissenters and latitude-men, if not to the foes of Christianity itself. They closed ranks. The London clergy were the most active, providing the Doctor with a blackgowned bodyguard, a hundred or more strong, for all his public appearances.

After two days of simmering discontent the London mob burst out in March. One of the main targets was the rich Presbyterian meeting house south of Lincoln's Inn Fields, which had opened in 1705. The Clerkenwell rioters burned a chapel's fittings and were about to scale the garden walls of a rich Presbyterian merchant when they were interrupted. In Blackfriars the mob meant, after dealing with a meeting house, to burn down the Bank of England in Grocer's Hall. Papers found on rioters bore the slogan: 'Down with the Bank of England and the Meeting-Houses; and God damn the Presbyterians and all that support them.'

The London Tories had clearly organised the outburst with greatest care. The chapels were not burned but had their fittings stripped and carried some distance into the open so that fires would not spread. From the outset the rioters appeared equipped with the tools they needed to deal with pews, floorboards, doors, gallery rails, casement, wainscoting, pulpits, candle branches and clocks. There was a sprinkling of gentlemen among them, but the main body seems composed of small masters, craftsmen, self-employed artisans, tradesmen. Two lawyers and a physician were among those arrested. On the other hand workers in industry do not seem to have joined in; the Spitalfields weavers, on the contrary, are said to have been ready to march against the mob.

The last years of Anne's reign were full of rumours and alarms of plots. The most frightening tales were those of disaffected persons calling themselves Mohocks or Hawkabites, who scoured the streets at night and attacked anyone they encountered. Citizens were afraid to go out after dark, and a reward of a hundred pounds was offered for the conviction of any member of the group. But no one was caught. There were also stories of Whipping Tom who haunted the fields round London and flogged women. It is instructive to follow the way in which the accounts of the Mohocks multiplied. The immediate panicked belief in their deeds testifies to the deep fears stirred in men's minds by a society that was growing in ways they could not understand or control.

In March 1712 Steele published a letter telling of the Mohock Club, who drank themselves into a frenzy, then assaulted people. 'Some are celebrated for a happy dexterity in tipping-the-lion upon them [the victims]: which is performed by squeezing the nose flat to the face, and boring out the eyes with their fingers. Others are called the dancing-masters, and teach their scholars to cut capers by running swords through their legs.' A third set are the Tumblers, 'whose office it is to set women on their heads, and commit certain indecencies, or rather barbarities, on the limbs which they expose'. They should all 'be taught to take warning from the Club of Duellists; and be put in mind, that the common fate of these men of honour was to be hanged'. (Steele is thinking of events like those recorded by Lapthorne on 18 August 1691: 'The Lord of Banbury fought with his brother-in-law, Capt. Laurie, and killed him. Young, clerk, fought Graham, clerk, and killed him. Lord Mohun killed Montfort the player. Reprieves used to be sent after the prisoners on their way to Tyburn. They were brought back on the Sheriff's horse, yet after all executed.')

On 8 April Budgell in the *Spectator* wondered if the Mohocks ever existed. 'The terror which spread itself over the whole nation some years since, on account of the Irish, is still fresh in most people's memories, tho' it afterwards appeared there was not the least ground for that general consternation.' Perhaps, he says, the Mohocks were like those spectres that frightened several towns and villages, though never seen by anyone; or they may have been 'a kind of Bull-Beggars, first invented by prudent married men, and masters of families, in order to deter their wives and daughters from taking air at unseasonable hours' – just as parents used 'to bid their children have a care of Raw-head and Bloody-bones'. (Shadwell wrote a play on the Scowrers, who specialised in window-breaking. He represented a Rake as very much surprised to hear someone saying that the breaking of windows was not humour.)

Swift carries on the tale. On 10 February 1712 he had written: 'Here are a parcel of drunken Whiggish Lords, like your Lord Santry, who come into chocolate-houses, and rail aloud at the Tories, and have challenges sent them, and the next morning come and beg pardon. General Ross was like to swinge the Marquis of Winchester for this trick the other day.' But on 8 March he is serious. 'Did I tell you of a race of rakes, called the Mohocks, that play the devil about this town every night, slit people's noses and bid them &c.' Next day he writes: 'Young Davenant was telling us at court how he was set upon by the Mohocks, and how they run his chair through with a sword. It is not safe being in the streets at night for them. The bishop of Salisbury's son is said to be of the gang. They are all Whigs.' Later, in his *History of the Four Last Years of Queen Anne*, he states as a fact that Mohocks were part of an extensive political plan to create riot and confusion at night, during which Lord Oxford might be assassinated. He ascribed the plot to Prince Eugene. Yet on 12 March 1712 he wrote to Stella: 'Grubstreet papers about them [Mohocks] fly like lightning,

and a list of near eighty put into several prisons, and all a lie;
and I begin almost to think there is no truth, or very little, in
the whole story.' However, his servant told him that 'one of
the lodgers heard in a coffee-house, publicly, that one design
of the Mohocks was upon me, if they could catch me; and
though I believe nothing of it, I forbear walking late'. On the
18th a proclamation was issued against them.[3]

Because Dr Radcliffe did not attend Queen Anne on her
deathbed, he was accused of disloyalty or even of causing her
death and a letter from a friend on 2 August 1714 states: 'I
presume that by tomorrow they will find other themes to talk
of but today the mob as well as quality have expressed so much
resentment that if your new house had stood at London or
Kensington they would scarce be restrained from pulling it
down.' An anonymous letter warned him that if he went to
'meet the Gentleman you have appointed to dine with, at the
Greyhound in Croydon, on Thursday, you will be most certainly murthered. I am one of the persons engaged in the
conspiracy with twelve more, who are resolved to sacrifice
you to the Ghost of her late Majesty, that cried aloud for your
Blood,' signed N.G. 'I am touched with remorse, and give
you this notice, but take care of yourself, lest I repent of
it.'

In 1715 the Riot Act was issued, with more precise definition of riotous behaviour. In 1719, a time of depression, there
were London riots, led by weavers, against wearers of printed
calicos. The early 1720s saw the Waltham Blacks, whose violent
protests and depredations swept over a wide area of Berkshire
and Hampshire. The Black Act of the Whigs in 1723 imposed
the death penalty for almost every conceivable form of rural
crime against property. The Blacks, rebels who often blackened
their faces, resisted; and in the Waltham area were directed
by a sort of Robin Hood called King John. In 1723 Habeas
Corpus was suspended and many suspected traitors arrested.
The government was active in pressing the authorities to take
steps 'to suppress all riotous assemblies' within their jurisdic-
tions, as was reported in May 1722. That year Secretary
Townshend wrote often to urge magistrates to act in specific
cases. Hearing of a riot in Hyde Park, he told the chairman

of the Westminster Sessions to go and read the Riot Act. When, in a riot at Greenwich over the election of a churchwarden, a man was arrested for failing to leave the scene as soon as the Act was read, Townshend ordered the Treasury to pay the cost: 'His Majesty finding it necessary for the preservation of public peace that some example be made.' A justice reported that he would 'take care of our next licensing not to license Papists, non jurors or any disaffected persons', so the Ministers need have 'no apprehension of danger from these quarters'.

In the 1730s there were riots against the Gin Act; in July 1736 in Spitalfields against Irish weavers said to be working 'at an under rate'. Sir Robert Walpole wrote that the trouble lay in the increased number of Irish come for hay and corn harvest, who also worked cheaply for weavers. More, they worked for a third less per day than the English at building a new church. Another account says Irish weavers offered to work at half the wages as bricklayers' labourers. There were pitched battles for two days, and the English wrecked two Irish public houses. The Riot Act was read with no effect; the Tower Hamlets militia was called out, but it took companies of Guards from the Tower to disperse the mob. A few days later the 'mob arose in Southwark, Lambeth and Tyburn Road and took upon them to interrogate people whether they were English or Irish, but committed no violence'. The conflicts of English and Irish went on well into the next century.[4]

In 1730 Gonsalez, probably an English writer pretending to be Portuguese, wrote of the common folk that in London and other big commercial areas they were well dressed on Sundays and holidays, 'and in their own phrase, look upon themselves to be as good as the best, that is, deserve to be treated with respect' – though cottagers were so dependent on the gentry and the farmers that they paid 'their masters the respect that is due to them'. Collective bargaining by riot had begun and was to be carried on into the next century. Clothiers of the West of England complained to Parliament in 1718 and 1724 that the weavers 'threatened to pull down their houses and burn their work unless they would agree to their terms'. In 1726–7 there were disputes in Devon, Somerset, Wiltshire, and Gloucester-

shire, during which we find weavers 'breaking into the houses'
of masters and black-legs, spoiling wool, cutting and destroying the pieces on the looms and the tools of the trade. In 1738
there were great textile riots at Melksham.

The period saw a large-scale increase in crime and its applications, with London as main breeding-ground. The spread of
thievery and robbery among the populace was matched by the
vast spread of bribery and corruption in the upper levels of
society made possible by the steady expansion of the administra-
tive system. Thieves were liable to cut open stealthily the back
of a hackney as it drove along at night, and make a sudden
grab at the wig or the head-gear of the occupants. Persons
obliged to walk in the streets at night carried a lantern, but
the thieves were adept at leaping out, snatching the lantern,
and knocking down the carrier. Both the town and suburbs
were infested with thieves, pickpockets, and highwaymen.
Fielding says that Constables often ignored a well-known
robber, afraid that at his signal 'twenty or thirty armed
villains' would rush to his aid. A new aspect was the development of well-organised crime; the racket accompanied the rise
of large-scale business, just as gambling, with its forms from
dice-throwing to public lotteries expanded with the new forms
of speculation. Hence too the growth of literature dealing with
crime in a much more specific sense than the old sort of low-
life narratives. Here Defoe is the great innovator, followed by
works like Fielding's *Jonathan Wild*.

The thieves took advantage of any tumult or any public event
when crowds gathered. Thus when George I entered London,
for the next week or so papers like the *Post Boy* or the *Daily
Courier* were full of advertisements in which people offered to
pay for the return of stolen goods and to ask no questions.
Among the articles stolen in or round Westminster Abbey
during the coronation were a blue cloth cloak, several watches
and seals, a 'silver-hilted sword, with a black string and
japanned about six or eight inches long on the blade', which
vanished 'on the north side of the choir, east of the organ
loft', a silver snuffbox with an agate lid and a picture and
gilding within, a 'brown wig tied at the bottom'. Thieves even

got away with many items from the Hall, so that for some time the advertisement appeared:

> Whereas, several pieces of plate, as dishes, trencher-plates, knives, forks, spoons, and salts, together with pewter of all sorts, table-linen, and several other necessaries which were provided and used in Westminster Hall at His Majesty's coronation feast on Wednesday the 20th inst, have been feloniously taken away from thence, and are yet concealed, all persons who have any of His Majesty's goods of what sort soever in their custody are hereby required forthwith to bring them to Whitehall, and there give notice of the same at His Majesty's Board of Greencloth, upon pain of being prosecuted ...

A reward was offered, but to no effect. When George went to the Guildhall there was confused violence among the gathered mob, as an advertisement in the *Post Boy* tells:

> A man had the misfortune on Friday, the Lord Mayor's Day, to have a violent fall in the entry of Guildhall at eight o'clock at night, after His Majesty was gone from thence. Several boards were beaten down at the end of the entry, and he lost his hat, with a mourning hat-band upon it, his periwig, and an oaken-stick. Whoever will bring 'em to George Nash, Corn Chandler, in Wood Street, near Cripple-gate, shall receive twenty shillings, or proportionable for either. If they have disposed of the periwig, send him word where, and he will return the money, and give 'em something for their pains; the wig being of his children's hair.

Despite the many violences and losses there was something of an admiring attitude towards the bold criminal, as was shown by the popularity of Gay's *Beggar's Opera*.

A story appeared in the *Weekly Journal* for 27 August 1723, which brings out this ambivalent attitude.

> A highwayman robbed a single gentleman at Newmarket t'other day, and, taking a watch from him that he set an extra value on, he entreated the gentleman that had made

so free with him to let him redeem it at any price he should be pleased to put upon it, and to appoint a time and place for yielding up the ransom and paying the money. 'You are upon honour, I hope,' says the thief. 'Yes, by my soul,' says the gentleman. 'Why, then,' says the robber, 'If you are acquainted with anybody hereabouts, I'll go with you now, and you shall have the watch again for two guineas.' So the gentleman named a house in Newmarket; but the other desired to be excused waiting on him thither, because it lay a little way out of his business. 'Why, then, we'll go to Bourne Bridge,' says the gentleman again. 'With all my heart,' says the other.

So away they rode together, and in their way met a nobleman's coach, with a great retinue, which they passed by without taking any notice, and at length came to the house at Bourne Bridge, where the gentleman borrowed some money, paid down two guineas, and had his watch returned, and, after the drinking of a bottle of wine, with mutual civilities they took leave of each other.[5]

In such a world with its inefficient police system, the treatment of criminals or of unfortunates who had collided with the law was brutal in the extreme. The retort of the government to the spread of crime was to increase the number of offences against property that incurred the death-penalty. There were about fifty such offences in 1688; by 1820 there were some two hundred and fifty. Wesley records that once he preached in a jail to fifty-two felons waiting to be hanged, among them a child of ten. Corpses were left to rot in chains in important city-quarters and along highways. One of the few checks on the barbarity of the law was the fact that juries often preferred to commit perjury than to convict for minor offences.

The procession of doomed men (along what is now Holborn and Oxford Street) to Tyburn drew huge crowds, and better-off citizens paid large sums for good seats or points-of-vantage from which to view the deaths. Foreigners were impressed. Misson says in 1719 that: 'The English are people that laugh at the delicacy of other nations who make it such a mighty matter to be hanged; their extraordinary courage looks upon it as a trifle.' A little later Murault, a Swiss traveller, wrote: 'The criminals pass through the streets in carts, dressed in their best clothes, with white gloves and nosegays, if it be the season. Those that die merrily, or that don't at least show any great fear of death, are said to die like gentlemen; and to merit this encomium, most of them die like beasts, without any concern, or like fools, having no other view than to divert the crowd.' Amid all the uproar and plaudits from the spectators, who waved sticks, hats, clubs, cloaks, kerchiefs, Murault admitted, 'A man cannot well forbear laughing to see these rogues set themselves off as heroes, by an affectation of despising death.' Men and women struggled round the death-carts to grasp the hands of the felons and to praise them; and at times the victims even fought among themselves about the order of precedence of their carts. The drop was not invented till 1760 and the hanged men were slowly strangled by the rope. Relatives often pulled at a man's legs to shorten his agony. Defoe, watching four men on their way to Tyburn amid the rampaging crowd, reflected, 'Many of the rest shall die in torture and terror, ten thousand times more grievous than those four. Nay, perhaps few of the thousands who go to see these four people die shall get so easy a passage out of life.' Gin or Sots' Comfort was sold from barrows, and there were hordes of hawkers, thieves, whores, barking dogs, children looking for a chance to pilfer; drunken brawls went on; women and children were trampled; and speech-vendors sold Ballads or Dying Speeches. 'Here's the right and true last speech and confession, birth, parentage, education, life, character, and behaviour' of the hanged man. Hogarth's harlot has an engraving of a hanged highwayman next to one of Dr Sacheverell as a pin-up in her room.

Till mid-century women were half-strangled and then burned in public for a number of crimes such as arson or husband-murder. Till 1771 prisoners who refused to plead were liable to be pressed to death with iron weights on their chests, though by then the law had not been enforced for some three decades. When in 1783 public hangings were ended, Dr Johnson was infuriated. 'The age is running mad after innovations ...

Tyburn itself is not safe from innovations.' He argued that 'The old method was satisfactory to all parties; the public was gratified by a procession; the criminal was supported by it; why is all this swept away?' Till the fifth decade of the century persons convicted of high treason were cut down from the gallows only half-dead, disembowelled, and their entrails burnt before the shouting mob.

Prisons were foul. A Parliamentary Committee of 1728–9 found that 'gross cruelties' were perpetrated upon debtors, amounting to 'deliberate torture'. Thus, in 1725 the uncle of the composer Thomas Arne, an upholsterer confined to the Fleet for debt, was unable to pay the fees demanded by the warden; he was 'carried into a stable, which stood, where the strong room on the master's side now is, and was there confined (being a place of cold restraint) till he died', though he was previously in good health. In 1728 Robert Castell, a well-known architect and author of *The Villas of the Ancients Illustrated*, was shut up for the same reason in a sponging house by the Fleet, which was raging with smallpox. He told the warden that he had never had the disease and 'that the putting him into a house, where it was, would occasion his death, which, if it happened, before he could settle his affairs, would be a great prejudice to his creditors and would expose his family to destruction'. He duly caught smallpox and died; and it was his death that brought about the parliamentary inquiry. When reputable persons were thus treated we can imagine what were the sufferings of ordinary criminals. The dead bodies of debtors were left to rot until the relatives could pay the rent and fees that were due, 'to the great endangering of the health of the whole prison by the nauseous stench'.[6]

4

Journalism and the New Reading Public

An important factor in helping along and spreading many of the changes now coming over society was the newspaper. News-sheets of one kind or another had a long history, going back to the early years of the seventeenth century; the Civil War gave a strong impetus to the purveyors of news. With the Restoration appeared the *London Gazette* in 1666, a two-page mixture of news, announcements, advertisements; but it was after 1688 that the crucial developments occurred. The first daily paper appeared in London in 1702; the first provincial paper at Norwich in 1706. Despite the stamp tax, levied in 1712 and carried on with alterations for a century and a half, there were printed in London in 1724 three dailies, five weeklies, seven papers coming out thrice a week, three thrice-a-week halfpenny posts – eighteen in all.[1]

The first periodical of literary journalism appeared in 1691, the work of John Dunton; and since it heralded so many important developments in this field, and tells us so much of the way people thought, worried, acted, it is worth some notice. Born in May 1659, 'son, grandson and great-grandson of a clergyman', Dunton fell in love at thirteen and did not become a clergyman; instead he was apprenticed to a bookseller and served his seven years. 'Had I not been overborne with head-strong passions, both to my own ruin and the loss of time, I might have made considerable improvements in so good a family.' He was absorbed in love and politics. Free, he set up 'with half a shop, a warehouse, and a fashionable chamber'.

In 1682 he married the daughter of a clergyman, Samuel
Annesley; Samuel Wesley married another of the girls. After
Monmouth's rebellion Dunton was in a bad way and voyaged
to New England in the hope of disposing of part of his stock
of books there. Back in 1688 he opened a shop at the sign of
the Black Raven in the Poultry, and got the idea of his periodical through being himself plagued with a problem which he
could not solve. He called his paper the *Athenian Gazette*, then
the *Athenian Mercury* in the second issue, no doubt through protests from the *London Gazette*. It was to answer 'all the nice
and curious questions proposed by the ingenious of either sex'.
Running for six years, it dealt with matters of religion, casuistry,
love, literature, manners, science, superstition.[2]

The first issue was on Tuesday 17 March 1691. On 5 May
Dunton announced that he had taken in 'a Civilian, a Doctor
in Physick, and a Chyrurgeon' to help. Persons with queries
were to send them by 'a penny post letter to Mr Smith at his
Coffee-House in Stocks-Market in the Poultry'. Among the
aiders were Richard Sault, a mathematician, who later went to
Cambridge, and Samuel Wesley, who, quarrelling with friends
in his youth, had walked to Oxford and entered himself as a
poor scholar at Exeter College. Sault and Wesley, now a curate
in London, held weekly discussions, guaranteeing Dunton
every Friday night 'two distinct papers', each of which would
make up half a printed sheet; in return they got ten shillings
for each number of the paper. Dunton reserved the right to
edit copy. Elkaniah Settle in his *New Athenian Comedy* depicts
the group. Sault is Joachim Dash, Wesley is Grub, author of
a poem *Maggots*, Dunton is Jack Stuff, while another col-
laborator Dr Norris is Jerry Squire. They meet and discuss
business over a dinner of black puddings. The queries sent
in to the paper are ridiculed in a scene where an under-turnkey
of Newgate brings a prisoner's question: Which is the more
noble animal, a louse or a flea?

The paper caught on. Dunton often had several hundred
letters to consider. Defoe, Motteux, and others wrote odes in
praise of his work; Swift sent in an early ode with a laudatory
letter of which he was later ashamed. At first the paper appeared
on Tuesdays, then on Tuesdays and Saturdays; thirty issues

made a volume; and with each early volume went a supplement containing the 'transactions and experiments of foreign Virtuosos; to which is added an account of the design and scope of most of the considerable books printed in all languages, and of the quality of the others if known'. After the fifth volume the book notices stopped, as there had appeared, edited by J. de la Crosse, a new monthly, *The Works of the Learned; or an Historical Account and Impartial Judgment of Books newly printed, both foreign and domestic; as also the State of Learning in the World.*[3]

The last number of the *Athenian Mercury* appeared on 14 June 1697. A week or two earlier Dunton's first wife had died; he then married Sarah Nicholas of St Albans, who brought him money and a troublesome mother-in-law, and after a while they parted. In 1705 he published *The Life and Errors of John Dunton, late Citizen of London, written in Solitude*; and round this time he took to writing on the Whig side. Notes by Edward Harley, second Earl of Oxford, state that he also wrote an *Essay proving we shall know our friends in Heaven*: 'to the memory of his wife, 8vo., 1698. This Dunton is the author of many libels.' He 'had a gold medal given him of about the value of £30, which he used to wear about his neck; but necessity obliged him to pawn it now and then. He died, as I have been informed, the beginning of 1733.'

In his journal's scientific section he dealt with Harvey's theory of the circulation of the blood and had some knowledge of gravitation. Do fishes breathe? What is the cause of Titillation (tickling)? Where does extinguished fire go? What causes earthquakes? Not so much wind struggling in deep caverns, he thinks, as the fact that the globe 'may be as subject to ruin and decay as the lesser particles of the Creation, and that earthquakes are but the convulsions of nature's frame'. Veins of fire meet deep channels of water, cause strife and motion in the earth's bowels and 'generate air by fumigation and rarefaction of the water'. Where do swallows go in the winter time? He repeats the belief they live in 'ruinous buildings and subterraneous caverns, where the cold makes 'em senseless'; and adds the old tale of a cluster of them found in a pond, but thinks they came from some hollow bank nearby, 'which broke and fell in with 'em'. Here the *Mercury* was ahead of

In the winter of 1683–4 a sharp frost set in; it froze the Thames so strongly that booths were set up along what was called Temple Street (the entry being from the Temple). All sorts of games and sports were carried on: bull-baiting, throwing at cocks, pigeon-holes, nine-pins, as well as sliding and skating; the most spectacular event was the roasting of a whole ox. The whirling sledge and the hutch moved by a stick seem inventions for the occasion.   *Museum of London*

Map showing the area of London that had to be rebuilt after the Great Fire.   *Radio Times Hulton Picture Library*

The Stocks Market, Poultry, and Statue of Charles II: on the site where now Mansion House is built. The Market for fish and vegetables took its name from a pair of Stocks. The Poultry Compter was one of the prisons of the Sheriff of London. Note how the architecture – the façades, the dome, the steeple – of the new London are wholly unmedieval. *British Museum*

The print, called the *Prentice's Boxing Day*, depicts a rowdy Christmas scene in Cheapside, with an orange barrow upset and a beadle trying to restore order. Some well known characters of the time, Captain Flash, Dr Rock, the Duke of Limbs, are included. Dr Rock sold his Anti-Syphilicon, Diuretic Cleansing Elixir, and 'the only Venereal Antidote', from the *Hand and Face* near Blackfriars Stairs. *British Museum*

Marcellus Laroon uses the effects of a High Wind on a Market Scene to depict a topsy-turvy world. In the right hand corner a bending girl has her dress blown right over her head. Hats are blown off, but the three heavy baskets on a porter's head are unaffected. Joints of meat and poultry are hanging in the shops. Note the odd sign of the Monkey and Cock.

Courtauld Institute of Art

When Defoe published his savagely ironical *Shortest Way with the Dissenters*, a warrant was issued for his arrest in January 1703; he went into hiding but in May was found in a French weaver's house. In July he was sentenced to stand three times in the pillory, pay a fine of 200 marks, and lie in prison at the Queen's pleasure. For five months he was held in Newgate. But when he was set in the pillory, the people, instead of pelting him with the usual rotten eggs, cheered him, drank his health, and set a guard round him, while girls hung the pillory with flowers. What had been meant as his disgrace became his triumph.

The Mansell Collection

Marcellus Laron, son of a Frenchman settled in The Hague, moved to England and worked in a Dutch style. (His son's name is generally spelt Laroon to distinguish him.) Laron's *Cryes of the City of London* depicted over seventy of the types to be seen in the streets, most of them crying their wares. They were 'drawne after the Life'. The woman selling the *Gazette* shows how newspapers were reaching a wide audience. (A)   *British Library*

The Mountebank was common in the streets and one of the most colourful of the shouters seeking to attract attention. Quacks, like astrologers, especially frequented Moorfields, selling, says Ned Ward, 'Nectar and Ambrosia, May Dew, Golden Elixirs, Popular Pills, Liquid Snuff, Beautifying Waters, Dentifrices, Drops, Lozenges, all as infallible as the Pope'. (B)   *British Library*

Laron's non-conformist Minister is discreetly clad in black, but cannot resist dandifying himself with laces. (C)   *British Library*

Laron's Salesman has a tray of assorted wares; he is one of the superior huxters. (D)   *British Library*

Hogarth's print shows a street, apparently Hog Lane, with the church of
St-Giles-in-the-Fields at the back, the clock marking half past twelve. Two
taverns on the left face a chapel used by French refugees in Soho, who now
emerge in modish finery. Opposite the fop in the front is a black man kissing
a plump girl with a pie-dish. Here everything symbolises 'Good Eating',
even the Baptist's head on a platter.   *British Museum*

Lady Mary Wortley Montagu is dressed in the Turkish clothes that caused a sensation after her return from the east. The neglected daughter of Lord Kingston, she educated herself eruditely in the family library; then eloped with Wortley Montagu who had common literary tastes. Four years later, in 1716, he became ambassador to the Grand Seigneur of Turkey; Lady Mary, with her inquisitive intelligence, described what she saw in her travel-letters.

Laroon produced several drawings and paintings of fashionable music parties. This one with the flautist and cello-player is dated 1735; as usual the conversationalists take little notice of the music, even when right up against the players.

Courtauld Institute of Art

In the early 1740s Francis Hayman painted a series of pictures (important for the creation of an English school of art) for display at Vauxhall Gardens, a popular place of resort. He depicted a large number of games or amusements. Here two couples play quadrille, with another couple looking on. The table has its corners hollowed to hold money or counters; and a maid and Negro boy are about to serve tea.   *British Museum*

Hayman's *Battledore and Shuttlecock* shows a boy and a girl playing in an upperclass house with ancestral portraits in the style of Van Dyck. A second girl watches, perhaps keeping the score.   *British Museum*

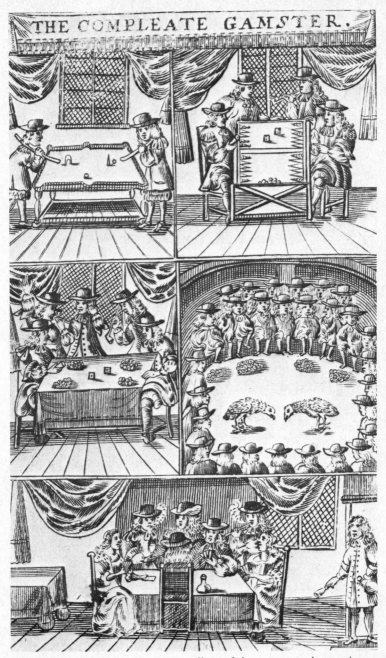

THE COMPLEATE GAMSTER.

'The Complete Gamester': a compendium of the most popular pastimes: billiards, backgammon, dice, bets on cockfights, cards. Only with cards do women as well as men come in. The pipe-smoking and the tapster at the door suggest a tavern or a bawdy-house, so that the women would be whores.

Radio Times Hulton Picture Library

'The Coffeehouse Mob': in the Coffee House a large fire heats the water, while before it stand six coffee-pots of different sizes. The girl at the counter is in charge. In the foreground a boy pours coffee from a pot into a small dish without a handle. The other guests drink from the same sort of dish while one of them, quarrelling over some argument, throws his coffee into his adversary's face. The sheets on the table suggest that the argument has been political, concerned with some news-report.

Radio Times Hulton Picture Library

'A Conversation': Laroon seems to have set his conversation in a brothel. The client and his girl are engrossed in one another while the attendant expertly pours out wine for himself and the bawd.

Reproduced by gracious permission of Her Majesty the Queen

Here at first glance we seem to have a moral print showing how at last the Modish Couple have met in love 'with Mutual Transports' after shaking off Mistress and Pimp. But in fact the print represents the marriage of Frederick Prince of Wales in 1736 to the Princess of Saxe-Gotha. He abandons his mistress, the Hon. Anne Vane, one of the Queen's maids-of-honour, who had borne him a son in 1732. The pimp seems to be Robert Walpole lolling in his seat between Prince and Throne. (The boy died this year and Anne died soon after.)

British Museum

Laroon liked the social contrast of riders and the lowly on the ground. He did several drawings showing riders and beggars, a fruitseller, and so on.
Reproduced by gracious permission of Her Majesty the Queen

'Kentish Election, 1734': the print shows the hustings or temporary stage where candidates stood for nomination and addressed electors. (The term hustings came into use about 1719.) Below, the supporters of the opposing sides shout and demonstrate: 'No Excise'. The labels identify the Country and the Protestant Interest. Walpole's most famous project in taxation aimed at extending the excise. In fact all that his Bill of 1733 attempted to do was to order tobacco (or wine) to be stored in warehouses on the quays, with duty to be paid if it was moved out for sale in England; it went free if re-exported. A furious opposition was worked up with violent large-scale demonstrations; the project was described as a deadly blow at the very root of property and freedom, sure to wreck the whole economic life of England. Walpole dropped the Bill. *Radio Times Hulton Picture Library*

Here we see the Courtyard inside the Royal Exchange with foreign brokers, merchants, and stockjobbers gathered. Ned Ward defined the Jobber: 'He is a compound of knave, fool, shopkeeper, merchant and gentleman. His whole business is tricking.'
British Museum

The fireworks of 1749 aroused little enthusiasm. One print showed 'the Jubilee Ball, or Masquerade, at Ranelagh, by his Majesty's Command, after the Venetian Manner in the Day-time, April 26th, the Day between the Thanksgiving and the Fireworks for the General Peace'. Another print (of 27 April) was entitled: 'The Grand Whim for Posterity to Laugh at: being the night view of the Royal Fireworks, as exhibited in the Green Park, St James's, with the Right Wing on Fire, and the Cutting Away of the two Middle Arches to prevent the whole Fabric from being Destroy'd.' Our print complains that the Dutch concentrate on business, while the English are impoverishing themselves with unnecessary display.
British Museum

The *Bubblers Bubbl'd* (advertised in the *Post-boy* for 21 June 1720) copied a
Dutch print dealing with Law's Mississippi scheme, with English inscriptions.
The building seems meant for the Stock Exchange with the Keeper pointing
to a list of the ridiculous Bubble Companies, while speculators exult or
lament: 'I have got £4,000 out of nothing.' 'A gaol must be my portion.'
'O, I live in hopes.' 'I have lost a thousand pounds this day.'

the times; Dr Johnson still held in 1768 the thesis that swallows wintered under water. The Rev Charles Norton, master of Newington Academy where Defoe went as a boy, wrote a treatise, *Whence come the Stork and the Turtle, the Crane and the Swallow when they Know and Observe the appointed Time of their Coming?* He rejects the pond-idea, as 'when they should awake, it is scarce conceivable how their feathers should be in trim to lift them out of the water', and so he decides that they winter on the moon.

Dunton accepts the existence of Mermen, thinking they were created at the beginning with other fishes, not that they are 'monsters got by unnatural copulation', devils (fallen angels who went into the sea), creatures got by devils on fishes, or the creation by fishes who saw so many drowned persons in the Flood that they 'by strength of imagination got something like 'em'. But he also deals with many subjects more within the scope of science: What is the cause of suction? Whether 'the reverse or recoil of a gun be at the firing in the chamber or before, or at the immediate departure of the fire from the muzzle'? (The questioner here adds: 'Gentlemen, three wagers depend upon this question; therefore the sooner you answer, the sooner we shall drink your health.') Boyle is cited. There are several questions about tobacco, its nature and effects. Two different answers are given about Light: that it is a body and that it is not one.

Questioners about superstitions ask if there is a phoenix, a basilisk, a salamander; they want advice on premonitory dreams, sleepwalking, the hag of nightmare, the omen of death-watches, witches, the fetch-light or deadman's candle. Dunton tries to be rational: 'This deathwatch is but a little worm in the wall.' But at times he falls down. He credits the imps of witches. Religious queries raise such matters as: Whether the substance of this earth shall be destroyed or only refined? Where was the soul of Lazarus for the four days he lay in the grave? Of what form was the serpent? What became of the water after the Flood? Is it probable there will be any sexes in heaven? Readers, worried about love, ask whether, if females went a-courting, there would not be more marriages than now? Whether there is or can be such a thing as Platonic Love? What is love? How far may singing and music be proper in making love? Whether interrupting discourse by repeated kisses is not rude and unmannerly, and more apt to create aversion than love? One casuistical point is whether a condemned man who, when a hangman was lacking, hanged himself to earn the fee for his wife, was guilty of suicide. Cockfighting is lawful. 'It's possible to delight in the valour of the creatures, who are given for our diversion as well as necessity, without being cruelly delighted in their hurting one another.' Poverty is 'but a suggestion of our fancy. Therefore those men are the poorest who think they want most, not those that possess least.'

The need for drink is well brought out by one anxious letter-writer:

> Gentlemen, there is a public house hard by me, which I do generally use every night for an hour or two to pass the time away, which is the last thing as I do; but the inconvenience I find in using this house is no small trouble to me; yet I am so bewitched to this house, that I cannot forbear going to it, though I meet with the greatest inconvenience imaginable; for there I hear a great deal of wickedness, swearing, and unseemly talk, and the like; though the first I am not guilty of, but the latter I cannot forbear; though I make promise before to the contrary, I am so strangely overtaken, though I do not swear, yet my talk is as filthy and unseemly as theirs to the full. He that keeps the house is reckoned to be a great professor [of religion]; therefore I do the more wonder at it, that he should suffer such discourse at his house.

Defoe and Tutchin were other important early journalists. John Tutchin was a strong Whig who wrote the twice-a-week *Observator*, a dialogue between Observator and Country-man, beginning in April 1702. He had suffered under Judge Jeffreys for his part in Monmouth's rebellion; and his opponents kept on threatening him. He often referred to the 'oaken towel' he carried when walking abroad for protection; but in the end it failed him. In September 1707 he was so badly beaten up by ruffians that he died a few days later. For years he in his journal, Defoe in the *Review*, and Charles Leslie in the

high-Tory *Rehearsel* kept up continual abuse of one another –
though Defoe is credited with having written several *Observators*
for Tutchin when the latter was in trouble. Swift, too, feared
being beaten up for his writings. In June 1711 he told Stella,
'No, no, I'll walk late no more; I ought less to venture it
than other people, and so I was told.'

These journalists prepared the way for Steele and Addison,
men of a higher social class. Richard Steele, son of a Dublin
attorney, came to know Addison at Charterhouse school.
Leaving Oxford without a degree, he enlisted in the Horse
Guards and became a captain. After an all-too-lofty treatise
on morals, *The Christian Hero*, he wrote three comedies and was
appointed Gentleman Waiter to Prince George of Denmark,
then, in 1707, Gazeteer. Joseph Addison, son of a Dean of
Lichfield, had been given a pension of £300 to travel abroad
with a view to a diplomatic post; and in 1703 he composed
a poem on the Blenheim campaign to please the government
and was appointed a Commissioner of Appeals. He wrote the
libretto of an opera, accompanied Halifax on a mission to
Hanover, and in 1708 was made Chief Secretary for Ireland.
In 1709 Steele started the *Tatler*, to which Addison almost at
once contributed; and in 1711 the pair began the *Spectator*. At
the end of his *Weekly Review* (started in February 1704) Defoe
had added 'a little diversion, as anything occurs to make the
world merry; and whether friend or foe, one party or another,
if anything happens so scandalous as to require an open reproof,
the world may meet it here'. The first diversion was an account
of a scandalous club. With the *Tatler*, Steele carried on this sort
of thing, taking from another paper, the *English Lucian* of 1698,
the idea of presenting news from different quarters of the town.
Accounts of gallantry, entertainments, pleasures, came under
the heading of White's Chocolate House; poetry and criticism
under that of Will's Coffee House; learning under that of the
Grecian; foreign and domestic news under that of St James's.
What we could call an editorial came 'from my own Apartment'. In his no. 48, following the *Female Tatler* (begun July
1709), he divided his paper less into sections and gave less news.
Following Dunton with his letters and Ned Ward with his
character sketches, he concentrated on people and their views,

taking from Dunton and Defoe the idea of grouping them in clubs. Thus, he invented a set of eccentrics, the Trumpet Club. On 17 December 1709 Byrom wrote to a friend, 'Is the *British Apollo* put down? or do you take in the *Tatler*, which is mightily admired here, or know you the author?' (The *Apollo* had as subtitle: Curious Amusements for the Ingenious.)

Steele was prolific in new periodicals; apart from the famous pair in which he collaborated with Addison, he launched *The Guardian, The Englishman, The Lover, The Reader, Town Talk, The Tea Table, Chit Chat, The Plebeian, The Theatre*, and Addison had also *The Freeholder* and *The Old Whig*. The general aim was that set out by Steele in *The Christian Hero*, 1701, of making wit useful, of turning religious folk polite, and polite folk religious. The *Tatler* and the *Spectator* were admired in the dissenting academies. At Spalding the village coffee-man took the *Tatler* in and every post-day the more educated members of the parish gathered to hear him read aloud the musings of Steele's character Bickerstaff. Then, seated round the fire, they discussed what they had heard. We hear also of squires founding a gentleman's society and aspiring to a village library. The culmination of the varied periodicals of the first three decades of the century, with their widening of the reading public, came in 1731 when the *Gentleman's Magazine* was founded by the journalist and bookseller Edward Cave. Here there was no fiction, but more solid literary fare, with lighter items ranging from conundrums to cooking recipes. It provided 'practical information about domestic life and a combination of improvement with entertainment', and was highly successful; but the inventive vitality of the earlier journals was lacking.[4]

Behind the periodicals lay a considerable expansion of the reading public, of printing establishments, and of literacy. After 1688 the number of university students fell; but there was a wide increase in primary education, largely through what has been called the charity-school movement. There were also the old endowed grammar-schools and non-endowed schools of various kinds such as the dame-schools. In the new development the dissenting academies played a key part. At the same time there was a strong drive for better morals and manners, concentrated in three powerful bodies: the Society for the Propagation of Christian Knowledge (founded 1698), the Society for the Reformation of Manners, the Society for the Propagation of the Gospel in Foreign Parts. Queen Mary had been horrified at the low tone of London society. When William was away, she issued a proclamation for the more reverent observation of the Sabbath, and against swearing and profanity. Directives were sent to magistrates throughout the land to use special severity against drunkards; and circular letters were read everywhere from the pulpits on the reform of manners. The climax came in the summer of 1692; orders were issued against hackneys on Sunday, constables were ordered to take away pies or puddings from anyone met carrying them, and so on. But the queen had gone too far, and the whole thing collapsed in ridicule. However, it was succeeded by the solid movements mentioned above.

Evelyn tells us about the origin of the Society for the Reformation of Manners. On 15 November 1699, 'There happened this week so thick a mist and fog that people lost their way in the streets, it being so intense that no light of candles or torches yielded any (or but very little) direction. I was in it and in danger. Robberies were committed between the very lights which were fixed between London and Kensington on both sides, and whilst coaches and travellers were passing. It began about four in the afternoon, and was quite gone by eight, without any wind to disperse it. At the Thames they beat drums to direct the watermen to make the shore.' On the 24th he says: 'Such horrible robberies and murders were committed, as had not been known in this nation; atheism, profaneness, blasphemy, amongst all sorts, portended some judgement if not amended, on which a Society was set on foot, who obliged themselves to endeavour the reforming of it, in London and other places, and began to punish offenders and put the laws in more strict execution, which God Almighty prosper.' On 24 March 1700 he notes: 'Divers persons of quality entered into the Society for Reformation of Manners; and some lectures were set up, particularly in the City of London. The most eminent of the clergy preached at Bow Church, after reading a declaration set forth by the King to suppress the growing wickedness; this began already to take some effect, as to common swearing, and oaths in mouths of people of all ranks.' The way of speaking which was considered so offensive is given by Defoe in his early *Essay on Projects*; two gentlemen meet:

> Jack, God damn me, Jack, how do'st do, thou little dear son of a whore? How hast thou done this long while, by God? and then they kiss; and the other as lewd as himself, goes on: 'Dear Tom, I am glad to see thee, with all my heart, let me die. Come, let us take a bottle; we must not part so, prithee let's go and be drunk, by God.'

In 1735 alone the Society took out 99,380 actions in the London area.[5]

The charity-school movement, which by George II's reign was dominated by High Anglicans and Tories, provided education for children of artisans and shopkeepers, and thus helped to meet the increasing demand for clerks in the world of trade. The schools were often built up by the pooling of subscriptions from the wealthy in the way of a joint-stock company. The impulse had been largely puritan: to reduce crime, reform manners, make the poor thrifty and hardworking. Reading and writing were taught, so that the Bible could be read; in some schools arithmetic and trade-skills too (e.g. knitting and spinning) to keep the poor off the parish rates. Girls as well as boys were taken in – a great innovation – and pupils were mostly given a distinctive dress, partly so that they might be clad decently, partly so that they and the public might be reminded that they were charity-children. Morning and afternoon there was a rollcall. *An Account of the Methods whereby the Charity-Schools have been Erected and Managed* was first issued in 1704. The 1711 edition states: 'And if any be missing, their names shall be put with a note for tardy, and another for absent. Great faults, as swearing, stealing, &c shall be noted down in monthly or weekly bills, to be laid before the subscribers or trustees every time they meet, in order to their correction or expulsion.'

A list of schools shows how varied were their origins. Besides personal subscriptions from the gentry, the local magistrates or corporation might help. At Leeds the corporation 'gave a large house for a school and supplies for repairing and fitting it'. At Kingston on Hull the children spun Jersey; at Launceston they knitted, sewed, and made bone-lace, and so on. On a higher level, at the dissenting academies, Norton at Newington (who later became the first vice-chancellor of Harvard College in New England) had his chiefest excellence 'in mathematicks, and especially the mechanick part of them'. Under him history, geography, and political science were also taught. Defoe proably began his study of French and Italian at Newington.

The charity-schools were much praised in sermons and orations. Addison was moved by the sight of the children in their charity-uniforms parading in the London streets. Nothing 'so much pleased and affected me as the little boys and girls who were ranged with so much decency and order in the Strand. Such a numerous and innocent multitude, clothed in the charity of their benefactors, was a spectacle pleasing both to God and man.' He had always looked at the charity-schools 'as the glory of the age'. (Evelyn in March 1687 at Christ's Hospital saw the children being trained. 'They sung a psalm before they sat down to supper in the great hall, to an organ which played all the time, with such cheerful harmony that it seemed to me a vision of angels.') Addison also wrote in complaint at the niggardly subscriptions to the schools, not £5000 in fourteen years for some 1600 children – but 'I shall readily compound with any lady in a hoop-petticoat, if she gives the price of one half yard of the silk towards clothing, feeding and instructing an innocent helpless creature of her own sex in one of these schools.' Then he more strongly turned on the men: 'It is methinks a most laudable institution this, if it were of no other expectation than that of producing a race of good and useful servants, who will have more than a liberal, a religious education.' It was 'common prudence' to support a movement that would add to a master's orders 'the weight of the Commandments to enforce an obedience to them'. More, as the children of the upper classes 'run too much among the servants', it was bad for them to see only lowliness in the latter. Thinking of the schools, he was stirred to an unusual breadth of sympathy. 'The crowds of poor, or pretended poor, in every place, are a great reproach to us, and eclipse the glory of all other charity.'

But though the upper class wanted the poor folk and the servants to be orderly and respectful, they were afraid that education would give them ideas above their station. Mandeville in his *Fable of the Bees* gathered all these doubts and fears, and gave them bold and witty formulation. Would the schools reduce the number of criminals? 'As to religion, the most knowing and polite part of a nation have every where the least of it; craft has a greater hand in making rogues than stupidity, and vice in general is no where more predominant than where arts and sciences flourish.' We find 'innocence and honesty no where more general than among the illiterate, the poor, silly country people'. As for the acquiring of manners, 'boys there may be taught to pull off their caps promiscuously to all they meet, unless it be a beggar: But that they should acquire in it any civility beyond that, I cannot conceive'. Parental example has more effect on children than anything taught at school.

The schools, indeed, will have disastrous economic effects, Mandeville sums up, for the poor will come to despise the labouring jobs on which society depends. 'It is manifest, that in a free nation where slaves are not allowed of, the surest wealth consists in a multitude of labourious poor; for besides that they are the never-failing nursery of fleets and armies, without them there could be no enjoyment, and no product of any country could be valuable. To make the society happy and people easy under the meanest circumstances, it is requisite that great numbers of them should be ignorant as well as poor. Knowledge both enlarges and multiplies our desires, and the fewer things a man wishes for, the more easily his necessities may be supplied.' The welfare and felicity of every state require that 'the knowledge of the working poor should be confined within the verge of their occupations'. At the same time the upper classes, by living luxuriously and prodigally, provide jobs for the labourers. (The poor themselves at times acted on Mandeville's principles. Stephen Duck, thresher and poet, was taken from school when fourteen by his mother 'lest he become too fine a gentleman for the family that produced him'.)[6]

With the increasing differentiations within the reading public and the expansion of that public itself, a new kind of writer

was emerging, as we have already seen with Dunton and Defoe.
Writers could no longer depend on noble patrons, though a
few in the eighteenth century, such as Thomson and Young,
continued to find them. The publisher or bookseller now took a
dominant role, and around him were gathered a varied assort-
ment of hacks, the inhabitants of Grub Street. Johnson in his
Dictionary defined that term as 'originally the name of a street;
near Moorfields in London, much inhabited by writers of small
histories, dictionaries, and temporary poems; whence any
mean production is called *grubstreet*'. In 1725 Defoe wrote that
writing 'is become a very considerable branch of the English
commerce. The booksellers are the master manufacturers or
employers. The several writers, authors, copiers, sub-writers,
and all other operators with pen and ink are the workmen
employed by the said master manufacturers.' Writing was effectively a part of the new bourgeois world, and the writer was,
in Savage's phrase, 'an author to be let'. Wesley thought Isaac
Watts was long-winded so as 'to get money', and the drawn-
out discursive aspects of the style of Defoe and Richardson were
similarly blamed, no doubt unfairly.[7]

In January 1713 Swift already gives us a glimpse of the
garret-poet. 'I was to see a poor poet, one Mr Diaper, in a
nasty garret, very sick. I gave him twenty guineas from Lord
Bolingbroke, and disposed of the other sixty to two other
authors.' Johnson in his *Life of Savage*, whom he had known
well, gives us a vivid picture of the new literary Bohemia,
which included both Steele and Savage. Once Steele took the
latter to a petty tavern at Hyde Park corner, where they retired
to a private room. Steele said he wanted to publish a pamphlet
and dictated it to Savage till a very poor dinner was put on the
table. After some hesitation Savage asked for wine, which Steele
reluctantly ordered. They then went on with the pamphlet,
which they finished in the afternoon; but instead of calling
for the reckoning and going home, 'Sir Richard told him that
he was without money, and that the pamphlet must be sold
before the dinner could be paid for; and Savage was therefore
obliged to go and offer their new production for sale for two
guineas, which with some difficulty he obtained. Sir Richard
then returned home, having retired only to avoid his creditors

and composed the pamphlet only to discharge the reckoning.'
Another time Steele invited to his home 'a great number of
persons of the first quality', who 'were surprised at the number
of liveries which surrounded the table; and after dinner, when
wine and mirth had set them free from the observation of
rigid ceremony, one of them inquired of Sir Richard, how
such an expensive train of domestics could be consistent with
his fortune. Steele confessed that they were bailiffs come with
an execution whom he couldn't send away and whom he therefore put into liveries.' In his early days, when working on
the *Gazette* for Tonson in 1708, Steele had been afraid to go
home because of the bailiffs. He wrote to his Prue from a
barber's shop opposite the Devil Tavern in Charing Cross,
'If the printer's boy be at home, send him hither; and let Mrs
Todd send me by the way my nightgown, slippers and clean
linen.'

The account of Savage's later life shows how even a talented
writer could get lost in Grub Street.

He spent his time in mean expedients and tormenting
suspense, living for the greatest part in fear of prosecutions
from his creditors, and consequently skulking in obscure
parts of the town, of which he was no stranger to the
remotest corners. But wherever he came, his address
secured him friends, whom his necessities soon alienated;
so that he had, perhaps, a more numerous acquaintance
than any man ever before attained, there being scarcely
any person, eminent on any account, to whom he was not
known, or whose character he was not in some degree able
to delineate. To the acquisition of this extensive acquaintance every circumstance of his life contributed. He excelled
in the arts of conversation, and therefore willingly practised
them. He had seldom any home, or even a lodging in
which he could be private; and therefore was driven into
public houses for the common conveniences and supports
of nature. He was always ready to comply with every
invitation, having no employment to withhold him, and
often no money to provide for himself; and, by dining with
one company, he never failed to obtaining an introduction

into another. Thus dissipated was his life, and thus casual his subsistence; yet did not the distraction of his views hinder him from reflection, nor the uncertainty of his condition depress his gaiety. When he had wandered about without any fortunate adventure by which he was led into a tavern, he sometimes retired into the fields, and was able to employ his mind in study, or amuse it with pleasing imaginations; and seldom appeared to be melancholy, but when some sudden misfortune had just fallen upon him, and even then in a few moments he would disentangle himself from his perplexity, adopt the subject of conversation, and apply his mind wholly to the objects that others presented to it.

In his pamphlet, *An Author To Be Lett*, Iscarius Hackney tells how he succeeded in getting away from the important bookseller, Curll, for some years, but then 'he arrested me for several months board, brought me back to my garret, and made me drudge on in my old, dirty work. 'Twas in his service that I wrote obscenity and profaneness, under the Names of Pope and Swift. Sometimes I was Mr Joseph Gay [so as to be mistaken for John Gay], and at others Theory Burnet, or Addison. I abridged histories and travels, translated from the French, what they never wrote, and was expert at finding out new titles for old books ... Had Mr Oldmixon and Mr Curll agreed, my assistance had probably been invited into Father Boneur's Logick, and the critical History of England.'

A quick success was often got by writing up the scandalously topical or by the pretence of secret memoirs or scurrilous exposures. In November 1712 when the Duke of Hamilton was killed in a duel with Lord Mohun, Swift objected to the duchess being removed. 'The lodging was inconvenient, and they would have removed her to another; but I would not suffer it, because it has no room backward, and she must have been tormented with the noise of the Grub Street screamers mentioning her husband's murder in her ears.' The middle-class and lower-class audiences were never tired of hearing how debauched their betters were. Fake-arguments were worked up. In Fielding's *Author's Farce* a bookseller sets his hacks to work:

Bookweight: Fie upon it gentlemen! What, not at your pens? Do you consider, Mr Quibble, that it is a fortnight since your letter to a friend in the country was published? Is it not high time for an answer to come out? At this rate, before your answer is printed, your letter will be forgot. I love to keep a controversy up warm. I have had authors who have writ a pamphlet in the morning, answered it in the afternoon, and answered that again at night.

Quibble: Sir, I will be as expeditious as possible: but it is harder to write on this side of the question, because it is the wrong side.

Bookweight: Not a jot. So far on the contrary, that I have known some authors choose it as the properest to show their genius.

Savage, despite his own experience of Grub Street, jeers at the inhabitants as mostly 'persons of very low parentage', who 'without any pretence of merit are aspiring to the rank of gentleman. Thus they become ill oeconomists, poverty is the consequence of ill oeconomy, and dirty tricks the consequence of their poverty. Tho' they are sad writers, they might have been good mechanicks; and therefore by endeavouring to shine in spheres, to which they are unequal, are guilty of depriving the publick of many that might have been its useful members.' The gentleman writer such as Pope thus affected an extreme disdain for the men who wrote for money. As the most effective of the satirical wits, who still considered fine writing the prerogative of the gentlemen and to be above the money-world, Pope became the archfoe of the Grubstreeters. The hacks were linked with the Whigs who were the men of the cash-nexus. Pope, though son of a linen-draper, moved in Tory circles and was friendly with Swift, Atterbury, Burlington, Bolingbroke; in the 1730s he was involved with the opposition to Walpole. His first troubles had come from Addison's group at the Whig coffee house, Button's; and in pamphlets the praise of Walpole was often linked with attacks on him, while the writers who attacked Walpole did not attack Pope. Thus, *An Essay upon the Taste and Writings of the Present Times* (in the *Evening Post* of 29 June 1728) is inscribed to Walpole and assails Pope as a malicious tyrant who has patched up his version of the *Odyssey* with other men's work. Richard Verney, in his poem *Dunces out of State* (1733) praises Walpole's Houghton but declares, 'Pope breathes his Satire without Wit,/And plainly in his Face dull Fool is writ.' *The Satirists* about the same time is strongly pro-Walpole and describes Pope as venal: ' 'Tis all for Gain ... T'enhance the Price of every Satire sold,/And wring from each Competitor more gold.' Thus the Grubstreeters tried to retort the charge of writing-for-money on the Wits, while themselves taking their stand with the Whigs.

The new kind of writer we are examining not only championed opposing political and social viewpoints, but also made an appeal to different levels of the new reading public. Defoe certainly widened the human interest of the weekly periodicals. Under his guidance *Mist's Journal* and *Applebee's* gradually won a wider and less educated public than any previous newspaper. In 1719 *Mist's* was reported in the *Weekly Medley* as 'mightily spread about among the vulgar', and A. Phyllips warned the writer of *St James's Journal* not to get into an argument with Mist. 'You will very much lessen your importance in several families of distinction where you are received, and be perhaps obliged to write only for porters and cobblers, and such dirty customers as are his greatest patrons' (2 August 1722). Charles Gildon jeered: 'There's not an old woman that can go to the price of it, but buys *Robinson Crusoe*.' An exaggeration (the original edition cost five shillings), but none the less significant. More amiably an epigram of 1720 remarked: 'Down in the kitchen, honest Dick and Doll/Are studying Colonel Jack and Flanders Moll.' Certainly a writer like Defoe had his works spread by group-reading. An opponent of his said: 'The greatest part of the people do not read books; most of them cannot read at all. But they will gather together about one that can read, and listen to an *Observator* or *Review* (as I have seen them in the streets).'[8]

Important changes in the attitudes to language and style were going on. Tom Brown and Ned Ward still used a

vigorous, colloquial and imaginative English that had affinities
with the work of the popular writers of the Elizabethan or
Jacobean worlds. In a few years with the *Spectator* we find a
style more controlled by a sense of the rules of grammar and
orderly composition, though still holding elements of the old
liveliness. There were coming to a head tendencies that had
been at work since spelling became relatively fixed in mid-
sixteenth century, and men began to argue whether English
words were too scanty, too rough, too confused with foreign
borrowings, for a serious literature. The advent of the Royal
Society in 1662 raised the question of an efficient form of writing that would be adequate to the new scientific precisions.
Wilkins in his *Essay towards a real character, and a philosophical
language* (1668) put these issues sharply. Latin was breaking
down as a *lingua franca* for scholars; men wanted a linguistic
system that would aid the progress of knowledge. And entangled
with the pragmatic considerations were fantasies of a primeval
language, the problems raised in devising systems of secret writing (used mainly for diplomatic purposes), and ideas drawn
from logic, hieroglyphics, and mnemonic systems, the art of
memory. Such elements in turn were mixed confusedly with
the new literary needs of the emerging middle class, which
wanted standards of correct behaviour here as elsewhere (for
instance, in business accounting) – standards that rose above
popular turbulence without succumbing to aristocratic or élite
notions of elegance.

At one extreme some scientists tried to fabricate an artificial
language without ambiguities. Thus, in Newton's notation *tor*
referred to temperature, the prefix *u-* referred to a point in the
positive extreme, *i-* to such a point in the negative, and *e-* to a
point halfway between. *Utor* meant hot; *itor*, cold; *etor*, tepid.
In the literary sphere such attitudes led to a search for more
definite principles of organisation in style and expression.
Dryden remarked on the lack of 'a more certain measure' for
the noble English language, and noted that the French had
an academy for dealing with such matters. The Royal Society
appointed a committee for 'improving the English language',
with Dryden on it. But nothing definite emerged; in 1693
Dryden was still asking for his measure.

The writer who took up this issue was Swift. In 1711 he discussed it with Addison, who in the *Spectator* explored the differences between English and the tongues of neighbouring countries. In talk the English were more given to pauses and intervals; in writing they showed more compactness. English abounded in monosyllables which lessened elegance but helped to set out ideas 'in the readiest manner'. English words sound like string music, short and transient; those of other tongues 'are like the notes of wind instruments, sweet and swelling, and lengthened out into variety of modulation'. The rapidity of English had been increased by turning the pronunciation of words like *drownēd* into *drown'd* and by dropping the ending *-eth* in favour of *-s*: which has 'added to that *hissing* in our language, which is taken so much notice of by foreigners'. Also there were abbreviations such as *may not* into *mayn't*. Such matters 'will never be decided till we have something like an Academy, that by the best authorities and rules drawn from the analogy of languages shall settle all controversies between grammar and idiom'.

In 1712 Swift published *A Proposal for Correcting, Improving and Ascertaining the English Tongue*. He found English very imperfect and daily corrupted; he wanted it fixed and purified by authority. We see the strong conviction that there were some sort of ideal or correct forms (with Latin somewhere at the back of the mind). One practical way of grappling with the problems was through dictionaries. There were some fifteen between 1700 and 1755 when Dr Johnson's came out. Gradually the concept of ideal rules gave way to a scientific approach.[9]

The idea of universal rules was strongly stimulated by the growth of mechanistic science and of the belief that Reason could solve all things – Reason being in the last resort identified with the idealised Nature believed to reveal itself in the Newtonian system. Shaftesbury was the apostle of such ideas in relation to artistic expression; in the religious field they appeared in Deism (merging at one end with Free-thinking and the argument, as in Toland and Collins, that Christianity must stand up against the rigorous tests of Reason). There was a wide feeling that there must be some 'pure and natural religion' (Tindal). Such matters were much debated. In 1723 Waterland declared that 'controversy on the Trinity was widespread among all ranks and degrees of men, and the Athenasian Creed became the subject of common and ordinary conversation'.

In such a situation it was inevitable that men would challenge the long-accepted position that the ancients were superior in all things to the modern world. In 1690 Sir William Temple published his complacent essay stating the superiority of the ancients and holding that the oldest books of all were the best, that is, the Fables of Aesop and the Letters of the Tyrant Phalaris. Four years later the grandnephew of the chemist Boyle, aged seventeen, produced an edition of the Letters. Bentley, born in Yorkshire of humble stock, the greatest scholar of his day, demolished the Letters and showed them to be late forgeries. The argument about Ancients and Moderns came out into the open, Swift contributing his *Battle of the Books* in 1704. (Bentley was well acquainted with the results of contemporary science both in the fields of chemistry and physics.)

Out of the various converging tendencies we get both Augustan elegance and the realism of Defoe. Augustan form in poetry expressed a balance between the aristocracy and the upper middle class. Its couplet, with its essentially symmetrical systems, took over the Newtonian idea of a mechanistic or symmetrical universe, in which action and reaction were equal and opposite, and interpreted it socially, producing the ultimate effect that all was for the best in the best of all possible worlds. Discords were slight and temporary, effaced in the overriding and reasserted symmetry. Metaphysical poetry (linked with the period of revolutionary stress in the earlier seventeenth century) had sought to build dialectical structures, emphasising opposites and yet uniting them. It expressed a society in deep inner conflict and sought for resolutions in terms of a new unity. After the Commonwealth there grew up a fear of imagination and the passions, which were linked with religious enthusiasm and the turbulent ideas still seething in the populace. We find a wish to get away from the merely rhetorical and ornate. Locke, at the end of the third book of his *Essay concerning Human Understanding*, dealt with the abuses of language, which included figurative writing. The great bulk of literature was excluded from what he saw as the proper use of language. 'Eloquence, like the fair sex', involves a pleasurable deceit. Shaftesbury in *A Letter concerning Enthusiasm* (1708) wanted: 'Justness of thought and style, refinement in manners, good breeding, and politeness of every kind'.

The new realism of a Defoe excluded Eloquence but it also excluded most of the things that Shaftesbury wanted. The ninth *Tatler* thought it was making a joke when it praised Swift's *Description of the Morning* for its realism, 'a way perfectly new' that 'described things as they happened'. But the comment had its deep truth. With Defoe we indeed see a complete rejection, or lack of knowledge, of the rhetorical or elegant control of material. The balanced symmetrical universe is gone, and the writer's whole effort is to make the things or events described as much as possible like what they would seem to someone directly involved with them.

Thus the Novel proper was born, with Bunyan as its forerunner and Defoe as its first mature exponent. Women played only a slight part in these robust origins, yet as an ever-growing section of the reading public they had powerful effects on the development of the novel. Addison in 1713 in the *Guardian* wrote that women have more spare time and lead a sedentary life, so 'learning is more adapted to the female world than to the male'. De Murault in 1694 noted that 'even among the common people the husbands do not make their wives work'; de Saussure in 1727 noted that the tradesmen's wives were 'rather lazy and few do any needlework'. Women in families who had money enough to take advantage of the new shopping facilities were relieved from many of the old labours. Isaac Watts, dissenter, commented on 'all the painful and dismal consequences of lost and wasted time'. He encouraged his flock, mainly feminine, to spend their leisure in reading and literary discussions, though among some puritanic religious groupings reading was still considered a waste of time (apart from the Bible). Dunton founded the first journal directly addressed to women, *The Ladies' Mirror*, in 1693, and later many were published.

Among the labouring classes and in the countryside women would still have had no time for reading. In general the decay of domestic industry was lowering the status of women, who formed a surplus in the labour market with wages going down. Hence for the first time the Old Maid becomes a joke, with many caricatures in literature, such as Mistress Tipkin in Steele's *The Tender Husband*. Defoe expatiated about 'the set of despicable creatures, called Old Maids'. The term Spinster for an unmarried woman past the usual age of marriage also comes up. In the first issue of the *Spinster*, 1719, Steele reminds readers that the word was originally not opprobrious. With the breakdown of the guilds, the old protections and privileges of widows went, and the entry of women into the trades became more difficult. Some trades that had been traditionally women's, such as brewing, were taken over by men. Textiles became women's work, though attempts were made to exclude them from weaving. Women surgeons faded out in the seventeenth century, and the status of midwives was downgraded.

The middle class provided the new leisured woman with time and inclination to read novels, though among the poorer sections there were apprentices and household servants who also had a certain amount of leisure. Pamela in Richardson's novel insists that the post she takes after leaving Mr B. allows her 'a little time for reading'.[10]

5
Women, Fashions, Assemblies

Legally, women had a very inferior position. *Angliae Notitia* pointed out: 'Women in England, with all their moveable goods so soon as they are married are wholly in *potestate viri*, at will and disposition of the husband'. Even 'her very necessary apparel, by the law, is not hers, in property'. So it was a high crime for a woman to kill her husband, her father, her master. 'That is Petit-Treason, to be burnt alive. So that a wife in England is *de jure* but the best of servants, having nothing her own, in a more proper sense than a child hath, whom the father suffers to call many things his own, yet can dispose of nothing. She loses even her very name.' Chamberlayne, however, insisted that such is 'the good nature of Englishmen towards their wives, such is the tenderness and respect, giving them the uppermost place at table, and elsewhere, the right hand everwhere, and putting them upon no drudgery or hardship, that they are, generally speaking, the most happy women in the world'. As comment we may cite Swift on 24 August 1711. Dick Tighe (later a privy councillor in Ireland) and his wife 'lodged over against us; and he has been seen, out of our upper windows, beating her two or three times: they are both gone to Ireland, but not together; and he solemnly vows never to live with her. Neighbours do not stick to say she has a tongue; in short, I was told she is the most urging, provoking devil that ever was born; and he is a hot whiffling puppy, very apt to resent.' On 30 June 1711 Swift writes of Dr Coghill losing his drab. Coghill was a judge of the Prerogative Court in Ireland, who decided in a case that moderate chastisement with a switch was one of a husband's privileges; so a lady whom he had long courted dismissed him, and he died unmarried.[1]

A wife's dependence could produce its problems for a husband. One man wrote to *Appleby's Journal* in 1724 about the difficulties resulting from his wife's infidelity. If he turned her out, she could take the house next door and make him pay the rent; if her associates lent her money, they could arrest him for debt. He was forced to own her bastards or at least pay for them. Even if she was proved to be a notorious adultress, she might be granted 'a large allowance out of her fortune, nay almost equal to it, for her subsistence. That is, she got back some of the money she had brought in as her portion. The annulment of a marriage by a private Act of Parliament was only for the powerful and wealthy. A separation granted by an ecclesiastical court did not allow the partners to remarry, and it was difficult to get. Such a court refused to accept as proof of adultery the fact that a wife and her lover were found naked together, though not in the act of copulation. De Murault declared that in England husbands 'must be posted behind their wives, and see all with their own eyes, for no other proof will do'.

The beginnings of a revolt about the low estimation in which women were held can be traced. Richard Baxter had declared that a man marrying must prepare himself to deal with 'the natural imbecility of the female sex'. Mary Astell, in *A Serious Proposal to the Ladies*, 1694, asked: 'How can you be content to be in the world like tulips in a garden, to make a fine show and be good for nothing?' She gathered a group of privileged women who supported her ideal of a female academy. Since access to the world of male activities was so totally barred, the main plea for greater freedom was directed towards education. But Mary added, 'To plead for the weak ... seemed a generous undertaking', thus linking the cause of women with that of other downtrodden persons or groups. The Quaker George Fox had held male domination came from sin and that in the new life men and women would be equals. What the few girls' schools were like may be gauged from Steele's comment in 1701, when he lodged at Wandsworth:

'At the other end of the house my landlady teaches girls to read, make bone-lace, and curtsy.'

A few women played their part in the new literary sphere. Aphra Behn (1640–89), daughter of a barber, was the first English woman professional writer who could hold her own in obscenity with the men. During her youth in Surinam she had met the slave Oronoko, whom she made the hero of a novel; she was thus among the very first attackers of slavery. Mrs Manley, who lived till 1724, belonged to the same school but she was also a lively political writer and conducted the *Examiner*. In her early years she had been decoyed into a bigamous marriage with a cousin. Susanna Centilivre was the daughter of a Lincoln-shire gentleman who was a keen Parliamentarian and lost his estates at 1660. She is said to have dressed as a young man and lived with a student at Cambridge; then after a short marriage she took as second husband an officer soon killed in a duel; her third marriage was with the chief cook of Queen Anne. A keen Whig, she expressed her views in her comedies and died in 1723.

Mrs Manley attacked the double standard for men and women in *The New Atlantis*, 1709, in which she satirised many Whig notabilities. In Lillo's play *London Merchant* (1731), Sarah Millwood, the whore, rounds on her accusers who have lamented her abuse of fine qualities: 'If such I had, well may I curse your barbarous sex, who robbed me of 'em, ere I knew their worth, then left me, too late, to count their value by their loss.' Laetitia Pilkington, writing in her *Memoirs* (1748) out of her own experience, asked, 'Is it not monstrous that our seducers should be our accusers?'

In the middle class generally there was a mixture of ideas of woman's inferiority, which at the same time rejected aristo-cratic ideas of gallantry (woman as a plaything), and puritan ideas of woman as a helpmate more or less equal in her own sphere of work and devotion. Steele in *The Lover* (no. 2, 1714) declared that notions of gallantry have of late been 'turned topsyturvy, and the knight errantry of this profligate age is destroying as many women as they can'. Defoe in *The Family Instructor* (1715) laboriously set out the puritan ideals. T. Salmon, in *Critical Essays Concerning Marriage* (1724) wrote of the dangers in ambiguous terms like honour and gallantry. Swift, in his *Letter to a Very Young Lady* (1727), warned against expecting the ridiculous passion that exists only in playbooks and romances; he advocates a 'match of prudence and common good liking'.[2]

The attack on aristocratic attitudes and the double standard reached its climax in Richardson, but not with any aim of liberating women. The heroine is made so delicate that she faints at any sexual advance and feels strongly about her wooer only when she is his wife. The middle-class wife is now cut off from any economic role except as the bearer of money-benefits.

As part of the new ideals of correctness merged with middle-class morality there is a sharp censoring of language. Jeremy Collier, an Anglican priest, not a dissenter, led the attack in his *Short View of the Profaneness and Immorality of the English Stage* in 1699, horrified that 'the Poets make *women* speak smuttily'. Soon the verbal taboos were unquestioned. Swift wrote on 9 December 1710: 'I had a letter from Mrs Long, that has quite turned my stomach against her; no less than two nasty jests in it with dashes to suppose them. She is corrupted in that country town with vile conversation.' A campaign began, aiming to clean up the marriage ceremony, leading to the Marriage Act that sought to regularise the event and make it public.

Despite the urgings of a moralist like Addison that women should improve their minds, the seriously educated woman was unpopular. Lady Mary Wortley Montagu said that a woman should conceal learning as she would conceal 'crookedness or lameness'. She remarked that 'we are educated in the grossest ignorance, and no art omitted to stifle our natural reason; if some few get above the nurses' instructions, our knowledge must rest concealed, and be as useless to the world as gold in the mine'. Swift said that not one young gentlewoman in a thousand was taught to read or spell; it was the male heresy that women's duty was to be fools in every article except what is merely domestic. He added that there were very few women 'without a good share of that heresy, except upon one article, that they have as little regard for family business as for the improvement of their minds'. Elsewhere he commented, 'The ladies in general are extremely mended both in writing and reading since I was young, only it is to be hoped that in proper time, gaming and dressing may reduce them to their proper ignorance.' In his correspondence with Stella he is fussy about spelling. 'Pray, Stella, explain those two words of yours to me, what you mean by Viloian and Dainger, and you, madam Dingley, what is Christianing?' The acceptable sort of talents in a woman were exemplified by Mrs Pendarvis. 'She reads to improve her mind, not to make an appearance of being learned; she writes with all the delicacy and ease of a woman, and the strength and exactness of a man; she paints and takes views of what is either beautiful or whimsical in nature with a surprising genius and art. She is mistress of the harpsichord and has a brilliancy in her playing peculiar to herself; she does a number of works, and of many of them is the inventor.' Thus she unobtrusively provided a decorative background for a male world.

Aristocratic manners still dominated the social scene, though they were being modified by middle-class views. The lady received abed in the morning. On 24 March 1712 Swift writes: 'I went to visit the duchess of Hamilton, who was not awake. So I went to the duchess of Shrewsbury, and sat an hour at her toilet. I talked to her about the duke's being lord lieutenant. She said she knew nothing of it, but I rallied her out of that.' The beau, too, lay abed most of the morning in a lace-trimmed cambric shirt, with his powdered periwig arranged on his pillow, receiving visitors. At noon he rose, bathed his face in beauty-washes, put on some patches, rubbed essence of orange or jasmine on his eyebrows, soaked his handkerchief in rose-water, and fixed his cravat for effect. He was then ready for a meal, after which a chair was called. 'No man of fashion can cross the street to dinner,' said the Rev John Brown, 'without the effeminate covering and conveyance of an easy chair.'

Steele describes the levee of a great man, that market for preferment. Army officers liked to appear half undressed, with open breast; ministers were buttoned up. My lord proved his parts by having something relevant to say to everyone. 'I have known a great man ask a flag-officer, which way was the wind, a commander of horse the present price of oats, and a stock-jobber at what discount such a fund was, with as much ease as if he had been bred to each of those several ways of life.' A great effect was got by the Silence and Order.

> The patron is usually in the midst of the room, and some humble person gives him a whisper, which his lordship answers aloud, 'It is well, Yes, I am of your opinion. Pray inform yourself further, you may be sure of my part in it.' This happy Man is dismissed, and my lord can turn himself to a business of a quite different nature, and offhand give as good an answer as any great man is obliged to. For the chief point is to keep in generals, and if there is any thing offered that's particular, to be in haste.

Fashion changed faster and involved a much larger number of persons as the middle class aped the upper class. Steele wrote: 'I do not doubt that England is at present as polite a nation as any in the world; but any man who thinks can easily see, that the affectation of being gay and in fashion, has very near eaten up our good sense and our religion.' Budgell in an essay of 1711 purports to give a letter from Exeter:

> A lady in this place had some time since a box of the newest ribbons sent down by the coach: Whether it was her own malicious invention, or the wantonness of a London milliner, I am not able to inform you; but, among the rest, there was one cherry-coloured ribbon, consisting of half a dozen yards, made up in the figure of a small head-dress. The foresaid lady had the assurance to affirm, amidst a circle of female inquisitors, who were present at the opening of the box, that this was the newest fashion worn at court. Accordingly the next Sunday we had several females, who came to church with their heads dressed wholly in ribbons, and looked like so many victims ready to be sacrificed. This is still a reigning mode among us. At the same time we have a set of gentlemen who take the liberty to appear in all publick places with several little silver hasps, tho' our freshest advices from London make no mention of any such fashion; and we

are something shy of affording matter to the button-makers for a second petition.

(There had been a petition bringing about a 1709 Act framed because 'the maintenance and subsistence of many thousands of men, women and children depends upon the making of silk, mohair, gimp, and thread buttons, and button-holes with the needle', and these had been ruined by 'a late unforeseen practice of making and binding button-holes with cloth, serge', and so on.) The letter ended with the mock suggestion of a Society to be set up in London for the Inspection of Modes and Fashions, so that 'no person or persons shall presume to appear singularly habited in any part of the country, without a testimonial from the foresaid Society, that their dress is answerable to the mode of London'.

Parnell in an allegory of 1712 describes three false Graces: 'Flattery with a shell of paint, Affectation with a mirror to practise at, and Fashion ever changing the posture of her clothes. These applied themselves to secure the conquests which Self-Conceit had got 'em, and had each of them their particular polities. Flattery gave new colours and complexions to all things. Affectation new airs and appearances, which, as she said, were not vulgar, and Fashion both concealed some home defects, and added some foreign external beauties.' Steele in another paper anticipates mildly the luxury-thesis of Mandeville. He had been with a friend shopping for his family.

I fancied it must be very surprising to any one who enters into a detail of Fashions, to consider how far the vanity of mankind has laid itself out in dress, what a prodigious number of people it maintains, and what a circulation of money it occasions. Providence in this case makes use of the folly which we will not give up, and it becomes instrumental to the support of those who are willing to labour. Hence it is that fringe-makers, lace-men, tire-women, and a number of other trades, which would be useless in a simple state of nature, draw their subsistence; tho' it is seldom seen that such as these are extremely rich, because their original fault of being founded upon some vanity, keeps them poor by the light inconsistency of its nature.

The variableness of fashion turns the stream of business which flows from it now into one channel, and anon into another; so that different sets of people sink or flourish in their turns by it.

He and his friends retire to a tavern and concoct the fancy of a Repository for Fashions 'as there are Chambers for Medals and other rareties'. The edifice is to have the shape of a woman's head, with two apartments, one for female fashions, one for male; there will be boxes instead of books, and babies (dolls) dressed up in past fashions. People can use the place to choose modes; young men need not travel abroad to see fashions; and scholars can study there.(3)

St James's Park was an important place for showing off one's clothes. Tom Brown stresses the military aspect: army men arguing about campaigns. 'Here is decided the price of commissions, which are openly bought and sold, as if a lawful merchandise.' We hear 'that colonel damned for being put over this captain's head; that agent cursed for tricking the regiment out of their pay, or by raising such contributions with the colonel's connivance, that estates are now got at this end of the town, as well as by stock-jobbing in the city'. Here money-lenders take 'their mid-day perambulation, to agree with the spendthrift officers for advancing their money at 30 per cent'.

Ned Ward drives thither in a hackney with perforated tin windows. He and his friend pass through the porch into the first court where some hobnailed boobies stare amazed at the whale's rib, which an Irishman insists is the ass's jawbone wielded by Samson. They enter the park at the time when the court ladies rise and go for an evening stroll. In the Mall 'the ladies looked like undaunted heroes, fit for government or battle, and the gentlemen like a parcel of fawning, flattering fops'. In Duke Humphrey's Walk many men, mostly non-commissioned officers, lie under the limetrees. 'I mean not such as have left their commissions, but such as never had any, and yet would be angry should you refuse to honour them with the title of Captain.' The Parade, which used in the mornings to be strewn with red-herring bones, is 'perfumed again with scents of English breath, and the scents of Oronoko tobacco no more offends the nostrils of our squeamish ladies'; a pregnant woman may stroll with the danger of being frighted at a terrible pair of Dutch whiskers belonging to one of William's followers. Our pair walk up the Canal where the ducks 'were striking about the water, and standing upon their heads'. (The lake is what now remains of the canal.) They look at the bronze statue of a naked Gladiator, as do two or three buxom ladies, one of whom asks, 'Is this the fine proportioned figure I have heard my husband so often brag on? It's true, his legs and arms are strong and manly, but that's all that can be said about him.' Our pair start up from the back of the pedestal and the ladies run off tittering.

Our pair then walk up by the Decoy, five or six parallel canals, linked with the big canal, 'where the water glided so smoothly beneath osier canopies, that the calm surface seemed to express that nothing inhabited this watery place but peace and silence.' Ned feels that he would like to live apart, 'purely to have enjoyed the pleasure of so delightful a luminous labyrinth, whose intricate turnings so confound the sight that the eye is still in search of some new discovery, and never satisfied with the tempting variety so artificially ordered within so little a compass'. (We see already the advent of strong elements of rococo sensibility.) Our pair turn into a long lime walk (Birdcage Walk) with its trees so ordered and similar that they seem to 'confine their leaves and branches to an equal number beneath the regular and pleasant shade'. (Here is the opposite of the rococo variety.) A place for lovers as well as for the children of the nobility with nurse or tutor. The walk ends under a knot of tall elms by Rosamund's Pond, a favourite rendezvous. A countryman, leaning on an oaken staff, stares at an elm-top. Ned asks what he's looking at. 'At yonder bird's nest.' What nest? 'What a foolish question you ask me! Why did you ever know any thing but rooks build so near the Queen's Park?' (Rookeries near country-mansions became the fashion.) Ned and his friend leave by a narrow passage for Westminster.

Swift gives us glimpses of the everyday uses made of the park. On 17 February 1711, 'I took some good walks in the Park today, and then went to Mr Harley.' On 2 April: 'We have such windy weather, 'tis troublesome walking, yet all the rabble have got into our Park these holidays.' On 11 January 1712: 'I walked lustily in the Park by moonshine till eight, to shake off my dinner and wine; and then went to sup at Mr Domville's with Ford and staid till twelve.'[4]

The new expansions of social life, the intrusion of city forms of entertainment into the countryside, appeared in the Assemblies, which in the 1720s Defoe considered to be recent. At Winchester, where he finds no trade, no manufacture, no navigation, he notes the abundance of gentry in the neighbourhood, which 'adds to the sociableness of the place'; the clergy, too, in general are very rich and numerous. 'As there is such good company, so they are gotten into that new-fashioned way of conversing by Assemblies,' which are 'pleasant and agreeable to the young people, and some times fatal to them'. He adds, 'Winchester has its share of the mirth: may it escape the ill consequences.' His index speaks of 'the pernicious tendency of Assemblies', and in dealing with Dorset he argues that such events are not necessary: 'Nor did I observe the sharp tricking temper, which is too much crept in among the gaming and horse-racing gentry in some parts of England,' though 'they sometimes play too, and make matches, and horse-races, as they see occasion. The ladies here do not want the help of Assemblies to assist in match-making; or half-pay officers to run away with their daughters, which the meeting called Assemblies in other parts of England are recommended for. Here's no Bury Fair, where the women are scandalously said to carry themselves to market, and where every night they meet at the play or at the Assembly for intrigues.'

London had its Gardens or Spas – Islington Spa, Bagnigge Wells, Marylebone Gardens, and so on. Evelyn in August 1699 'drank the Shooters Hill waters'. But it was at places like Bath and Tunbridge Wells that the new fashionable gatherings took place. Hampstead was considered so high with its fine views that it was unsuited 'for any but a race of mountaineers', said Defoe, 'whose lungs have been used to the rarified air'. The neglected mansion of Bellsize, north of London, had been taken over by a projector and turned into a true House of Pleasure, with all sorts of sports in the gardens and gaming of all sorts inside. 'The wicked part at length broke in, till it alarmed the magistrates.' A large room was fitted for balls, 'and had it gone on to a degree of Masquerading as I hear was actually begun, it would have bid fair to have half the town run to it.' Despite the reduction of liberties there, the concourse had not lessened. At Richmond, after it became the retreat of the Prince of Wales, George I's son, many fine houses were built; there were wells and a mineral water; and the company, though less than at Epsom or Tunbridge Wells, was of a higher quality, with the waters drunk in the morning and with music in the evening.

At Epsom over the downs the company was greatest round July. Business was not talked of (except in 1720, the Bubble year); even the London men of the Exchange, the Alley, the Treasury-office, or the Court 'look as if they had left all their London thoughts behind them, and had separated themselves to mirth and good company; as if they came hither to unbend the bow of the mind'. The houses were detached, 'with gardens and ground about them, that the people who come out of their confined dwellings in London, may have air and liberty, suited to the designs of country lodgings'. As soon as you enter your lodgings, you walk out again; for everyone says, 'Come, let's go see the town; folks don't come to Epsom to stay within doors.' Next morning 'you are welcomed with the musick under your chamber window; but for a shilling or two you get rid of them and prepare for going to the Wells'. There you become a Summer Citizen of Epsom by paying another shilling, or, if you please, half a crown. 'Then you drink the waters, or walk about as if you did; dance with the ladies, tho' it be in your gown and slippers; have musick and company of what kind you like.' After the morning diversions you walk home; the town is quiet with nobody on the Green, in the Great Room, or the Raffling Shops. 'There's little stirring, except footmen, and maid servants, going to and fro of errands, and higglers and butchers, carrying provisions to people's lodgings. This takes up the town till dinner is over, and the company have reposed for two or three hours in the heat of the day; then the first thing you observe is, that the ladies come to the shady seats, at their doors, and to the benches in the groves, and covered walks (of which, every house that can have them, is generally supplied with several). Here they refresh with cooling liquors, agreeable conversation, and innocent mirth.' As the sun goes down, those with coaches or horses take the air on the downs; the others wait, then walk out in the shade of hedges and trees. Towards evening the bowling-green fills and music strikes up in the Great Room, 'every night being a kind of ball; the gentlemen bowl, the ladies dance, others raffle, and some rattle; conversation is the general pleasure of the place'. By eleven 'the dancing generally ends, and the day closes with good wishes, and appointments to meet next morning at the Wells, or somewhere else.' Often businessmen 'place their families here, and take their horses every morning to London', returning at night. 'I know one citizen that practised it for several years together, and scarce ever lay a night in London during the whole season.' On race days the downs were thick with coaches, ladies, horsemen, gentlemen and citizens, 'the racers flying over the course, as if they either touched not, or felt not the ground they run upon; I think no sight, except that of a victorious army, under the command of a Protestant King of Great Britain could exceed it'.

Carshalton was another site on the downs where the city folk built fine houses. This movement of the rich citizens out into the country was a characteristic of our period. A writer in the *Spectator* (perhaps Hughes) tells how Sir Andrew Freeport 'divides himself almost equally between the Town and Country'; after three or four days in the city he retires for the same period to a seat a few miles from London. 'Thus business and pleasure, or rather, in Sir Andrew, labour and rest, recommend each other.' Defoe remarks on the families of wealthy Londoners inhabiting the villages round about. At Eltham in Kent, 'Abundance of ladies of very good fortune dwell here, and one sees at the church such an appearance of the sex, as is surprising; but 'tis complained that the youths of these families where most beauties grow, are so generally or almost universally abroad, either in Turkey, Italy, or Spain, as merchants, or in the army or court as gentlemen; that for the ladies to live at Eltham, is, as it were, to live recluse and out of sight.' On the other hand, among the beaux, says Steele, were the Loungers, who 'shift coffee-houses and chocolate-houses from hour to hour, to get over the insupportable labour of doing nothing'. One of these, whom he knows, comes with a variety of dresses to public Assemblies, then drives fast, 'now to Bath, now to Tunbridge, then to Newmarket, and then to London', achieving the fact 'that his coach and his horse have been mentioned in all those places'.

Bristol had its Hot Well at the foot of a rock that had been levelled to take a large building; a pump had been fixed in the well. As for Bath, says Defoe, 'we may say that it is the resort of the sound rather than the sick'. The town is taken up 'in raffling, gameing, visiting, and in a word, all sorts of gallantry and levity'. In the morning 'you (supposing you to be a young lady) are fetched on a close chair, dressed in your bathing clothes, that is, stript to the smock, to the Cross-Bath. There the musick plays you into the bath, and the Women that tend you, present you with a little floating wooden dish, like a basin; in which the lady puts a handkerchief and a nosegay, of late the snuff-box is added, and some patches though the bath occasioning a little perspiration, the patches do not stick so kindly as they should. Here the ladies and gentlemen pretend to keep some distance, and each to their proper side, but frequently mingle here too, as in the King's and Queen's Bath, though not so often; and the place being but narrow, they converse freely, and talk, rally, make vows, and sometimes love; and having thus amused themselves an hour or two, they call their chairs and return to their lodgings.' In the middle of this bath was a Cross, Celia Fiennes tells us, with seats for the men; seats for ladies were in arches round the walls, while round the top was a gallery for spectators. A woman's gown was loose and bellied out with the water; the men wore drawers and waistcoats of the same canvas. 'The rest of the diversion here,' adds Defoe, 'is at the walks in the great church, and at the raffling shops, which are kept (like the Cloister at Bartholomew Fair) in the churchyard, and ground adjoining. In the afternoon here is generally a play, though the decorations are mean, and the performances accordingly; but it answers, for the company here (not the actors) make the play, to say no more. In the evening there is a ball, and dancing at least twice a week, which is commonly in the great town hall, over the market house.'

Tunbridge Wells was also very fashionable. The main diversion was in the Walks. 'Here you have all the liberty of conversation in the world,' says Defoe, 'and any thing that looks like a gentleman, has an address agreeable, and behaves with decency and good manners, may single out whom he pleases, that does not appear engaged, and may talk, rally, be merry, and say any decent thing to them; but all this makes no Acquaintance.' That must be by proper introduction. There is less slander here than at Hampstead, Epsom, and other places, but 'some say no lady ever recovered her character at Tunbridge, if she first wounded it there'. However, Thomas Baker in his play *Tunbridge-Walk* (1703) gives a less flattering picture. 'That People should come hither for air, a damn'd hole amidst a parcel of confounded hills more stifling than a bagnio, and stinks worse than the Upper Gallery in hot weather.' Lovewell says that London is a perfect solitude in the season, lawyers gone on their circuits, tradesmen to cheat at the fairs, courtiers dodging off to avoid creditors, no plays and no one in the park, the whores forced to live virtuously. Reynard says that Tunbridge Wells is full of fops from the lordly ones with long flaxen wigs to the merchant's apprentice who's always neat about the legs, squires come to court some fine town-lady and town-sparks to pick up a russet-gown, country-ladies with ruddy cheeks, fat city-ladies with tawdry silk-satins, and court-ladies with everything about them French. For pastimes there are raffles, dances, nine-pins, bowls, back-gammon, a lottery. Rakes scour the Walks, bully the shop-keepers, and beat the fiddlers, while men of wit rally over claret.

We see then, in the region round London, a transformation of country-towns with new urban pleasures and amenities. The moving-out of richer London citizens to the country completed the breakdown of the old type of city-family in which residence and place-of-work were combined. The womenfolk were now quite cut off from the work world and secluded in what was more and more considered their proper domestic isolation.[5]

6

The Landed Gentry and the Labourers

We are mainly concerned with London, but we cannot wholly omit a consideration of the rest of England. All the while the developments going on in London were having effects in varying degrees all over the country; and the country-changes in turn had their impact on London. London was the seat of government, the great financial and commercial centre, but it was in the countryside and its towns that the first stages of the industrial revolution were occurring. We realise how essential were the two elements, London and the countryside, when we compare what was happening in England with what was happening in Holland. The Dutch had a great centre of trade and money-dealings, Amsterdam; but from now on Holland fell steadily behind England because Amsterdam was not backed by anything like the manufacturing and agricultural hinterland of London. Defoe put the situation hyperbolically but with a core of truth:

> The whole kingdom, as well as the people, as the land, and even the sea, in every part of it, are employed to furnish something, and I may add, the best of every thing, to supply the city of London with provisions; I mean by provisions, corn, flesh, fish, butter, cheese, salt, fewel, timber etc, and cloths also; with every thing necessary for building, and furniture for their own use, and for trade.

He saw London so clearly as the centre of the whole system that he thought all goods should pass through it. 'If Norwich trades with Exeter, if Exeter trades with Leeds, if Leeds trades with Canterbury directly, and not by London, a model too much practised', then the goods pass through fewer hands and cause unemployment. 'The circulation of trade is ruined, and things go in straight lines that formerly took large circles.' He saw the London markets, like London itself, as monsters: for instance the corn-markets of Bear Key and Queen Hith, which were 'monsters for magnitude, and not to be matched in the world'.

We can get a fair idea of the components of this world; for the study of what was called Political Arithmetick had been coming up, applied to economic matters by such practitioners as John Gaunt, Sir William Petty, Charles Davenant, Gregory King. King made an estimate of the population in 1668, based on taxation returns, especially those of the hated hearth-tax. His unit was the family household, and he arrived at the estimate of five and a half million inhabitants, a figure that has been generally accepted by later investigators. There had therefore been an increase of about two and a half million since 1500. King's range extended from the vagrant with no family at all to the big households in which were included all the servants, even the chaplain.

He considered that half the population (some 2,795,000) were 'decreasing the wealth of the kingdom'. He meant that they needed more than they earned in order to live; the deficiency was made up by poor relief, charity, thefts. Between a third and a half of the people carried on at subsistence level, continually underemployed. These were the cottagers, paupers, labouring people, and outservants. Many were copyholders living in their own small tenements, but many more were mere wage-labourers. The labourers and outservants consisted of some 364,000 families, each averaging three and a half persons; the total was some 1,300,000 souls. The cottagers and paupers made up 400,000 families, some 1,300,000 souls. Comments by Davenant show that they did not consist of idle or useless folk, but were badly paid and underemployed. They were not immune from taxation, since they felt the effects of the duties on commodities like salt, malt, leather. And the taxes on other classes helped to depress their condition. 'If the gentry upon whose woods and gleanings they live, and who employ them to day labour, and if the manufacturers for whom they card and spin are overburdened with duties', they could neither pay so well, 'nor yield them those other reliefs which are their principal subsistence, for want of which these miserable wretches must perish with cold and hunger.'

Common seamen made up some 50,000 families, and common soldiers some 35,000: in all about 220,000 souls. Only those children who were living with their families were counted by King; others came in as servants in the households of gentlemen, freeholders, farmers, where they lived. Of vagrants there were some 30,000. The farmers made up some 150,000 families: some 750,000 souls. The average farmer earned £44 a year and spent £42 10s. His standard of living was lower than that of tradesmen, shopkeepers, artisans. Freeholders, with a better basis, numbered 180,000. Richard Baxter, writing about the same time as King, in *The Poor Man's Advocate to Rich, Racking Landlords*, declared that in all counties most farmers were small men with a rent of £60 to £80 a year, many of them worse off than their own servants by £5 to £30. The condition of these servants, 'could they but contain themselves from marriage, is far easier than of the poor tenants who are their masters. For they know their work and wages and are troubled with no cares for paying rents, or making good markets, or for the loss of corn or cattle, the rotting of sheep or the unfavourable weather, for providing for wife and children and paying labourers' and servants' wages.' What worries Baxter is that they have to work so hard 'they cannot have time to read a chapter in the Bible or to pray for their families'. Many were illiterate.

'The poor tenants,' says Baxter, are themselves 'glad of a piece of hanged bacon once a week and some few that can kill a bull eat now and then a bit of hanged beef enough to try the stomach of an ostrich. He is a rich man that can afford to eat a joint of fresh meat (beef, mutton or veal) once in a month or fortnight. If their sow pig or their hens breed chickens, they cannot afford to eat them but must sell them to make their rent. They cannot afford to eat the eggs that their hens lay, nor the apples or pears that grow on their trees (save

some that are not vendible) but must make money of all. All
the best of their butter and cheese they must sell, and feed
themselves and children and servants with skimmed cheese and
skimmed milk and whey curds.' They are so dependent on their
landlords that he thinks they may well be described as enslaved.
'They dare not displease them lest they turn them out of their
houses or increase their rents.' They are indeed so humbled
that a poor tenant takes 'every footboy or groom or porter of
his landlord to be a gentleman whose favour seemeth a preferment to him'. Defoe, we may note, described the agrarian
areas as the 'unemployed counties'. Baxter's account helps us
to see the realities behind Addison's idealisation of the feudal
Sir Roger. All over the north of England, Roger North said,
working people went barefoot.[1]

Yet in King's system the farmers were on the prosperous
side of the nation. Not all of them indeed were among the
Rackt Poor, who mostly cultivated land in the old common-
fields. The rich farmers near London would have ranked elsewhere as gentry; and other farmers did well near big towns
like Bristol. Round Epping dairy-farms were doing well by
1700; by 1750 they were quite large. There were also the groups
who owned freehold land besides their farms, and those who
had some trade that helped them to meet the rent. Such men
might be 'a weaver, a butcher, a taylor, a joiner, a carpenter'.
In some areas we even find small men turning from industry
in difficulties to farming, or trying to combine the two. Thus,
Essex clothiers round 1700 saw more Londoners than ever
taking up Essex estates and farms as a step upwards in the
social scale. One Bocking clothier's accounts start with records
of bay-making and end with farming transactions. Some
clothiers in this way turned into squires; others acquired house
properties and invested in bank or government stock.

Baxter considered the artisan or industrial (domestic) worker
to have a preferable lot to the small farmer: 'A joiner or a
turner can work in the dry house with tolerable and pleasant
work and knoweth his price and wages. A weaver, a shoemaker
or a tailor can work without the wetting or the tiring of his
body and can think and talk of the concerns of his soul without
impediment to his labour.' Again, 'though the labour of a

smith be hard, it is in a dry house, and but by short fits, and little, in comparison of threshing and reaping, but as nothing in comparison to the mowing which constantly pulls forth a man's whole strength'. Even a carrier's work is better, for he knows what it is and what he'll earn; and as for the domestic iron-workers of the Midlands, 'the nailors, spurriers [spur-makers], sithsmiths [scythe-makers] and all the rest about Dudley and Stourbridge and Brummicham [Birmingham] and Walsall and Wedgbury [Wednesbury] and Wolverhampton', they 'live in poverty, but not in the husbandman's case: they know their work and wages and have but little further cares'.

The landowners and professional classes, said King, made up some five per cent of the population; yet they enjoyed a larger proportion of the national income than did all the lower classes put together.

Our period was full of extreme contradictions, of transitions between two systems in which outlooks and relationships were sharply opposed. Looking at London, we have seen forces at work that were breaking down old bases and beginning a new sort of social mobility; but the contrary forces were still very strong. The ties of kinship over much of the country still had their old binding power. An estate was felt to belong to a family rather than an individual; it provided sources of income not only to the man who by law and custom was the owner, but also to the womenfolk, connected by blood or marriage, through jointures and portions. Entails ensured the continuity of this block of property. For the securing of place and privilege kinship was of crucial importance, in the government, the law, the church. Lower down the social scale we meet the farm, still the most common or at least the most approved agricultural unit, which was worked by a man and his family. Merchant houses were often made up of small groups of close relations. The family-head might run the head-business in London while sons, brothers, cousins were the representatives abroad. Some trades were open only to the sons of tradesmen. Weavers, stockingers, sailors, and many other such workers were helped in their work by wives and children. Later in factories wages were generally paid, not to a woman or child, but to the husband as head of the family. The Bubble Act of 1720 forbade the formation of jointstock companies except under charters not easy to get; but even without such a prohibition industrial enterprises would probably have gone on drawing on a family-group for finances.

In many rural areas a man seldom went far afield to find a wife; and since in any given parish or hundred the numbers of men and women were usually unequal, there would always be some who failed to marry. Defoe says that the gentry of Cornwall rarely stepped outside their region for a wife, or the ladies for a husband. Hence the proverb: All Cornish gentlemen are cousins. Class-divisions also hedged people in when the question of a marriage choice came up. Preston was famed for its old maids, since there were many families too poor to marry into the gentry, but too proud to marry tradesmen. Scottish colliers were more or less restricted to the daughters of other colliers for wives. There were also classes that were generally prevented from marrying at all: servants in husbandry were expected to live with the masters in the farmhouses. And apprentices had to stay single till they served out their time.

But the old restrictions were weakening. With enlarged agricultural estates, more labourers had cottages of their own; and towns with fairs attracted young people as visitors or residents. Regional economies took over from more local ones. Thus we find some of the effects of immemorial interbreeding overcome. Height increased. In the seventeenth century skeletons from London cemeteries show an average height of five feet five inches; two centuries later the average male was three inches taller.

As part of the contradictions we are tracing there was much difference in the forms of organisation of labour. Some areas had industries with corporate systems and regulations that went far back: the tin-miners of Cornwall, the coal-miners and iron-smelters of the Forest of Dean, the cutlers of Sheffield, the lead miners of Derbyshire. Elsewhere there were no such systems of control: for instance, among textile workers almost everywhere, the manufacturers of the Black Country and Birmingham, the copper miners of Anglesey and the coal miners of Northumberland. Again, we find great corporations controlling sea-trade in London and merchant adventurers still active at Hull, Bristol, Newcastle; but other outports such as Liverpool lacked such organisations. While the domestic workers in textiles arranged things as best suited themselves, in the iron industry we find wage-earners working a fixed number of hours daily under supervision. Despite the steady growth of central state-power, the JPs still remained master of much of the rural areas, where products were sold and articles bought without concern for what was being done in London. Local resources were called upon for most local enterprises, from building a harbour to a hospital.

Ideas about trade inherited from medieval days still obstructed the free play of the new money-forces. It was felt that it was wrong for a man to dispose of things if he did not alter their form. 'We have a wise law,' said Charles Townshend, 'which says no man shall sell beef who does not kill beef.' The miller was forbidden to sell corn unless it had been turned into flour, meal, malt. A man should have one sort of work, it was felt, and not meddle with the sphere of others. Townshend considered it right that 'no one who fats cattle shall follow the business of a butcher'. Drovers, concerned with transport, should not act as dealers; the common brewer, the wine-importer, the spirit-distiller should not sell by retail – though a brewer-victualler in country towns might act also as publican. But the new capital coming into inland trade worked mainly along lines that ignored law and tradition. The distinction of dealer and factor became more and more obscured. A grazier might buy cattle in a market or stop a drover in the road and come to terms with him; and so on. Early in the century the Thames lightermen became crimps or coal-factors; the hoymen of Kent, once restricted to shipping business, got stalls on the Corn Exchange; tallow chandlers, with or without licence, sold spirits. Dealers bought and sold grain, cheese, and the like in various markets on the strength of samples, so that buying and selling, with contracts for future delivery, were speeded up.[2]

Thus from the first years of the eighteenth century trade was growing in volume and finding new outlets and systems; the population was slowly growing as well. The expansion of the towns gave the farmers more markets, and there was a bigger demand for textiles, which provided employment in carding, spinning, weaving. The wives and children of small farmers and cottagers thus found work; and by the 1720s Defoe took the amount of jobs available for women and children as a measure of prosperity. John Locke thought it a scandal that children above three years should be maintained in idleness and their labour 'lost to the public till they are twelve or fourteen years old'. Defoe was delighted when he found that round Halifax 'hardly anything above four years old' was unemployed. In his 1797 report for the Board of Trade on Poor Relief, Locke had advised that children should be taught to earn their livelihood at work-schools for spinning or knitting where they should be given bread; 'what they can have at home from their parents is seldom more than bread and water, and that very scantily too'.

In general for the first half of the century wages rose and corn was cheap. But the man depending on small farming or odd jobs still found his conditions worsening in an age of enclosures. The squires and the big landlords were those who did best out of the situation. In 1709 Defoe divided the population into seven social levels: '(1) The Great who live profusely. (2) The rich who live very plentifully. (3) The middle sort who live well. (4) The working trades who labour hard but feel no want. (5) The country people, farmers, etc, who fare indifferently. (6) The poor that fare hard. (7) The miserable that really pinch and suffer want.' He always wanted to praise and encourage trade and industry, and he may have exaggerated, though he had substantial truth in saying of his fourth class: 'If the gentleman eats more puddings, this man eats more bread, if the rich man drinks more wine, this drinks more ale or strong beer, for it is the support of his labour and strength.' The same idea about beer inspires Hogarth's hearty *Beer Street*. 'If the rich man eats more veal and lamb, fowl and fish, this man eats more beef and bacon, and add to it has a better stomach. As to the milk, if the rich man eats more butter, more cream, more white meats ... our workman eats more hard cheese and salt butter than all the other put together.'

But there could be ups and downs in the trades. The bayes

(baize) of Essex depended on markets in Portugal, Spain, and Latin America, and it was believed that as a result of the war the crafty French 'prejudiced our interest and the sale of our woollen goods' in Spain, and 'began to steal our wool and to make manufactures of the same kind and also to underwork and undersell us in many countries'. In 1728 Defoe, in his *Plan of the English Commerce*, says,

> I remember after the late plague in France and the Peace in Spain, the run for goods was so great in England and the price of everything rose so high that the poor women in Essex could earn one shilling to one shilling and sixpence per diem by spinning. What was the consequence 'twas too plain to be concealed. The poor farmers could get no dairy maids, the wenches told them in so many words they would not go to service for twelve pence a week when they could get nine shillings a week at their own hands as they called it. So they all run away to Bocking, to Sudbury, to Braintree and to Colchester and other manufacturing towns in Essex and Suffolk. The very plowmen did the same and the alehouses in the great towns were thronged with them, young fellows and wenches together, till the parishes began to take cognizance of them upon another account, too dark to talk of here. While the hurry lasted the bayes were called for in prodigious quantities and the price rose from 12*d* per ell to 16*d*.

But as soon as the demand from abroad slackened, 'the parishes were left thronged with bastards which was all we may say was got by that bargain ... Nothing followed but confusion; the demand stopped, yet the makers run on as long as they were able, the bayes were pawned in every moneyed man's hand in the county, and the price sunk to 11*d* per yard at London so that a considerable deal of money was lost, bay makers broke by dozens, and ... now they, as well as the West Country men, tell us that the trade is declined.'[3]

The gentry hated the taxes that were linked with the new developments and so they were often entangled with smuggling, which made good profits and made them feel boldly independent, opposed to the tyrannies of central government. Robert

Walpole, JP of Norfolk, used to have smugglers knocking at his backdoor at Houghton and went so far as to use Admiralty barges to carry his wine up the Thames while he held government office. Robert Harley, a member of the Lord High Admiral's Council in 1706, when war held up trade with France, had his favourite claret brought over duty-free by a smuggler disguised as a secret-service agent. In 1708 at Wigtown the magistrates were involved with a big gang of smugglers who attacked and wounded customs officers, and seized a large cargo of brandy. Yet the Patent creating the Customs Board in 1671 had insisted on the cooperation of 'Justices of Peace Mayors Sherriffs Constables Bailiffs Headboroughs & all other our Officers & Ministers Whatsoever' with the collectors 'under pain of our high displeasure and the utmost peril that may fall thereon'. Such commands had little effect. What the Sunderland collector complained of to the Board in 1734–5 was generally applicable: 'We fear here many gentlemen of the county who are not friends to Officers of Customs.' Further, 'we are humbly of opinion the juries in this county are not friends to Officers of the Customs nor have they very great encouragement from many Justices of the Peace.' [4]

Lady Mary Wortley Montagu in October 1718 gives an amusing picture of a woman trying to smuggle some point-lace on a Channel packet in bad weather.

> She was an English lady that I had met at Calais, who desired me to let her go over with me in my cabin. She had bought a fine point-head, which she was contriving to hide from the custom-house officers. When the wind grew high, and our little vessel cracked, she fell very heartily to her prayers, and thought wholly of her soul. When it seemed to abate, she returned to the worldly care of her head-dress, and addressed herself to me – 'Dear madam, will you take care of this point? if it should be lost! – Ah, Lord, we shall all be lost! – Lord have mercy on my soul! – Pray, madam, take care this head-dress.' This easy transition from her soul to her head-dress, and the alternate agonies that both gave her, made it hard to determine which she thought of greatest value.

Defoe in his *Tour* remarks that Faversham, Kent, has

the most notorious smuggling trade, carried on partly by
the assistance of the Dutch in their oyster-boats, and partly
by other arts, in which they say, the people hereabouts
are arrived to such a proficiency that they are grown
monstrous rich by that wicked trade; nay, even the Owling
Trade (so they call the clandestine exporting of wool) has
seemed to be transposed from Romney Marsh to this coast,
and a great deal of it has been carried on between the
mouth of the East-Swale and the North-Foreland. As to
the landing goods here from Holland and France, such as
wine and brandy from the latter, and pepper, tea, coffee,
calicoes, tobacco, and such goods ... that black trade has
not only been carried on here, as I was informed, but on
both sides the river, on the Essex as well as the Kentish
shores.

The full ramifications were brought out in 1744 by George
Bridges in his book, *Plain Dealing*. He had been a smuggler
for nine years before settling down as 'a destroyer of bugs'.
The Irish, he tells, were supposed to export wool only to
England, but they sent a great deal to the continent. English
graziers despatched wool to Scotland and the Orkneys, whence
it went with no trouble to Holland, Flanders, France. Combed
wools and shearings were taken to 'men of fortune' with houses
or cellars on the south coast; these men had specially-built
vessels to convey the supplies to ships lying offshore. Large
quantities of wool were floated down rivers to the estuaries
where ships, already cleared by customs, took it aboard at
night. Much wool and yarn was compressed in bales and went
through the customs as drapery, or was carried abroad, tight-
packed, in baggage. The smuggled goods were those with
special import duties: tobacco, wines, spirits, tea, lace, silk.
(Tea had its legal sale controlled by the East India Company,
which limited supplies and kept prices far above those charged
at Hamburg and Amsterdam.) Tobacco was brought ashore
by seamen in small parcels, or, after being passed by customs
with a drawback for re-export, was unloaded by night off the
coast and carried ashore. In London it was sold in coffee houses,

in the country by pedlars. No clear line distinguished thefts from ships in port, smuggling, privateering, and piracy. Privateers, when there were no wars, carried illicit cargoes or convoyed smuggling luggers; at times even revenue cutters were so employed. There was no public opinion condemning such activities. Adam Smith saw only that laws 'made that a crime which nature never meant to be', and a man who had scruples about buying smuggled goods suffered from pedantic hypocrisy, exposed as 'a greater knave than most than most of his neighbours'.

In 1700 England was made up of villages and hamlets; the few big towns were mainly on the coast, though new ones were growing up in Lancashire, the West Riding, the West Midlands. But big changes had occurred in many areas, dating from the period of revolutionary struggle, when new fallow crops (clover, lucerne, sainfoin), asparagus and artichokes were brought in to supplement the corn that was now a valuable export to Europe. Clover revolutionised the use of heath and other wastes that had been previously unproductive: a result especially important in the North and West where people were moving in as industry followed low wages and cheap food. Market-gardening and intensive fruit-growing developed with outlets in the big towns, particularly London, and tended to change diets. Turnips were grown as a field crop, and more potatoes. Characteristic of the new turn were also marsh-draining, the floating of water-meadows, manuring and stock-breeding. New plants and trees were introduced, such as the weeping willow and acacia of the Duke of Argyle. (Tobacco, grown widely by the 1650s, was forbidden in the interests of colonial production.) Blyth's *English Improver* of 1649 showed ideas and attitudes that were to carry on and transform agriculture in the later seventeenth and eighteenth centuries. The effective development of capitalist farming meant the worsening of the lot of the small free farmer and finally his destruction, hence the growth of enclosures and the tricks of jobbers who lent small-holders money, then seized their land.

The enclosing of commons robbed the poor of a source of fuel and pasture, and drove them to seek employment by wages. Traditional sources of food were cut off. Tell the Fenmen, says

Fuller, 'of the great benefit to the public, because where a pike or a duck fed formerly, now a bullock or sheep is fatted; they will be ready to return that if they be taken in taking that bullock or sheep, the rich owner indicteth them for felons; whereas that pike or duck were their own goods, only for their pains of catching them'. Hence the way in which the gentry's triumph in 1688 led to ever harsher penalties for poaching. Squatters were driven from forest-holdings as land was deforested and put under cultivation.

In the Commonwealth, with Cromwell himself a keen hunter, the confiscation and breaking-up of the deer-parks of the king and of royalists, together with the abolition of the game-laws, led to a drastic decrease in the number of deer. Charles II tried to reverse things, but, apart from the revival of the game-laws, with little effect. Deer-hunting for venison gave way to fox-hunting for sport: a change that took over a hundred years to complete. In Stuart times fox-hunting had been a plebeian sport with no purpose beyond the pleasures of cruelty; it was linked with the various baitings, especially with badger-digging. The hunt was followed on foot so that everyone would be in at the maltreatment of the dug-out creatures. For a while the gentry, lacking deer, turned to the hare, which was considered sweet-smelling unlike the malodorous fox. But the sport was boring, as hares tended to run in circles while foxes provided a good run. So more and more gentry left the hare for the fox, harriers for packs of foxhounds. From the late seventeenth century the change was going on in Yorkshire, but Midland grass was found to provide the best setting for fox-scents. Squire Boothby founded the Quorn in 1697, and his successor, Meynell, set the seal of fashion on the fox-hunt. The Midland meetings attracted London swells. Meynell hated smart thrusters, but they crowded to Melton Mowbray to gallop after and over the hounds.[5]

For the gentry hunting became an ever more important pursuit. Steele describes the horrors of living in the country among the ardent hunters. 'It is to me an insupportable affliction, to be tormented with the narrations of a set of people, who are warm in their expressions of the quick relish of that pleasure which their dogs and horses have a more delicate taste of. I do also in my heart detest and abhor that damnable doctrine and position of the necessity of a bumper.' A man was not permitted to drink modestly. Worst of all was the conversation. 'To attend without impatience an account of five-barred gates, double ditches, and precipices, and to survey the orator with desiring eyes, is to me extremely difficult, but absolutely necessary, to be upon tolerable terms with him: but then the occasional burstings out into laughter, is of all accomplishments the most requisite. I confess at present I have not the command of these convulsions, as is necessary to be of good company.' The Roarers 'think they themselves, as neighbours, may come into our rooms with the same right, that they and their dogs hunt in our grounds'. He suggests that these persons should be kept apart in a Club.

> Their attire should be the same with their huntsmen's, and none should be admitted into this green conversation-piece, except he had broke his collar-bone thrice. A broken rib or two might also admit a man without the least opposition. The president must necessarily have broken his neck, and have been taken up dead once or twice: For the more maims this brotherhood shall have met with, the easier will their conversation flow and keep up; and when any of these vigorous invalids had finished his narration of the collar-bone, this naturally could introduce the history of the ribs. Besides, the different circumstances of their falls and fractures would help to prolong and diversify their relations. There should also be another Club of such men, who have not succeeded so well in maiming themselves, but are however in the constant pursuit of these accomplishments.

Elsewhere he jokes at the obsession with poachers by depicting a country gentleman of between five and six thousand pounds a year, who has scarcely enjoyed a moment's rest through fear of the poachers in his deer-park and the fops wooing his daughter. 'I have indeed pretty well secured my park, having for this purpose provided my self of four keepers, who are left-handed, and handle a quarter-staff beyond any other fellow in the country.' Further, 'I have blunderbusses always charged, and fox-gins planted in private places about my garden.' He suggests that daughters as well as deer should be secured by law, and hopes that 'some honest gentleman of a publick spirit, would move for leave to bring in a Bill *For the better preserving of the Female Game.'* [6]

Women were now riding to hounds. Addison on 5 May 1711 describes a country girl

> who came up to town last winter, and is one of the greatest fox-hunters in the country. She talks of hounds and horses, and makes nothing of leaping over a six-bar gate. If a man tells her a waggish story, she gives him a push with her hand in jest, and calls him an impudent dog; and if her servant neglects his business, threatens to kick him out of the house. I have heard her, in her wrath, call a substantial tradesman a lousy cur; and remember one day, when she could not think of the name of a person, she described him in a large company of men and ladies by the Fellow with the Broad Shoulders.

This fashion must have been recent; for on 10 August of the same year Swift tells how he and Dr Arbuthnot, overtaking Miss Forester, went to see the place 'they have made for a famous horse race tomorrow, where the queen will come. We met the queen coming back, and Miss Forester stood like us, with her hat off, while the queen went by.' As for Miss Forester, 'she is a silly true maid of honour, and I did not like her, although she be a toast, and was dressed like a man', in a riding habit, according to the recent fashion. (In 1701 she had married Sir John Downing, he fifteen and she thirteen; they were soon divorced by mutual consent on the grounds of mutual aversion.)

The small landowner to the best of his ability followed the ways of his betters and felt himself raised above the level of the common folk who committed a crime when they killed animals for food. 'He, that has a spaniel by his side, is a yeoman of about an hundred pounds a year, an honest man. He is just within the Game Act, and qualified to kill an hare or a pheasant: He knocks down a dinner with his gun twice or thrice a week; and by that means lives much cheaper than those who have not so good an estate as himself. He would be a good neighbour if he did not destroy so many partridges; in short, he is a very sensible man; shoots flying; and has been several times foreman of the Petty-Jury.'

Some big landlords led the way in the farming changes: Lord Townshend with his turnips and fourfold rotation of crops, Jethro Tull with his seed-drilling and horse-hoeing. Not that the facts quite followed the legend. Tull's ideas were little imitated for about a century; and Townshend, though a talker about turnips, was not their introducer. Robert Bakewell, famed for developing barrel-shaped Leicestershire sheep, was not the only breeder of more profitable flocks; and Coke's Norfolk system of large farms let on long leases to capitalist farmers (who increased yields with soil-fertilisation and four-course rotation of crops) was beginning to operate in fact by the early century. Nor did the mass of farmers follow quickly in such trails. The medieval open-field strip-system still was pre-valent. Generally two or three big open fields lay round a village, the strips individually owned but the crops and stock controlled by the community of owners according to im-memorial usage. Enclosures brought in smaller fields where the stocking or cropping was under the control of a single owner. Large sums could be made from the land despite the poor breed of cattle and sheep in many areas; there was an increasing demand for wool and there was the corn-bounty. The enriched sections of the gentry wanted ever larger estates, and enclosure was the main way to getting new land. The Dukes of Bedford owned almost all the productive land of Bedfordshire; the Duke of Newcastle, with a yearly income of £40,000, had estates in twelve counties and used dubious methods to get hold of royal forests.

Such men wanted to build noble mansions. The great ones could do this with ease, and the construction of large country houses went on through the eighteenth century, turning soon to Palladian models. A new standard was set by Castle Howard, begun in the spring of 1701 and taking five years to build, with Vanbrugh as architect. There was a central cupola and a bold array of towers, pinnacles, domes, on a scale not previously used for a private dwelling. New problems had to be tackled and solved; and Vanbrugh was delighted that, despite the height and size of the rooms, there was comfort.

> I am much pleased here (amongst other things) to find Lord Carlisle so thoroughly convinced of the conveniencies of his new house, now he has had a year's trial of it. And I am the more pleased with it, because I have new proof that the Duchess of Marlborough must find the same conveniency at Blenheim. For my Lord Carlisle was pretty much under the same apprehensions with her, about long passages, high rooms etc. But he finds what I told him to be true. That those passages would be so far from gathering and drawing wind as he feared, that a candle would not flare in them. Of this he has lately had the proof, by bitter stormy nights in which not one candle wanted to be put in a lanthorn … He likewise finds, that all his rooms, with moderate fires are ovens.[7]

Walpole consolidated his position by buying more land and rebuilding his house. Then he built a mansion at Houghton in Norfolk (begun 1721), which he used to strengthen his place among the East Anglian gentry and to entertain visitors from London. The parties were called his Norfolk Congresses: sessions of hard drinking, hunting, bawdy conviviality. He used the best architects and the best craftsmen, and put in the best art-collection of the time as evidence of his power, wealth, culture. Thus he angered his brother-in-law, Lord Townshend, once a greater man than he, who had started him off on his road to success. Lord Hervey was amused: 'Lord Townshend looked upon his own seat at Raynham as the metropolis of Norfolk, was proud of the superiority, and considered every stone that augmented the splendour of Houghton as a diminution of Raynham.' The new country houses had their rural aspect of hunting and farming, but they were more importantly attempts to bring as much as possible of city-life into the country. Thus, when the Duke of Devonshire rebuilt Chatsworth at the end of the seventeenth century, he was leaving London for political reasons and wanted a sumptuous palace in the midst of what Defoe called the howling wilderness of the Derbyshire moors.

The upper classes were spending more and more time in London. Many were there four months in the year, with a month in Bath or some such spa, a month travelling, and perhaps six months at home. The richer sections created such towns as Bath, Clifton, Edinburgh, Dublin, Brighton; the lesser gentry built such urban centres as Nottingham, Newcastle, York, Norwich, Exeter. The absentee landlord and the boozy bumpkin squire became types in plays and other writings. The ruling class showed a cross-fertilisation of town and country, with important power-roots in the country; the towns provided jobs, contacts, ideas. Men involved with the government had to spend much time in London; Walpole could give Houghton only a month a year, though most members of parliament and men with lesser posts were not so tied. But for all the gentry the city was the place to meet friends from other regions, arrange marriages, carry on lawsuits, borrow money, get the latest news at first hand, and stock up with fashionable clothes and furniture.

Estate-villages were already being laid out on principles that carried on through the century, for example at Chippenham in Cambridgeshire (1702–13). They were formally planned with more or less identical cottages all set in straight lines: a system that held till the advent of the Picturesque theory, when a haphazard effect was sought.

Lesser landowners often overstrained their resources in building. Roger North's granddaughter says that he 'pulled down the old house and built one too large for the estate, unfortunately. He loved and understood architecture, and drew it well.' He included a gallery sixty feet long to hold an organ, and made a collection of pictures, being very fond of Lely's work. He played about as a chemist in his laboratory, 'but I never heard that he did anything but found a method of bleaching bees' wax, from which he had candles made in the house'. Lesser gentry also often failed in trying to get profits from the land. Prices and rents were falling in the later century; and the disillusioned squires were liable to become diehard Tories. The northern gentry, often Catholic and desperately hard up, supported the Jacobite cause in 1715. Though others were averse to such drastic steps, a cleavage was beginning between large sections of the gentry on the one hand and on the other the successful landlords and the mercantile class with which they were coming to terms. Thus the party-line between Tory and Whig deepened, though it was long before a clear-cut party-system emerged.

The lesser men were afraid, unable to fathom what was happening, but disliking what they could make out. The big men were those with capital and the resources for improvements; they captured the heiresses who had land worth grabbing, were able to draw funds from the profitable places they held in the administration, and knew where to get good advice about the investment of their surplus money. Besides falling rents, the small men had to meet many bad seasons in the 1690s, and then, after some bettering under Anne, a very bad crop failure in 1709. They could not pay the increasing taxes. William Bromley wrote in a letter of 1707, 'I believe all country gentlemen are under the like pressure and uneasiness, and all cannot so well bear them. Tenants are breaking every day, and the quarterly payments of the taxes takes away the little money we receive.' The great burden was the land tax, which after 1688 was the most important single source of revenue voted yearly by Parliament; it had become a rate on land, fixed in 1693 by an assessment of rental value; and the rate stayed high from 1693 to 1713 save for a brief space under William.

An Act of 1714 set out the state of things: 'The heavy burden of the late long and expensive war hath been chiefly borne by the owners of the land of this kingdom, by reason whereof they have been necessitated to contract very large debts, and thereby and by the abatement on the value of their lands are become greatly impoverished.' So the landed gentry in general felt themselves menaced by the strange new money-power which operated as a force in itself – something unlike money made directly from agriculture or trade – and by the long-drawn-out wars. They suspected that the City, the Whigs, the politicians who insisted on fighting out the war to the bitter end, were all in some sort of villainous plot. Though legal machinery was growing ever more expert, they found it hard to mortgage their lands in a helpful way. In 1707 Lord Harvey stated that estates in Suffolk had fallen in value and that he was now refusing to buy lands that he would earlier have taken up. In 1711 the agent of the Duke of Newcastle declared that 'land about London and all other parts of England is fallen at least 4 or 5 years' purchase'. He considered that this drop resulted from 'the great difference of advantage between money and land'.[8]

Addison's Sir Roger de Coverley typifies the sort of character that had emerged among the more backward gentry, who stood out flatly against the way the world was going. From the account of the money he spent in wooing the widow we see the sources of his income. 'He has disposed of an hundred acres in a diamond-ring, which he would have presented her with, had she thought fit to accept it; and upon her wedding-day she should have carried on her head fifty of the tallest oaks upon his estate. He further informed me that he would have allowed her a coal-pit to keep her in clean linnen, that he would have allowed her the profits of a windmill for her fans, and have presented her once in three years with the shearing of his sheep for her under-petticoats.' He is depicted as a sort of feudal patriarch, commanding the complete devotion of his servants. 'As the knight is the best master in the world, he seldom changes his servants; and as he is beloved by all about him, his servants never care for leaving him; by this means his domesticks are all in years and grown old with their master.' They show unreserved joy when he arrives back at his country seat.

> Some of them could not refrain from tears at the sight of their old master; every one of them pressed forward to do something for him, and seemed discouraged if he were not employed. At the same time the good old knight, with a mixture of the father and the master of the family, tempered the enquiries after his own affairs with several kind questions relating to themselves. This humanity and good nature engages everybody to him, so that when he is pleasant upon any of them, all his family are in good humour, and none so much as the person whom he diverts himself with. On the contrary, if he coughs, or betrays any infirmity of old age, it is easy for a stander-by to observe a secret concern in the looks of his servants.

This idealised picture is however relieved and given force by the various oddities attributed to him, which are well observed. Thus, at church,

> as Sir Roger is landlord to the whole congregation, he keeps them in very good order, and will suffer nobody to sleep in it besides himself; for if by chance he has been surprised into a short nap at sermon, upon recovering out of it he stands up and looks about him, and if he sees anybody else nodding, either wakes them himself, or sends his servant to them. Several other of the old knight's particularities break out upon these occasions. Sometimes when he will be lengthening out a verse in the singing-psalms half a minute after the rest of the congregation have done with it, sometimes when he is pleased with the matter of his devotion, he pronounces *Amen* three or four times to the same prayer; and sometimes stands up when everybody else is upon their knees, to count the congregation, or see if any of his tenants are missing. In the midst of the service he calls out to an idle fellow, who is kicking his heels, 'to mind what he was about, and not disturb the congregation.'

We thus see him a man who wants his own way in everything and imposes what he considers decorum, without the least idea that he is despotic; Addison's gently humorous style makes it all seem very harmless and likeable. The characteristics which Addison idealised in his Sir Roger reappear in such characters as Richardson's Lovelace in *Clarissa*. 'It was a maxim with his family, from which he would by no means depart, never to rack-rent old tenants, or their descendants.' He liked to see all his tenants sleek and contented, even if his rent-roll were £300 or even £400 the worse for it. Such an attitude was even more antique in 1748 than in 1711–12 when Addison wrote. It represented a Tory ideal which was less and less rooted in reality.[9]

7

Marriages and Elections

After 1688 there was an increasing subordination of marriage to the building-up of landed wealth, and other motives for marrying played a minor role. In the sixteenth and seventeenth centuries royal favour had been a major factor in status and wealth; now political power more than ever depended on land. Behind the new attitudes to marriage among the upper class there lay the new laws of entail whereby the father became in effect the life-tenant of the estate, with the eldest son given a special role of authority. The family property had thus grown more important than any individual owner, while at the same time the gentry had more and more to adapt themselves to a situation where the standards of expenditure were for the first time set by men who drew their wealth from other sources and where landowners had to meet heavy taxes. The gentry had to consolidate estates if they were to survive and they used marriage as an important means for doing so.[1]

The reigns of William III and of Anne were characterised by wide and deep antagonism between the landed gentry and the big men of the City. A landowner or his son might condescend to marry a City heiress in order to get her money; but it was still unacceptable for his daughter to marry into a City family. All the while the needs of the gentry were driving up the price of husbands and swelling the size of marriage portions. Lord Nottingham had to pay out £52,000 to get rid of his girls. Daughters or sisters were thus liable to be a burden for the landed gentry, who had to ponder carefully every alliance they entered into. On 3 May 1703 Sir William Massingberd, second baronet of Gunby, wrote to his second cousin, a fellow-commoner of Emmanuel College, Cambridge,

> There goes a report about the country that you are court-ing a young lady. What truth may be in it, I know not. But before you engage in such a concern I hope you will seriously consider how far your own happiness, as well as that of your family, depends upon your discreet manage-ment of so important an affair ... You are too well acquainted with the unfortunate circumstances of your family to stand in need of any information, and unless you marry a prudent person with a considerable fortune I fear you will let slip the most likely opportunity of retrieving it ... A discreet wife with five or six thousand pound (and if she have more 'tis the better still) would put you in a condition to pay your brother and sisters' portions, clear the estate, furnish you wherewithal to build or repair, and give you a comfortable prospect of living easy in the world. Such matches there are to be had, and should you stay a while ere you meet with one, yet the future success would compensate for the delay, and I believe you will grant that 'tis more eligible to be happy at last than to repent at leisure. 'Tis your advantage I am at in what I write, though I must confess there is something of self-interest too in the case, but no more than this (viz) that your welfare will always contribute to my satisfaction.

Sir William Temple, writing in the late seventeenth century, declared that the custom of making marriages 'just like other common bargains and sales by the mere esteem of interest or gain, without any love or esteem' was 'of no ancient date'. In the next century the newspapers carried advertisements offer-ing or demanding specified dowries and jointures. In the *Athenian Mercury* a correspondent inquired, 'Whether it is lawful to marry a person one cannot love only in compliance to rela-tions and to get an estate?' The editor, Dunton, replied, ' 'Tis beyond all doubt and must be answered in the negative, since such a practice would be both the most cruel and imprudent thing in the world' – but he must have known that he was denouncing a common and approved practice. Marriage-settlements were important items of gossip. Thomas Wilson noted in his diary on 8 October 1731: 'Went to Aston Parks to see Egerton Leigh, not at home. Dined with Hamlet Yates. George Leigh of Highleigh made but an indifferent bargain for himself at his marriage. Agreed to pay off debts and mortgages and sister's fortunes to the amount of £8000. Had only £6000 with his lady and is to pay £550 *per ann.* to his father, and the estates not worth above £1200 *per ann.* Came home at night and supped at Cousin Worseleys.' Clearly he and Yates had discussed Leigh at length over dinner.

Sometimes a man was too mean to finance his sisters. Dr John Radcliffe, dying in 1714 worth £140,000 (according to Hearne), wrote in repentance a few days before his death to his sister Millicent: 'You will find by my Will, that I have taken better care of you, than perhaps you might expect from my former treatment of you, for which with my dying breath, I most heartily ask pardon. I had indeed acted the brother's part much better, in making a handsome settlement for you while living than after my decease; and can plead nothing in excuse, but that the love of money, which I have emphatically known to be the root of all evil, was too predominant over me.' (He himself had once negotiated for the hand of a rich city-merchant's daughter, but found that she was already compromised with her father's book-keeper.)

As soon as a man had a chance to rise in the world, he thought of an advantageous marriage to lift him yet further. Mrs Adams, wife of the rector of Great Baddow, Essex, wrote in January 1700, in her odd spelling, of one of her many cousins: 'Mr Abdy that was the Minister dieid, and left my Lady Abdy exectricks, and my cosen Jack Niklas is to have the living, so he is to go into orders with all speid, this good living has mad him declar his resolutions of being A Minister and now the next business must be to get a good fortune with a wife, his parsing will be A very good provision for A younger brother, his own porsion besids.' The chief triumph of Mrs Adams's later years was to gain from the local bigwigs, the Pascalls of Great Baddow Hall, a highly suitable bride for her great nephew, the heir of the Verneys. How unusual or even undignified a man of any quality felt it to be to live on his own earnings rather than by inheritance or marriage-portion may be read in a note from Steele to his mother-in-law. 'You are well acquainted that I have had no fortune with your daughter: that I have struggled through great difficulties for our maintenance: that we live now in the handsomest manner supported by my industry.' He added, 'My posterity is yours also: you will be, I doubt not, inclined that your estate should pass to them.' His note was carried by the lawyer Diggle who had been warding off bailiffs and who would tell Mrs Scurlock how best to leave her estate to the Steeles.

The way in which a girl could be forced into a marriage that she loathed is exemplified by Mary Granville. When she was seventeen, the family produced the man she was to marry. 'I expected to have seen somebody with the appearance of a gentleman, when the poor old dripping, almost drowned, Pendarvis was brought into the room, like Hob out of the well. His wig, his coat, his dirty boots, his large unwieldy person, and his crimson countenance, were all subjects of great mirth and observation to me.' He was nearly sixty. 'He was fat, much afflicted with gout, and often sat in a sullen mood, which I concluded was from the gloominess of his temper.' She left the room when he entered, and took care to let him see why she did so. He approached Lord Lansdowne, who pleaded his cause with Mary. 'He took me by the hand, and after a very pathetic speech of his love and care of me, of my father's unhappy circumstances, my own want of fortune, and the little prospect I had of being happy if I disobliged those friends of mine who were desirous of serving me. He told me of Pendarvis' passion for me and his offer of settling his whole estate upon me.' She burst into tears, but the family's relentless pressure, with threats of retaliation on a young man whom she liked, ended by breaking her down. 'I was sacrificed. I lost not life, indeed, but all that makes life desirable—joy and peace of mind.' Pendarvis was extremely jealous. She lived with him at Roscrow Castle where he drank heavily and groaned with gout. Worse, his finances turned out to be in a poor way through 'bad tenants and a cheating steward'. She comments in restrained chagrin. 'I thought myself at least secure of an easy fortune.' In 1724, after some eight years of marriage, he died, leaving her only a few hundred pounds a year. (Among her later wooers was Wesley.)[2]

As the century wore on, alliances between the landed gentry and mercantile families grew more common. 'We have so many of the first titled families,' says Mr B. in *Pamela*, 'who have allied themselves to trade (whose inducements were money only) that it ceases to be either a wonder as to the fact, or a disgrace to the honour.' The situation is fully worked out in *Clarissa*. The Harlowe family have already increased their wealth by careful marriages, but they want to go further. The two uncles (one enriched by minerals found on his lands, the other by East India trade) decide not to marry; the eldest child and only son, James, considers that his sisters may be married off with ten to fifteen thousand pounds each; then all the real estate (that of their grandfather, father, and uncles) will come to him. He also expects a big estate from his godmother. All together he will be in a position to obtain a peerage.

This neat arrangement is badly disturbed by the grandfather leaving his estate to Clarissa. She lets her father manage this inheritance, taking only what he allows her; when she leaves home, he keeps possession of her property. The family smiles on the aristocrat Lovelace's proposals to the elder daughter; but when he turns to Clarissa, the whole scheme of Harlowe aggrandisement is threatened. If he marries her, the uncles might switch over to his side. So the family decides to marry her off to the coarse and repellent Mr Soames, who represents the rising middle class, upstart and mercenary, grown rich by 'land-jobbing and husbandry'. If he and Clarissa have no children, the Harlowe family will benefit enormously. Miss Howe sums up: 'You are all too rich to be happy, child. For must not each of you, by the constitutions of your family, marry to be *still* richer?'[3]

This permeation of marriage by the money-ethic affected all the levels of society above the working class. With it goes the idealisation of women that grows throughout the century, especially among the middle classes, to whom the family seems more and more an enclave or refuge from society. James Bonnell, married in 1693, set out the ideal: 'Upon marriage,

let us immediately remove from the mixt company in which
we hitherto have lived, to enjoy each other in more solitary
retirement, where all things about us are our own, and to be our
own care: and here, let us be sufficient company to each other,
as Adam was to Eve in Paradise.' This ideal, which seems to
exclude the cash-nexus from the family, is in fact a submission
to it, accepting its socially divisive force.

The terms Whigs and Tories were old nicknames given now a
new force and breadth. The Tories were dispossessed Irish
become outlaws, bogtrotters: the name was given to the men
opposing in 1679–80 the exclusion of James Duke of York from
the throne; after 1688 it was applied more widely to the con-
servative landed gentry and their supporters. The Whigs in the
seventeenth century were the adherents of the Presbyterian
cause in Scotland. The name was applied to the exclusionists
and then to the men who remained strong for the Protestant
succession and who largely represented the commercial and
financial interests. Not that a strict line could thus be drawn
between landed and commercial interests, but in a broad way
the division existed and determined the main lines of political
conflict. The use of the distinguishing terms soon become
habitual, though without much precision of definition. The
very idea of a political party was still something with extreme
odium attached to it. Halifax puts cogently in his *Political,
Moral and Miscellaneous Reflections* what was the accepted
viewpoint:

> The best Party is a kind of conspiracy against the rest of
> the nation. They put everyone else out of their protection.
> Like the Jews to the Gentiles, all others are the offscourings
> of the world.
>
> Men value themselves upon their principles, so as to
> neglect practice, abilities, industry, &c.
>
> Party cutteth off one half of the world from the other,
> so that the mutual improvement of men's understanding
> by conversing, &c, is lost, and men are half undone when
> they lose the advantage of knowing what their enemies
> think of them.

Party is generally an effect of wantonness, peace and plenty, which beget humour, pride, &c, and that is called zeal and public spirit.

Ignorance maketh most men go into a Party, and shame keepeth them from getting out of it.

Addison, like all the moralists, attacked parties. 'There cannot a greater judgment befall a country than such a dreadful spirit of division as rends a government into two distinct people, and makes them greater strangers and more averse to one another, than if they were actually two different nations. The effects of such a division are pernicious to the last degree, not only with regard to those advantages which they give the common enemy, but to those private evils which they produce in the heart of almost every particular person. This influence is very fatal both to men's morals and their understandings; it sinks the virtue of a nation, and not only so, but destroys even common sense.' He sees it ending, if carried to its full extent, in civil war and bloodshed. Elsewhere he called on 'the honest men of all parties' to enter into an 'Association for the Defence of one another, and the Confusion of their Common Enemy'. They would seek 'to extirpate all such furious zealots as would sacrifice one half of their country to the passion and interest of the other; as also such infamous hypocrites, that are for promoting their own advantage, under colour of the publick good'. He feared that party-spirit 'may in time expose us to the derision and contempt of all the nations about us'. We see that the development of the class-struggle in England was far ahead of the rest of Europe.

The line of reasoning by Halifax and Addison leads on to the positions of Bolingbroke in his *Patriot King*, where all parties are denounced as factions and the hope of the nation set in a dominant king who rules impartially for the good of everyone. Feudal concepts of hierarchical unity are thus carried on into the bourgeois world that is busy disintegrating all such concepts by means of the cash-nexus; and a ghost of feudal order is used to disguise the reality of warring egoisms and interests. Indeed Bolingbroke in a letter of 1710 to a Jacobite friend gave away the facts behind the Tory pretences. 'I am afraid that we came to Court in the same disposition as all parties have done; that the principal spring of our actions was to have the government of the state in our hands; that our principal views were the conservation of power, great employment to ourselves, and great opportunities of rewarding those who had helped to raise us, and of hunting those who stood in opposition to us.'

Addison tried to ridicule women out of holding political views. Party-rage is a spot or blemish that has crept into their conversations, a male vice.

When I have seen a pretty mouth uttering calumnies and invectives, what would not I have given to have stopt it? How I have been troubled to see some of the finest features in the world grow pale, and tremble with party-rage? Camilla is one of the greatest beauties in the British nation, and yet values her self more upon being the virago of one party, than upon being the toast of both. The dear creature, about a week ago, encountered the fierce and beautiful Penthesilea across a tea-table; but in the height of her anger, as her hand chanced to shake with the earnestness of the dispute, she scalded her fingers, and split a dish of tea upon her petticoat. Had not his accident broke off the debate, nobody knows where it would have ended.

He tries to frighten women by saying that nothing is so bad for the face as party-zeal.

It gives an ill-natured cast to the eye, and a disagreeable sourness to the look: besides, that it makes the lines too strong, and flushes them worse than brandy. I have seen a woman's face break out in heats, as she has been talking against a great lord, whom she has never seen in her life; and indeed I never knew a party-woman that kept her beauty for a twelvemonth.

The London ladies had become much interested in political events. Justinian Isham records of Dr Sacheverell, who was impeached for his sermon attacking the principles of 1688, 'All the conversation in town runs upon the trial, the ladies get up by four a clock in the morning to go to it, and all foreign or home news relating to publick or private concerns are quite laid aside.'(4)

Defoe gives us an example of the way in which the local landlord imposed his political will on people. Coleshill in Warwickshire, he says, is a small but handsome market town. 'It chiefly, if not wholly, belongs to the Lord Digby, who is Lord of the Mannor, if not real owner of almost all the houses in the town, and as that noble person is at present a little on the wrong side as to the government, not having taken the oaths to King George, so the whole town are so eminently that way too, that they told me there was but one family of Whigs, as they called them, in the whole town, and they hoped to drive them out of the place too very quickly.' Lord Clare in 1714 wrote to the electors at Boroughbridge, Suffolk: 'Being now in the quiet possession of the estate devised to me by my late uncle, the Duke of Newcastle's will, I hope I shall meet with no opposition in your town. I hope by your ready compliance with my desires you'll show how well you deserve of me. And you may be sure according to your deserts I shall endeavour to confer my favours.'

Elections determined who was to have the power of patronage and therefore they stirred up strong party feelings. In 1708 the twelfth general election since 1694 was held, and Defoe in his *Review* argued that while the Triennial Act had a 'complication of advantages ... lodged in the bowels of it', it yet had 'this fatal consequence in it, which all England feels ... viz: that the certainty of a new election on three years is an unhappy occasion of keeping alive the divisions and party strife among the people which would otherwise have died of course. Had the election to come been remote and uncertain, the interest of this or that person had been equally uncertain, and men had not applied themselves so much to the cultivating their interest and riveting themselves in the opinion either of people or parties.' He is a man of his period who feels that parties are pests, and yet he knows that without a fixed term for the life of a parliament there would be an ossification of certain strong interests. 'This beautiful rose has its prickle: this certainty of the return of an election occasions a constant keeping alive of innumerable factions.' In a deeply divided society there was no escape from parties. 'Parties are ever struggling; they contend on every occasion, choosing their parish officers, their Recorders, their magistrates, and everything that has the least face of public concern; all runs by parties, all eye the grand election ... and have that occasion in view.' (5)

Steele, in his long struggle to escape from debts, tried standing for parliament. In 1713 he tackled the borough of Stockbridge, Hampshire, on the river Test, with sixty odd village families and some hovel-dwellers in the marsh to the rear, who had become electors by building a door and a hearth, the costs of which they would recover in election bribes. Under Anne, as no lord got profits from the borough, an attempt was made to disenfranchise it, but failed by one vote. The burgesses had appointed two managers to find who would pay best, and they thought Captain Steele a likely man. The bailiff Snow led the candidates to the hustings on polling day, with constable, hayward, and sergeant (carrying the mace), and ensured that adverse voters got too drunk to vote. While the candidates stood on a platform, the bailiff recited their merits amid yells, laughs, groans; and when he counted the votes he put in fifty for Steele, seventy-one burgesses voting.

In 1722 Steele was sent by the Earl of Sunderland to stand for Wendover: a mean dirty corporate town, said Defoe. A few years before, the vicar had denounced the 'toping days and nights' at elections, the 'dismal swearing and ranting', and the electors 'selling their souls for a debauch'. Steele was returned. A tale was told:

Sir Richard Steele got his election by a merry trick. He scooped an apple and put ten guineas into it, and said it should be deposited for the wife of any of the voters that should be first brought to bed that day nine months. Upon this, several that would have been against him, and who lived some miles from the town, posted home to capacitate their wives to claim the apple, and the next morning the election passed in his favour before they returned.

King William himself was not above making a royal progress that was in effect an electoral stunt. At the time of the general elections of 1695 he went around to influence the gentry, visiting Newmarket, Althorp, Stamford, Lincoln, Welbeck, Warwick, Burford, Woodstock, Oxford. At Newmarket he hunted and attended horse-races for four days. Wherever he could, he hunted and flattered the gentry. To the fox-hunting notables of Northamptonshire he declared that their county was the finest in England and perhaps the whole world, adding, 'Nothing made a gentleman look like a gentleman but living like one.' At Sherwood, hunting with four hundred gentlemen, he was appalled at the open sawpits and pleased the others by ordering them to be filled up. On his forty-fifth birthday at Warwick Lord Brooke gave a fireworks display and an 129-gallon bowl of punch for the townsfolk. Evelyn noted: 'The King made a progress into the north, to shew himself to the people, against the elections, and was every where complimented, except at Oxford.' [6]

The gentry dominated the electoral system. The inflation that been steadily going on for a long time had made the property qualification (a forty shilling freehold) apply to an ever larger number of persons, small farmers, shopkeepers, craftsmen, small freeholders. At the same time the increase in the population swelled the numbers. This development affected both country seats and boroughs with wide franchises. But though often two to three thousand men in an area had a vote, the gentry, if they agreed among themselves, could control elections. However, they often were at loggerheads, and points of disagreement came up in the country as well as among merchants and professional men in the large corporate towns. During the 1690s nearly 4000 polled in Norfolk, and by 1710 the number reached 6000. Here every general election under William was contested. The other counties showed similar changes. Some 200,000 men (about a thirtieth of the population) now had the vote, so that for the first time there was something like a large electorate. William, like James II, realised that this unruly and argumentative element must be somehow controlled if he was to have the sort of stability he wanted. So there emerged new ways of electioneering and propaganda, direct attacks by the Crown and every sort of rigging and corruption by nobles and gentry. Merged with the political ways of expressing opinions and gaining a share of power were the various traditional forms of self-assertion among the gentry which ranged from plots and shows of force to open rioting and revolt. The year 1688 represented the victory of groups and individuals who resented a strong executive and wanted to affirm their independence. The situation was complicated by the huge number of freeholds and liberties which were the source all over England of pride and profit. They included large and lesser posts, ranging from the stewards of hundreds to the beadles of corporations or clerical positions such as those of the precentors of cathedrals. These offices were held for life, and the men who enjoyed them often wielded considerable political influence when brought together as in boroughs, universities, cathedral towns. They did much to form opinion outside London and the great towns. The victory of common law had strengthened their role against the Crown; and though the judiciary was ready to support the latter, juries were hard to browbeat.[7]

Vanbrugh in his *Journey to London* depicts Sir Francis, a rustic squire who found himself a Member of Parliament.

James: Sir, here's John Moody arrived already; he's stumping about the streets in his dirty boots, and asking every man he meets if they can tell him where he may have a good lodging for a parliament man ... He tells them his lady and all the family are coming too, and that they are so nobly attended, they care not a fig for anybody, Sir, they have added two cart-horses to the four old geldings, because my lady will have it said, she came to town in her coach and six, and heavy George the plowman rides postilion.

Uncle Richard: The Lord have mercy upon all good folks! what work these people will make. Dost know when they'll be here?

James: John says, Sir, they'd have been here last night, but that the old wheezy-belly horse tired, and the two fore-wheels came crash down at once in Waggonrut Lane. Sir, they were cruelly loaden, as I understand, my lady herself, he says, laid on four mail-trunks, besides the great deal-box, which fat Tom sat on behind ... Then within the

coach there was Sir Francis, my Lady, the great fat lap-
dog, Squire Humphry, Miss Betty, my lady's maid Mrs
Handy, and Doll Tripe the cook.

They carry for protection against highwaymen the family
basket-hilt sword, a Turkish scimitar, an old blunderbuss, a
bag of bullets and a horn of gunpowder; as provision against
faintness between inns, baskets of plumcake, Dutch gingerbread, Cheshire cheese, Naples biscuits, macaroons, neats'
tongues, and cold boiled beef, with bottles of usquebaugh,
blackberry brandy, cinnamon water, sack, tent (a Spanish
wine), and strong beer.

After the confused turmoil of the first twenty years after 1688
the gentry, feeling themselves badly threatened, tried to get
parliamentary action to secure their position. In 1711 they
managed to get an Act passed which laid down that knights of
the shire were to own estates worth £600 per annum, while
borough members had to own real estate worth £300 per
annum. They thus hoped to exclude the money interest and
reserve Parliament for the landed men. St John (Bolingbroke),
moving the commitment of the Bill, declared that he had heard
of societies 'that jointed stocks to bring in members'; without
such a Bill he foresaw the time when 'the monied men might
bid fair to keep out of that house all the landed men'. Sir W.
Massingberd, happy, hoped for a further Bill that would qualify
JPs on the same lines. 'For when landed gentlemen represent
us in Parliament and do our business at home in the country,
we may justly look for better times, and that our tottering constitution may be once more fixed to the confusion and amaze-
ment of all its adversaries.' But no such Bills could stem or
deflect the money power and its wielders.[8]

Defoe gives us some vivid pictures of the way that the system
worked. Decayed borough sites sent members to Parliament
while the thriving new towns were unrepresented. In Sussex,

in the compass of about six miles are three borough towns,
sending Members to Parliament, (viz.) Shoreham, Bramber and Stenning; and Shoreham, Stenning are tolerable
little market-towns; but Bramber (a little ruin of an old
castle excepted) hardly deserves the name of a town,

having not above fifteen or sixteen families in it, and of them many not above asking you an alms as you ride by: the chiefest house in the town is a tavern, and here, as I have been told, the vintner, or ale-house keeper rather, boasted, that upon an election, just then over, he had made £300 of one Pipe of Canary.

Queenborough he found

a miserable dirty, decayed, poor, pitiful, fishing town; yet vested with corporation privileges, has a mayor, aldermen, &c, and his worship the mayor has his mace carried before him to church, and attended in as much state and ceremony as the mayor of a town twenty times as good: I remember when I was there, Mr Mayor was a butcher, and brought us a shoulder of mutton to our inn himself in person, which we bespoke for our dinner, and afterwards he sat down and drank a bottle of wine with us. But that which is still worse is that this town sends two burgesses to Parliament, as many as the Borough of Southwark, or the City of Westminster.

The new importance of elections and the growing interest in political argument appear both in the increase in pamphlets and books dealing with the issues and in the larger number of people demonstrating their concern at moments of significant struggle. Between 1689 and 1715 there were more general elections and more contested seats than in the rest of the eighteenth century. There were groups pulling in so many directions that stability seemed impossible, and the pessimists condemning party and faction could command wide assent. Yet all the while the forces were at work that were to produce Walpole's long reign under a virtual one-party system.

Defoe, who responded so strongly to all the main trends of his time, reveals the full contradictions of the situation. On the one hand he reviles the growth of parties: 'I have always thought the only true fundamental maxim of politics that will ever make the nation happy is this, That the Government ought to be of no party at all ... Their work ought to be to scatter and disperse parties, as they would tumults; and to keep a balance among the interfering interests of the nation with the same care as they would the civil peace.' Again he writes: 'I have seen the bottom of all parties, the bottom of all their pretences, and the bottom of all their sincerity ... all is a mere show, outside, and abominable hypocrisy, of every party, in every age, under every government, in every turn of government; when they are OUT to get IN, when IN, to prevent being out.' And yet about the same time, near the end of Anne's reign he depicts gleefully the way in which political arguments are going on everywhere – arguments that he himself is doing his best to stimulate with his journalism.

> Why, the strife is gotten into your kitchens, your parlours, your shops, your counting-houses, nay, into your very beds. You gentlefolks, if you please to listen to your cookmaids and footmen in your kitchens, you shall hear the scolding, and swearing, and scratching, and fighting among themselves; and when you think the noise is about the beef and the pudding, the dish-water, or the kitchen-stuff, alas, you are mistaken ... the feud is about the more weighty affairs of the government ... The thing is the same up one pair of stairs: in the shops and warehouses the 'prentices stand, some on one side of the shop, and some on the other (having trade little enough), and there they throw High Church and Low Church at one another's heads like battledore and shuttlecock. Instead of posting their books they are fighting and railing at the Pretender and the House of Hanover; it were better for us certainly that these things had never been heard of.

But they had been heard of, and he was doing his best to make them more heard of, and the very way in which he describes the situation shows how he glories in it.[9]

8

Projectors and Quakers

John Houghton, Fellow of the Royal Society and dealer in tea, coffee, and chocolate, of Bartholomew Lane, found in 1700 that a change was coming over the washing of clothes. 'Formerly, bucking with lees made of our English ashes and hogs' dung were very much used for the washing of clothes, but, for aught I can learn, wherever soap comes it gets ground of these, as being more neat, sweet, and less troublesome.' It was 'extraordinarily dear', but he hoped that the increasing use would bring the price down. Earlier in 1694 in his weekly pamphlet he had described the process of soap-making and explained why soap cleansed. In good citizens' houses, he found, washing was done once a month; in big households washerwomen were employed, but in smaller ones the mistress and the maid did the washing together.

An inquiring spirit was abroad and we keep coming across Projectors who had some invention or new method to sell. The word *Engine* takes on new meanings. About 1673 it came to mean an apparatus for applying mechanical power, which consisted of a number of parts, each with its own function; about 1704, an instrument for transmitting force or modifying its application. About the same time we find *engineer* as inventor or plotter. These more limited meanings emerge from the general connections of *engine* with mind, war, theatre, or literature. We now find it often used in relation to fire-fighting and water-supplies. On 28 April 1712 Swift writes: 'A projector has been applying himself to me to recommend him to the ministry, because he pretends to have found out the longitude. I believe he has no more found it out than he has found out mine arse. However I will gravely hear what he says, and discover him a fool or a knave.' He was also plagued by the inventor Joe Beaumont. We are reminded of the projectors in Hogarth's *Rake's Progress*, in the debtors' prison and in Bedlam. Addison tells how in a coffee house not far from the Haymarket he listened to 'the discourse of one, who, by the shabbiness of his dress, the extravagance of his conceptions, and the hurry of his speech, I discovered to be of that species who are generally distinguished by the title of Projectors'.

Evelyn records on 20 June 1696: 'I made my Lord Cheney a visit at Chelsea, and saw those ingenious water-works invented by Mr Winstanley, wherein were some things very surprising and extraordinary.' Winstanley was the architect who designed Eddystone Lighthouse and who died when it was blown down in the great storm of 1703. His structure was built by private enterprise; it was followed by one that Rudyerd and others designed, which was financed by Trinity House out of levies on shipping. Defoe describes the engines used in providing the London water-supply. In Lincolnshire he further tells us of 'some wonderful engines for throwing up water'. One, he was informed, threw up 1200 tons of water in half an hour, worked by twelve windsails to a mill. 'This I saw a model of, but I must own I did not see it perform.' On 25 October 1695 Evelyn writes that he and the archbishop

> went to Hammersmith, to visit Sir Sam Morland, who was entirely blind; a very mortifying sight. He shewed us his invention of writing, which was very ingenious; also his wooden kalendar, which instructed him by feeling; and other pretty and useful inventions of mills, pumps, &c, and the pump he had erected that serves water to his garden, and to passengers, with an inscription, and brings from a filthy part of the Thames near it a most perfect and pure water. He had newly buried £200 worth of music books six feet under ground being, as he said, love songs and vanity. He plays himself psalms and religious hymns on the theorbo.

(Evelyn uses the term engines for bombs. 'I saw a trial of those devilish murdering mischief-doing engines called bombs, shot out of the mortar-piece on Black-heath. The distance that they are cast, the destruction they make where they fall, is prodigious.' – 16 March 1687.)

In the Scillies engineers and projectors were working to get treasure from wrecks. Defoe tells us: 'Some, I say, with one kind of engine, and some another; some claiming such a wreck, and some such and such others; where they alledged, they were assured there were great quantities of money; and strange unprecedented ways were used by them to come at it. Some, I say, with one kind of engine, and some another; and though we thought several of them very strange impracticable methods, yet, I was assured by the country people, that they had done wonders with them under water, and that some of them had taken up things of great weight, and in a great depth of water.'

Alchemists did not fail to appear. In 1703, Steele, hard up as always, met a plausible experimenter and paid the rent for a laboratory in Poplar at the end of a big hanging garden. He would have spent more on the man, but he met Mary Manley, who had had two comedies produced and hoped to be Aphra Behn's successor. She set up a salon and engaged more in love-making than in literary work. Now she somehow convinced Steele that he was being cheated and that if he sold his army commission to finance the alchemist he was done for.

There was much ingenuity in toys. In the *Tatler* we find an advertisement on 30 November 1710 for Mrs Salmon's Waxworks, among which were a Turkish Seraglio, the Fatal Sisters that reel and cut the thread of a man's life, 'an Old Woman flying from Time, who shakes his head and hour-glass with sorrow at seeing Age so unwilling to die. Nothing but like can exceed the motion of the heads, hands, eyes, &c, of these figures'. Addison's projector asserts that he can bring all the shows of the town together in one grand opera; a raree-show, a ladder-dance, 'a posture-man, a moving picture, with other curiosities of the like nature'. Men were trying to improve or mechanise all sorts of everyday instruments. We read: 'The inventors of the straps for razors have written against each other for years, and that with great bitterness.' An advertisement in the *Athenian Mercury* reads:

> The Writing Engine, or taking several copies of the same thing at once, invented by Mr George Ridpath, being now brought to perfection by the assistance of Mr Alexander Urwin, Clock-Maker in St Martin's Lane, over against the Church, such as have occasion for any of the said Engines may see the same at Mr George Ridpath's, at the Blue Ball in Little Newport Street, near Leicester-fields, and be accommodated according to agreement, with Engines for 2, 3, 4, 5, or 6 copies.

John Byrom had Jacobite scruples about taking the oath to the Hanoverians, so he lost his fellowship at Trinity College by omitting to enter holy orders; but he made money with his shorthand system. He studied the methods in vogue, and 'was so disgusted with the absurdity and awkwardness of the contrivance' that he invented his own. He charged a fee of £5 and had many pupils at home in Manchester, in London, Cambridge, and Oxford. Shorthand was one of the privileges of the educated classes. Locke thought it should form part of the education of youth. Among Byrom's pupils were Charles and John Wesley, David Hartley, Horace Walpole, and many lords. He formed a shorthand society, and in 1724 was elected to the Royal Society. He saw shorthand as 'the most easy, concise, regular and beautiful manner of writing English'. It fitted in with the ideas of a regular scientific form of language.[1]

In the background were the growth of scientific experiment and theory, and the needs of industry. Byrom in 1738 writes: 'Thence into the park, met Mr Lloyd there walking with a Scotchman, who it seems had invented a way of making a bridge to lessen expenses by a machine:' (that is, a machine which made bridges). Spinning done by hand could not keep pace with weaving or knitting, even if Irish yarn, for example, was imported. Several men tried to invent a spinning machine. In the 1730s a factory with one at Nottingham was tried, but did not do well. These attempts, however, led on in time to the work of Arkwright and Hargreaves. In 1733 came Kay's flying shuttle. The demand for coal meant that it was not enough to find new surface deposits; and to make deeper mines men had to have effective pumps to avoid flooding. The steam pump of Savery and Newcomen, perfected in 1712, met this problem. In 1715 John Lombe went to Italy and managed to steal the plans of a machine used there for making silk yarn; he built a big factory on a site near Derby. In many ways the fine work being done on clocks and watches turned men's thoughts to precision-machinery.

By 1752 we are told of 'the infinite numbers daily inventing machines for shortening business', and in 1754 a writer, comparing France and Britain, says that in the main manufacturing towns of the latter 'almost every manufacturer hath a new invention of his own, and is daily improving those of others'. Control of the water supply was a prime need, to make more efficient the mills for corn and malt, fulled cloth, slit iron, rags for paper. Large sums were spent on dams, ponds, culverts, troughs, water-wheels. Early in the century came the overshot for the undershot wheel, by means of which a small volume of water could supply far more energy than a large volume could do with the latter. Later, at Coalbrookdale the atmospheric engine threw water back from below the millrace, with great savings. Then the rotary engine of Watt replaced the water-wheel.

All the mechanical applications and inventions were made possible by the great advances achieved on the theoretical level since Galileo, with Newton as the outstanding contemporary exponent. On the practical side we see the steady convergence of a need, a scientific idea, a slow devising of an effective model, then an adaptation to workshop or factory. One aim of the inventions was to get rid of the large number of unskilled workers which most systems of production still involved, especially in the mines and in the textile industries, to simplify and concentrate the processes or stages of work. The largest units of production were at first those controlled by the public authorities, such as the royal arsenal at Chatham, which Defoe described with much interest. Local authorities also, in the workhouses, from 1705 on, brought about an aggregation of labour. The workhouses, generally let out to contractors who undertook to keep the paupers at so much a head, were at times mere barns; but others were built in the form of a square, and with their workshops, stores, offices served later as models for privately owned factories. The state further helped the rise of large-scale production by its need of weapons, cannon, equipment, and so on, for the armed forces and the navy; it placed orders with firms that could guarantee quality and delivery on time.

Among the most important innovations were those made by the Quakers; for here it was not merely a matter of brilliant individual achievements, but of a closely knit group steadily advancing productivity. In the sphere of clock-making, for instance, three Quaker craftsmen played an outstanding role: Tompion, Quare, and Graham. Tompion did much to put into practical form the inventions worked out theoretically by Barlow and Hooke. In 1695, in conjunction with Barlow and William Houghton, he made and patented the cylinder escapement for watches. Extreme precision in the cutting of wheels was the secret of much of his success, e.g. on his twelve-month grandfather clocks. He made a clock for Flamstead which recorded decimal time. Quare invented the repeating movement for watches. In 1695 he turned to barometers and made a portable and unspillable one. In 1687 he made a unified drive for the minute and hour hands on watches which is still in use. In 1726 Graham published one of his twenty-one papers in the *Philosophical Transactions* of the Royal Society: *A Contrivance to avoid Irregularities in a Clock Motion by the Action of Heat and Cold upon the Pendulum*, in which he described his mercurial pendulum. The mural arc he constructed at Greenwich enabled the observatory to carry out more accurate and vitally important recordings of star positions and movements. In the transit telescopes he made for Molyneux and Bradley in 1727 he used a micrometer for fine readings.[2]

The Quakers were the group who, while preserving their sense of difference from people who conformed to the systems of State and Church, set themselves to master practical knowledge and to develop production. As trade was the dominant force in the economic world they gave much attention to it, but before long concerned themselves also with industry. They could not enter the universities or the large trade-guilds; they rejected many professions such as the army or the law; they turned their backs on the arts, which seemed to pamper the worldly. In education, where possible, they liked children to be taught foreign languages that would be useful in trade. In the domestic market, for instance, they saw that the southern ironmasters made cannons and ship-armaments, and exported arms; they themselves would not have produced such things, and they found the way clear for manufacturing for home-consumption iron pans, smoothing irons, sickles, and so on.

The whole society was literate. The businesses into which they moved were often wholly or largely run by their own members, who were forward-looking and well trained. Their capacity for discipline and their interest in rational systems facilitated the introduction of new schemes for controlling work-conditions and industrial processes. Christopher Story, a Cumbrian farmer who roamed much in the ministry, said that at first their creed seemed 'as it would have hurt their trades', but they persisted and prospered; through diligence and reliability 'they gained credit in the country'. Even when persecuted they managed to keep working in gaol; thus in York Castle they wove on looms provided by the Monthly Meeting. Their movements as preachers helped them as traders. John Gratton in 1678 said: 'I went abroad as much as I could, and kept my trade going too; my family also grew bigger and bigger, and my care was great to pay all I owed to everybody, so that I was often constrained to ride many miles after meetings to gain my markets on the second day of the week.' Aaron Atkinson, pedlar with linen pack on back, preached as he went. In 1689 came the Toleration Act and in 1696 the Act allowing affirmation instead of oath, which the Quakers would on no account take. There was then relief from much persecution and gaol; but they still had to face the demand for tithes and church dues. So the levying of fines and distraint of goods went on; heavy fines were paid for not attending church.

Because of the closely entwined loyalties, they were against mixed marriages, which involved church rites. All marriages were closely scrutinised and they might be forbidden if thought unsuitable. Also a community watched the behaviour of all its members and cast out the unworthy, though a properly contrite sinner, even if found out in fornication, might be re-admitted. At the Monthly Meetings queries were answered in writing for the whole membership, thus compacting the sect and helping to keep it on the correct path. Quaker trade and industry became a close network of firms linked by family relationships. A small firm did not stand on its own, but had friends to help it over difficulties. Among the ironmasters there even seems a policy of marrying daughters to the owners of small works so as to bring them into the general orbit. Further, as an Advice of 1697 advocates, the children of Friends were apprenticed to 'honest friends that they may be preserved in the way of truth'. Members of the Monthly Meeting were deputed to inquire into the suitability of each applicant for an apprenticeship. Many Friends left money or property for the apprenticing of poor children; and the Quaker attitudes were set out by John Bellers in 1697 in a scheme for helping the poor. 'Two hundred of all trades I suppose sufficient to find necessities for three hundred, and therefore what manufacture the other hundred make, will be a profit for the founders.' The proposals thus combined benevolence and profitability. Bellers thought £18,000 enough capital for a college of 3000 persons, and wanted a college in each big textile town. No college was ever set up, but the scheme stimulated various social projects. London Friends took over a workhouse in Clerkenwell and put in it some thirty aged folk who could still work, with some boys added later; but after a while the system broke down, and the house was used for educating poor children (finally becoming the Friends School at Saffron Walden). Bellers and others tried to get a Bill through Parliament for 'Imploying the poor', but failed. In Bristol by 1700 a workhouse was in operation, and the profits were used to build more such houses, though in 1720 the manager took over the Bristol concern on condition of employing poor Friends recommended by the committee. Bellers published more pamphlets, advocating a more humane treatment of criminals as well as an international organisation for the avoidance of war. (Penn had already in 1693 published his *Essay towards the Present and Future Peace of Europe*, in which he proposed 'an European Dyet, Parliament or Estates'.) By the time of George I's accession there were approximately half a million nonconformists in England and Wales, the congregations having increased by some thirty per cent since 1690; and it was held, apparently with much truth, that at least a hundred thousand of them were now in London, Westminster, Southwark and their out-parishes. *Angliae Notitia* estimated that one in twelve of the population did not go to the national church and cited five main types of dissenters: Libertines or Freethinkers, Papists (not so numerous as might be thought), Quakers, Independents, Presbyterians. British Anabaptists were not so wild and extravagant as those of Flanders or Germany, but they abhorred 'paying of Tithes and affect Parity', allowed laymen to administer sacraments and expected the Universal Monarchy of Christ on Earth. Among odd sects there were those named Brownists, the Family of Love, Antinomians, Traskites or Seventh-day-men, Antisabbatarians, and Muggletonians. Presbyterians came closest to the Anglican Church, but 'denied the civil magistrate any authority in Church government'. Independents had no over-all government, 'but each particular congregation is ruled by their own laws and methods'. They were mostly Millenarians, dating 'the last thousand years of Christ's Kingdom from the beginning of Independency'.

Quakers

practised formerly abstinence and self-denial, but now of late none are prouder and more luxurious than the generality of them. They formerly wore plain and coarse clothes, now the men wear very fine cloth, and are distinguished from others only by a particular shaping of their coats, a little pleated cravat, and a slender hat-band; the women nevertheless wear flowered, or striped, or damask silks, and the finest linnen cut and pleated in imitation of lace, but they wear no lace or superfluous ribbons; however they are extremely nice in the choice of tailors, seamstresses and laundresses. Those of the men who wear periwigs, have 'em of genteel hair and shape, though not long. They are as curious in their meats, and as cheerful in their drink, and as soft in their amours, and as much in the enjoyment of life as others.

Tom Brown, Ned Ward, and other satirists draw much the same picture. Tom, however, admits them to be 'the most sociable society of all without the pale; for here everyone may speak nonsense in his turn; and the women are not excluded'. He adds that they 'are more just than the other dissenters, because, as they pull not off their hats to God, so they pull them not off to men, whereas the others shall cringe and bow to any man they can get sixpence by, but ne'er veil their bonnets to God, by whom they may get to heaven; it may be indeed because, contrary to Christ's, their kingdom seems to be of this world'. He stresses their close-knit relationships. 'They are a sort of Jews, and not only trade and fornicate amongst themselves, but marry likewise in their own tribe ... A long cravat or wig in a man, or high topping and lace in a woman, they abominate as signs of vanity; but they will wear the best favours and richest alike, use the leather convenience [contraceptive] and be prouder in their plainness than the haughtiest lady at court.'

Ned Ward tells of a tavern in Finch Lane kept by a Quaker (an Aminadab as the nickname went). All was quiet there, 'no ringing of bar-bell, bawling of drawers, or rattling of pot-lids'. In the entrance he meets 'two or three blushing saints, who had been holding forth so long over the glass, that had it not been for their umbrellas [a kind of loose cloak], puritanical coats, and diminutive cravats, shaped like the rose of a parson's hat-band, I should have taken them by their scarlet faces to be good Christians'. They pass by with no touch of the hat. There is nothing unlikely in the Quaker tavern; not till 1797 did the sect issue a warning against the frequenting of public houses 'after the purpose of business or of refreshment, is accomplished'.

Steele in 1711 tells some stories that bring out the class-feeling of the dissenters when coming up against the established church. A distinguished dissenter, prevailed on to visit one of the large London churches, said that he liked 'the little ceremony which was used towards God Almighty', but feared he could never rise to that used by the congregation to one another. 'He was not well-bred enough to be a convert.' A Quaker, looking into a church, 'fixed his eyes upon an old lady with a carpet larger than that from the pulpit before her, expecting when she would hold forth. An Anabaptist who designs to come over himself, and all his family, within a few months, is sensible they want breeding enough for our congregations, and has sent his two eldest daughters to learn to dance, that they may not misbehave themselves at church'.[3]

But the wits failed to notice the practical work being done by the Quakers and other dissenters. Why did these men take such a leading role in the construction of industrialism? We may point to the element of thrift, the need to justify oneself before the world, the exclusion from the systems of church and state that made the groups especially cohesive in their resistance and their compensating activities. Instead of the inner world of the saint withdrawn from the world, the dissenters had what has been called an inner-worldly attitude. There were a few Catholics in the English world of industry and finance, but things would have been no different if they had not been there. Voltaire and other observers were much impressed by the role of the nonconformists despite their relatively small numbers. Certainly their concern with education played an important part in bringing about their vanguard role, but we see the same inner drive in the educational developments and the use to which they put their capacities. The author of *Reflections on various subjects relating to Arts and Commerce* in 1752 remarked, 'It is a point frequently urged by politicians and divines that the Protestant religion is better calculated for trade than the Catholic', and he somewhat basely adds, 'The great and religious Mr Boyle gives it as one argument for propagating the Gospel in foreign parts that if the converts could but learn so much of Christianity as to go clothed, it would greatly add to the sale of our manufactures.'

Protestants then were better suited for industry and trade than Catholics, and among the Protestants the dissenting groups had a special drive towards trading and industrial developments. Further, among those groups the Quakers had a special place. By 1700, indeed by 1690, they were much involved with ironworks: small furnaces for smelting, forges for bar and rod iron, wire-drawing forges, blacksmith businesses. During the next century their small firms gradually came together in the hands of a few large families, and through these ramifications developed the key-structure on which the industry rested. The large-scale foundry emerged in such firms as Darby's at Coalbrookdale. The pattern remained that of many converging family units, small plants and partners, with much fluidity. If one area turned out unsuitable for expansion, it was easy to move to another. The work carried on by some other member of the family kept things going as a new forge or furnace was set up. Losses in one unit were made up in another, and the units were held together in a single community, aware of itself, its purpose, and its achievements.

The Midland ironmasters provided the basis of practice on which the Boulton-and-Watt and the Smeaton steam-engines were worked out, and which became decisive for the industrial revolution. By 1789 the Quaker influence was lessening, but the essential impetus had been given. Meanwhile, ironworks had declined in the south, partly through Royalist devastations of the Weald and the Forest of Dean, and new works were started by Quakers in the wooded areas of the north and west, where ironstone also could be found. Disused monastic sites, in Furness and Yorkshire, were tried afresh. During the Quaker period there was a change from the use of forest woods for charcoal to the use of coppice woods only about fifteen years old. Coppice areas could be replanted in a system of rotation.

Sweden had stepped in to supply iron when British production fell; but troubles there in the second decade of the eighteenth century gave the Quakers their chance to produce raw iron. There were, however, many problems. The Quaker firm of Darby discovered how to smelt iron with coke fuel, and opened up a new epoch of iron-making. The slitting mill was brought in for the easier manufacture of rod and bar iron, and much progress was made in wire-drawing. A further development came by linking furnace, forge, slitting-mill, and the distributive system – though furnace and forge were still at times separated for reasons of water and fuel supplies. The discovery that coal and charcoal could be mixed proportionately for use in the forges made the latter move towards coal-fields, while furnaces preferring charcoal iron moved to areas where wood was handy.

The Rawlinsons and Lloyds represented the bloomer-forge associations, with the start of charcoal blast-furnaces. The Yorkshire group showed the strongest combination of charcoal furnace–forge–slitting-mill units, with big advances in management and organisation, while the Darby group mainly dealt with coke-furnace and foundry industry. The four groups covered all the transitional stages between the isolated bloomery and the full-grown blast-furnace–foundry plant. Further, the Friends had succeeded in taking over old systems and in bringing about the Quaker or London Lead Company, which soon extended its influence over lead-mines in most of Britain and revived the moribund mining industry. For two hundred years it was the biggest mining corporation in the country, with many contributions to technical advances in mining, social organisation, town planning, and education. Here was industry on a modern scale. From 1705, led by Wright and Haddon, the Company went on expanding, mainly in Wales and the North Pennines; in 1727 it tackled Derbyshire.

Later there were big Quaker activities in a large number of fields, from china-clay and china manufacture to chemical production and chocolate-making, from devising iron ploughs to projecting the first Gas Company, from road-making to canal-building. Important too was the part played by Edward Pearce in initiating the railway era through the Darlington and Stockton Railway. But in these later years many non-Quakers were also playing big roles. It was above all in the early crucial stages of industrialism that the Quakers played a dynamic and adventurous part. Without their devoted labours, their keen practical sense and readiness to innovate, their close-knit organisations, it is hard to see the industrial system developing as rapidly and decisively as it did in England.

But we must also glance at the part they played in developing the banking system. The Bank of England had been founded in 1694, growing out of a loan of £1,300,000 to the State, on which the lenders were to get 8 per cent interest, £4000 a year for management expenses, and a charter for ten years. The charter was renewed from time to time, and the Governor and Company of the Bank had come to stay. 'I looked into the Great Hall where the Bank is kept,' said Addison in 1711, 'and was not a little pleased to see the Directors, Secretaries, and Clerks, with all the other members of that wealthy corporation, ranged in their several stations, according to the parts they act in that just and regular economy.' But it was some time before there were private banks to play their part in the capitalisation of trade and industry. These developed mainly from the ironmasters and the mining corporations. In the previous century the provision of large loans and the custody of valuables had been the work of the goldsmiths, whose membership of their Company was considered security for their staying solvent. Advanced thinkers began to feel the need of banks proper. Barbon in *A Discourse of Trade*, 1690, wrote: 'Public Banks are of so great a concern in trade that the merchants of London for want of such a Bank have been forced to carry their cash to goldsmiths, and have thereby raised such a credit upon goldsmith's notes that they pass in payments from one to another like notes upon the Bank.'[4]

But the Bank of England wanted to keep as much a monopoly of banking business as possible, and an Act of 1697 forbade further banks, though allowing goldsmiths and other corporations to issue promissory notes and bills. An Act of 1707, however, allowed only bodies of more than six partners 'to borrow, owe or to take up any sum or sums of money in their bills or notes, payable at demand or at any less time than six months from the borrowing thereof'. So small local banks grew up, country-banks, mostly limited to a partnership of a few members of a family. It was through these banks that Quakers played their parts and soon rose to a dominating position. Looking after the finances of the large concerns in which they were involved, such persons were naturally interested in banking and its possibilities. Some of them, such as the Fox group, came in through the small woollen dealers. Out of the combination of families engaged in trade and industry there emerged the houses of Barclay, Lloyd, Gurney, Backhouse, and other firms belonging to Quakers, which played key-roles in the foundation of a modern banking system.

Out of the developments we have been considering there came a new complexity in the division of labour: more sub-divisions of processes and larger forms of organisation encompassing all the parts. This was observed (by Hughes or Henry Martyn) in the *Spectator*. Sir Andrew Freeport, besieged by beggars, gives some alms and then moralises. Of all men merchants, who live by buying and selling, should never encourage beggars. 'The goods which we export are indeed the product of the lands, but much the greatest part of their value is the labour of the people; but how much of these people's labour shall we export while we hire them to sit still?' He goes on: 'It is the very life of merchandise to buy cheap and sell dear.' What is needed above all is 'the reduction of the price of labour upon all our manufacturers. This too would be the ready way to increase the number of our foreign markets: The abatement of the price of the manufacture would pay for the carriage of it to more distant countries; and this consequence would be equally beneficial both to the landed and the trading interests. As so great an addition of labouring hands would produce this happy consequence both to the merchant and the gentleman, our liberality to common beggars, and every other obstruction to the increase of labourers, must be equally pernicious to both.'

The listener is surprised. Sir Andrew assures him that he is not advocating a mere beating down of wages. 'It may seem a paradox, that the price of labour should be reduced without an abatement of wages, or that the wages can be abated without any inconvenience to the labourer, and yet nothing is more certain than that both these things may happen. The wages of the labourers make the greatest part of the price of everything that is useful: and if in proportion with the wages the prices of all other things should be abated, every labourer with less wages would still be able to purchase as many necessaries of life; where then would be the inconvenience? But the price of labour may be reduced by the addition of more hands to a manufacture, and yet the wages of persons remain as high as ever.' He then cites Sir Willy Petty, thinking of his *Discourse on Taxes* (1689). One example that Petty gave was that of a watch.

It is certain that a single watch could not be made so cheap in proportion by only one man, as a hundred watches by a hundred; for as there is vast variety in the work, no one person could equally suit himself to all the parts of it; the manufacture would be too tedious, and at last but clumsily performed: But if an hundred watches were made by a hundred men, the cases may be assigned to one, the dials to another, the wheels to another, the springs to another, and every other part to a proper artist; as there would be no need of perplexing any one person with too much variety, every one would be able to perform his single part with greater skill and expedition; and the hundred watches would be finished in one fourth part of the cost, though the wages of every man were equal. The reduction of the price of the manufacture would increase the demand of it, all the same hands would be still employed and as well paid. The same rule will hold in the clothing, the shipping, and all the other trades whatsoever.

The labourers will be able to buy more: 'so every interest in the nation would receive a benefit from the increase of our working people'.

The whole concept here is modern and holds the germ of the idea of mass-production. What it directly expressed and prefigured was the growing specialisation and division of labour, with new applications of capital in fixed forms during the century. There were steady efforts to develop efficiently specialised jobs in coal-mining, in the iron industry and brass-founding, with new time-saving processes.

9

Merchants and Slaves

During the seventeenth century the work of the merchant proper had grown more complex. He began to be differentiated from the itinerant salesman who carried goods about. Now he specialised as merchant resident and employed agents to carry, buy, and sell abroad. He was a member of a Company of Merchant Adventurers, setting up factories and trading stations in foreign lands; and he might concentrate on certain goods and certain markets. Generally the merchant's work had four sections. He bought and sold for himself or others on commission; he speculated in time and place on merchandise; he dealt in money and credit; he insured goods and ships in transit. But by 1760 he did not necessarily do all four; he kept to whichever line suited him.

(In practice the term was loosely used, applied to bankers and stock-jobbers, loan-contractors and bullion-dealers. As employers often gave out work, bought raw materials, and marketed products, they called themselves merchants. The term manufacturer was also used ambiguously, for the small craftsmen who made things and the man who employed large numbers of such craftsmen.)

Among tradesmen in general there were many varieties. Some stayed in a shop; others roamed around; some did only wholesaling, others did retailing as well. Some carried their own goods, some used other means, whether carriage was by land or river, or along the coast. The exporter himself bought wares or used factors and packers to do it, at Blackwell Hall,

at the packer's place, in the draper's house, at the Leeds
market, or straight from the clothier's house in the country. At
times much ingenuity was used. In Lincolnshire, Defoe noted,
fish was carried alive in 'great butts filled with water in
waggons'. The butts had small square flaps instead of bungs,
which were opened to give the fish air; and each night at the
inn, the water was drawn off and fresh water run in. The fish
thus carried were tench, pike, perch, and eels.

With the growth of population and of traffic, more towns
had grown up; limited town economies were giving way to
regional systems linked with London. Daily or weekly markets
helped a more steady exchange, but all the while there was a
transfer of business from markets to shops through the increased
volume of production and trade, the specialisation of wares.
Middlemen flourished in ever larger numbers in all branches
of trade. In the late seventeenth century tolls for bridges,
causeways, ferries, and certain roads rapidly came in, with the
system of toll-gates. Tolls were payable by all vehicles on highways of the home counties, which bore the heaviest traffic. But
travellers often managed to dash past the collector; so, in 1695,
local authorities were given the right to set across the road a
defensive barrier of pikes fixed to a frame. When the toll was
paid, the frame turned on a central pivot and made a clear
way. With the eighteenth century the turnpike was replaced
by the ordinary tollgate. The milestone and the signpost also
came in. Waggoners brought wool and cloth to London by
regular time-schedules; in 1706 this was mentioned as a
'wonted practice'. Stage-coaches had long been common. By
1688 there was a system of services between London and important centres all over England, and even with Edinburgh.
Schedules of times and rates were advertised. Opposition had
made much of the threat to the breeding of good horses,
horsemanship, and revenues, but in the eighteenth century the
stage-coach became the most common way of travelling.
Chamberlayne in the late seventeenth century saw the coach as
still an innovation:

There is of late such an admirable commodiousness, both
for men and women of better rank, to travel from London

to almost any great town of England, and to almost all
the villages near this great city, that the like hath not been
known in the world, and that is by stage-coaches, wherein
one may be transported to any place, sheltered from foul
weather and foul ways, free from endamaging one's health
or body by hard jogging, or over-violent motion; and this
not only at a low price, as about a shilling for every five
miles, but with such velocity and speed, as that the posts
in some foreign countries make not more miles in a day;
for the stage-coaches, called flying-coaches, make forty or
fifty miles in a day; as from London to Oxford or
Cambridge, and that in the space of twelve hours, not
counting the time for dining, setting forth not too early,
nor coming in too late.

But despite the increased use of roads, for bulky materials the
coastal shipping and river-barges remained by far the cheapest
method of transport, with canals soon to be added. For this
reason some industries (e.g. coal in the north-east, tin- and
copper-mining in the south-west) were created within reach of
the sea. Cloth-making, however, rarely flourished near the
coast, partly through the political conviction that such a loca-
tion would facilitate smuggling.

At Bristol sleds were used, which, says Defoe, kill 'a multitude of horses; and the pavement is worn so smooth by them,
that in wet-weather the streets are very slippery, and in frosty
weather 'tis dangerous walking.'[1]

The big fairs became places where wholesalers met their
chap-men, made up accounts and got payment, chiefly in bills.
Such transactions at Stourbridge in 1722 were estimated to
'exceed by far the sales of goods actually brought to the fair
and delivered in kind'. Defoe reports 'the prodigious resort of
the trading people of all parts of England to this fair; the
quantity of hops that have been sold at one of these fairs is
diversely reported, and some affirm it to be so great, that I
dare not copy after them; but without doubt it is a surprising
account, especially in a cheap year'. Much wool was also sold
there, and 'all sorts of wrought iron, and brass ware from
Birmingham; edged tools, knives, &c, from Sheffield; glass

ware and stockings, from Nottingham and Leicester; and an infinite throng of other things of smaller value, every morning. To attend this fair, and the prodigious conflux of people which come to it, there are sometimes no less than fifty hackney coaches, which come from London, and ply night and morning to carry the people to and from Cambridge.' Also, there are wherries brought from London 'on waggons to ply upon the little river Cam, and to row people up and down'. Cambridge could not lodge the visitors, so

> all the towns round are full; nay, the very barns, and stables are turned into inns, and made as fit as they can to lodge the meaner sort of people. As for the people at the fair, they all universally eat, drink and sleep in their booths, and tents; and the said booths are so intermingled with taverns, coffee-houses, drinking-houses, eating-houses, cooks-shops, &c, and all in tents too; and so many butchers, and higglers from all the neighbouring counties come into the fair every morning with beef, mutton, fowls, butter, bread, cheese, eggs, and such things; and go with them from tent to tent, from door to door, that there's no want of any provisions of any kind, either dressed, or undressed. In a word, the fair is like a well fortified city, and there is the least disorder and confusion (I believe) that can be seen any where, with so great a concourse of people.

Near the end the gentry came for diversion and to buy from the milliners, mercers, toy-shops and the like, also to patronise the puppet-shows, drolls, rope-dancers. On the last day was a horse fair, with races on horseback and foot.[2]

Here was the old tumultuous fair with a new business network on top of it. More purely commercial were the weekly markets such as that at Exeter for serges. At Leeds the cloth-market was held twice a week, starting at the bridge and carrying on up the street as it sloped northwards. Trestles were set out early in two rows, sometimes two rows on a side; boards were laid across, so that they 'lie like two long counters on either side, from one end of the street to the other'.

The clothiers bring their cloth early too, mostly a single piece, so they go into the inns and set it down there. At 7 am (a little earlier in summer, a little later in winter) the market-bell rings. 'It would surprise a stranger to see how in a few minutes, without hurry or noise, and not the least disorder, the whole market is filled; all the boards upon the tressels are covered with cloth, close to one another as the pieces can lie long ways by one another, and behind each piece of cloth, the clothier standing to sell it.' As the bell stops, 'the merchants and factors, and buyers of all sorts, come down, and coming along the spaces between the rows of boards, they walk up the rows, and down as their occasions direct. Some of them have their foreign orders, with patterns sealed on them, in rows, in their hands; and with those they match colours, holding them to cloths as they think they agree to: when they see any cloths to their colour, or that suit their occasions, they reach over to the clothier, and whisper, and in the fewest words imaginable the price is stated; one asks, the other bids; and 'tis agree, or not agree, in a moment.' In little more than an hour all the business is done. 'In less than half an hour, you will perceive the cloths begin to move off, the clothier taking it up upon his shoulder to carry to the merchant's house; and by half an hour after eight a clock the market bell rings again; immediately the buyers disappear, the cloth is all sold, or if here and there a piece happens not to be bought, 'tis carried back into the inn.' In a quarter of an hour all is cleared, with ten or twenty thousand pounds value of cloth, and sometimes much more, bought and sold.

Defoe is particularly impressed by the way the bell is obeyed in 'the most profound silence', nobody speaking above a whisper. The silence is kept mainly to prevent the clothiers nearby hearing the prices discussed. By nine the boards and trestles are all gone. Defoe makes out three sets of dealers: first, Leeds merchants who go all over England with pack-horses through the summer and when necessary in the winter despite the bad roads; secondly buyers 'who buy to send to London; either by commission from London, or they give commissions to factors and warehouse-keepers in London to sell for them'. (The factors sell not only to shopkeepers and wholesalers in

London, but also to merchants who export to the American colonies or the Baltic, to Petersburg, Riga, Danzig, Sweden and Pomerania.) And thirdly, merchants buying on commissions from Hamburg, Holland, and other parts, who 'correspond as far as Nuremberg, Frankfort, Leipsick, and even to Vienna and Ausburgh'. Wool for export goes by the rivers Aire and Calder, made navigable by Act of Parliament, to Hull for shipment.

In London a special role was played by shops in the Royal Exchange. The place was rebuilt after 1666 on the original quadrangular plan, with walks for each nation. There were 160 shops (100 above stairs) and vaulted cellars. The rents (totalling £4000 in the early century) were used for upkeep. Here met the merchants and brokers. Addison stresses his pride and excitement at such a gathering. 'It gives me a secret satisfaction, and in some measure gratifies my vanity, as I am an Englishman, to see so rich an assembly of countrymen and foreigners consulting together upon the private business of mankind, and making the metropolis a kind of emporium for the whole earth. I must confess I look upon the High Change to be a great council, in which all the considerable nations have their representatives. Factors in the trading world are what ambassadors are in the politick world; they negotiate affairs, conclude treaties, and maintain a good correspondence between those wealthy societies of men that are divided from one another by seas and oceans.' He adds, 'I am infinitely delighted in mixing with these ministers of commerce, as they are distinguished by their different walks and different languages.' He goes on to say that he is happy 'to see such a body of men thriving in their own private fortunes, and at the same time promoting the publick stock; or in other words, raising estates for their own families, by bringing into their country whatever is wanting, and carrying out of it whatever is superfluous'. He communicates to us the thrill that men of the time could feel at the busily and decisively expanding trade.[3]

He develops the fancy which later became part of the creed of the Liberal Freetraders and which was easy to believe if one was a member of an advanced manufacturing nation trading with less developed areas: the notion of an harmonious interdependence of all the lands of the earth in a trading nexus.

> Nature seems to have taken a particular care to disseminate her blessings among the different regions of the world, with an eye to this mutual intercourse and traffick among mankind, that the natives of the several parts of the globe might have a kind of dependence upon one another, and be united by their common interest. Almost every degree produces something peculiar to it. The food often grows in one country, and the sauce in another. The fruits of Portugal are corrected by the products of Barbadoes: the infusion of a China plant sweetened with the pith of an Indian cane. The Philippick Islands give a flavour to our European bowls. The single dress of a woman of quality is often the product of a hundred climates. The muff and the fan come together from the different ends of the earth. The scarf is sent from the torrid zone, and the tippet from beneath the Pole. The brocade petticoat rises out of the mines of Peru, and the diamond necklace out of the bowels of Indostan.

A supercargo was an agent sailing with a cargo to make the sales abroad; he then bought, prepared, shipped and brought home a return cargo. In 1707 the first Glasgow tobacco merchants appointed the ship's captain as supercargo; in later voyages one of the partners did the job. Supercargoes were paid by salary or commission, generally the latter – the East India Company paid five per cent. They carried an invoice detailing the primary costs and charges of the wares to guide them as to prices. Their main work was the buying of return cargoes, but they also carried out insurance, exchange, packing and lading, payment of customs, collection of debts, and secured the favour of foreign princes and merchant houses.

A factor was a merchant's agent who resided abroad, holding a letter of attorney, to transact the business of buying, selling, transporting, and exchanging as directed. Unlike a supercargo he could act for more than one principal: in which case the risk of his actions was joint. A broker was a local man who facilitated exchange, and carried out deals between merchants. He was usually licensed.

By 1696 trade had gained a great new impetus and the organisation of the mercantile system was completed. That year came the final Navigation Act, setting out all the statutory regulations as to colonial trade. That year also the Board of Trade and Plantations was created to supervise the country's trade interests, with an office of Inspector General of Imports and Exports, which kept ledgers in a vain effort to get an exact computation of the balance of international payments.[4]

Factors were trained by a practical apprenticeship. Travelling was considered a big advantage, and most factors went round in early years. Henry Gerway, who rose from being a factor in the Levant to governorship of the Levant Company, claimed that he voyaged 'in all parts of Christendom'. Such experience abroad might be gained as a supercargo. In the colonies there was lack of capital; a young merchant, himself suffering that lack, might get his start by settling and selling consignments from friends in England on commission; then with experience and money he could return to England and act there as a merchant of the colony. A factor corresponded regularly with his principals. At times he played a part in political changes in his area which might benefit his business. His functions varied with his place of work. Thus at Havana his sole business was to sell slaves and make returns of the moneys received. The distance from England and the problems of supervision made factors very much their own masters, and frauds were hard to detect. As some protection a principal might insist on their entering into bonds of 'caution', or the factory abroad might have a governor and board. Qualifications were scrutinised on their appointment, and they had to keep to prescribed systems of accounting and reporting.

To avoid such controls they might marry a woman of the land where they worked, and so become foreign subjects; then go bankrupt and hand over the goods they held to confederates, who later gave them back. When they died, all their property was seized by the foreign wife. (There was no way of making wills in Turkey.) Merchants and companies tried to stop such abuses by laying down that only unmarried men might act as factors, with strict regulations to ensure this provision. But factors often faked accounts, e.g. of local customs. They were helped in their tricks by carrying on as merchants in their own right as well as acting as factors. They gave their own wares priority and sold them in the best markets. These abuses were specially common among officers of the East India and other such companies. A trader in India wrote in 1711: 'All private trade, either in Europe or Country ships, had been so long ingrossed by the Company's servants, that they really think they have a right to it at their own rates. The Agent at Ispahan is concerned one-third, the chief of Gombroon one-third, and the rest of the factors of Persia the other third in all investments; so that there's scarce an Englishman in place will give a true account of the value of goods against his own interest.'

We saw that newspapers had helped the manufacturing expansion. The first business advertisements date from 1658. Papers spread the latest political news of events at home and abroad, helping merchants to take decisions. They also printed consular letters, essays on trade, reports of the market and shipping movements. In 1675 a *Mercury* devoted to Advertisements Concerning Trade appeared; in 1679, a free sheet of advertisements for 'promoting Trade', getting its finances from the advertisement fees. The 1712 tax on newspapers applied to advertisements as well and checked their growth; but they were too important to be held back for long, and in 1745 came the *General Advertiser*, with items classified and separated by rules.

The Post Office, too, played an important role in trade and manufacture. It had begun as a political and military organisation, using the carriage of private mail to meet the cost of royal mail. During the Commonwealth it was farmed out, with a single Post Office under a Postmaster General. All letters passed through London. In 1661 eight Clerks of the Road dealt with letters sent along the four great roads (Northern, Chester, Eastern, Western); in 1677 the Kent and Bristol Roads were added; in 1696 Cross-post Roads were brought in. In 1711 sub-centres were set up at Edinburgh, Dublin, New York, the West Indies, and other American colonies; and the Scotch Post

Office, set up in 1695, was brought under the London Post-master-General. Packet service to the West Indies began in 1702, and the service to Holland, Flanders, France, and Spain was improved.

In England the service had been much extended by bye-posts and cross-posts. The former, introduced in 1689, ran between market-towns and the nearest post-towns. The success of the Exeter–Bristol cross-post led to more being set up by the government and private persons. In 1721 Ralph Allen obtained the lease of the cross- and bye-posts for seven years at £6000 a year; he provided a thrice-a-week service for the next two decades, and a daily service in the east and south-west directions from London after 1741. An important cross-post had branches from Plymouth, Exeter, Taunton, Bridgewater, and Bristol meeting and going along the Severn through Gloucester, Worcester, Shrewsbury, Chester, Liverpool, Warrington, Manchester, Rochdale, Halifax, Leeds, and Hull. Through it Hull merchants could learn much more quickly of their ships seen in the Channel; and dealers and manufacturers of the western and northern towns could keep in touch.

The mails were also used for light packages, e.g. of laces, diamonds, and so on. Further in 1738 the Bank of England brought in Bank Post Bills to speed up the transmission of large sums of money. The notes were payable at seven days' sight, so that the parties might stop payment in case of robbery. Also mercantile papers and bills receivable and payable were carried, with special forms of endorsement or assignation used to insure against robbery or loss of mail. Samples and patterns were sent. The franking privilege that an MP owned – much abused in the eighteenth century – was quite an inducement to a merchant to enter public life.

Chamberlayne sums up the advantages of the post round 1700:

All gentlemen, country-chapmen, and others, may hereby speedily and cheaply give notice of their arrival at London; shopkeepers and tradesmen may send to their workmen for what they want; bills may be dispersed for publication of any concern; summons or tickets conveyed to all parts;

brewers entries safely sent to the excise-office; appointments of meetings among men of business; much time
saved in solicitation for money; lawyers and clients
mutually correspond; patients may send to doctors,
apothecaries, and chirurgeons, for what they shall want;
besides many other advantages.

Letters 'that come from all parts of the world by the general
post, directed to persons in any of those country towns to which
the penny-post does go, are delivered by the messengers
thereof, the same day they come to London; and the answers
being left at their receiving-houses, are by them safely carried
every night to the office in Lombard Street'.

The increasing number of disputes over property in one
form or another had led to a considerable expansion of the
law practices. Solicitors, first mentioned in an Act of 1605,
had been attacked as 'a new sort of people'. *The Compleat
Solicitor* (edition of 1683) remarked: 'We are very sensible how
some Attorneys at this day do Abominate the Name of a
Solicitor.' The sort of description that was popular ran: 'A
solicitor is a pettyfogging sophister, one whom you may style
a lawyer as a pedlar is a merchant.' He 'can instruct with
the Counsellor, plead as an attorney; he has all the tricks and
quillets of an informer, nay, and of a bailiff, too, for a week ...
The best of his profession have been forlorn tailors, outcast
brokers, drunken cobblers, or the offspring of such a rabble
rout'. Despite various Acts the legal profession was in a confused state, with vagabond attornies whose address was not
known (till 1768). In 1707 attornies urgently asked for the profession to be limited to gentlemen's sons above tricks and petty
foggeries; and an Act of 1730 directed judges to examine
candidates. In 1733 there were 2236 attornies (893 in the King's
Bench as against 342 in 1683), with 1759 solicitors in Chancery
(though many of these counted as attorneys) – the total number
thought to be some 4000. (Not till 1730 did Parliament enact
that legal proceedings should be in English.)[5]

Among important items of the export trade were men and
women: indentured labour and slaves. It is one of the paradoxes

of history that the growth of capital necessary for the industrial revolution was substantially helped by the slave-trade. In the correspondence of Christopher Jeaffreson we meet a man who had many dealings with the West Indies, both in negro slaves and English deportees. Writing to Col. Hill, Governor of St Christopher's Island on 5 August 1685 after Monmouth's defeat, he says: 'The gaols are full of prisoners, and some hundreds will be transported. But they are not yet condemned. I hope that St Christophers will have a share of them. His Majestie has ordered that they shall be dispersed to several colonies. I have been several times to Whitehall and with Mr Blathwait about them; desiring that the King would send some of them in one of his frigates to St Christophers.' He was worried that his steward in the plantations was killing off the slaves by driving them too hard. 'You know, it is the old, sturdy and hard slaves that are to be driven to work, and not the new comers; but I was always sensible of John Steele's churlish and brutal humour, in that he was usually a companion of the old, and a tyrant over the new negroes; as if the extraordinary work gained by over straining them would countervail the loss sustained by their deaths.' A little later he finds that the agent Thorn has lost four horses and fourteen slaves; the slaves were overworked and lacked food and clothing. To another planter he writes: 'John Steele knows that I never worked my negroes by night, when they were not well fed by day, and that, instead of wasting my time at Sandy Point, or elsewhere, as I am informed Edward Thorne daily does, I was constant at almost every meal upon the plantation, not trusting to false, deceitful servants, with my own eyes saw the provisions distributed in order to the poor negroes, especially to those who could not shift for themselves; which I believe with the blessing of God, saved several of their lives in the hard time after the hurricanes.'

At the same time Jeaffreson was pressing Secretary Blathwait about the white transportees, glad that a bribe was being used –that Mr B.

is likely to receive a present from the island. It may make him willing, who, we know, is in the way of doing more service to those parts than another can; and I have fear that he has been disobliged by the want of it. For he hath not given me such encouragements to wait on him, as might induce me to hope for an advantage by giving him those troubles. He told me plainly, that I must take the women as well as the men, if I will have any of the malefactors; which has made me to expect your Honour's pleasure, which by a former letter I requested you would signify to me, if we should take them upon those terms ... Not but that the women might work, and in time help to people the island. The last gaol delivery, Mr Panden, Mr Cary, Mr Symkins, &c, thought to have the malefactors. But Captain Richardson was too hard for them, though they had given fifty shillings for each prisoner. Which it seems was too little, though for us it had been too much, seeing we must pay five pounds per head passage; which they could not do by I suppose at least one half, by reason they would victual the ship themselves, so that a passage would not stand them in above three pounds at most. However, the act that they shall serve nine years will be a great encouragement.[6]

When men were ready to chaffer in the persons of their own countrymen, we cannot wonder that they had no compunction in selling negroes. The crucial moment came in 1713, with the Asiento clauses of the Treaty of Utrecht. Through these Britain wrung from Spain and France the virtual monopoly of the slave trade, and contracted to supply to the Spanish West Indies alone 144,000 negroes within thirty years. The trade had been begun by Spaniards and Portuguese, but already in Elizabethan days England took her share. Stuart policy after 1660 made the traffic a recognised section of English commerce on the high seas, and members of the Royal Household shared in the profits. But only from 1713 did Britain become the great slave-trading nation, winning huge profits. Under the Treaty she had the monopoly-right of supplying Spanish America with 4800 negroes yearly till 1743; but in fact the agreement was used as a cover for smuggling in far more slaves. Liverpool became a great city out of the traffic;

and by the end of the century the white population was a small minority in the West Indies. Later cotton-growing by slaves in the southern states of America was linked with Lancashire textiles in which child-labour was used. It is hard to estimate how many Africans were seized, bought, and transported, since so many died on the voyages in their terrible conditions, or on the plantations with their harsh treatment. Horace Walpole wrote on 25 February 1750: 'We, the British Senate, that temple of liberty and bulwark of Protestant Christianity, have this fortnight been pondering methods to make more effectual that horrid traffic of selling negroes. It has appeared to us that six and forty thousand of these wretches are sold every year to the plantations alone.'

All sorts of tricks were used by crimps, decoys, sharks, to get sailors for the slave-ships. A tenant or lodger was lured into debt, then offered the choice of gaol or work on such a ship; a young man was let run up a bill in a ginshop, then given the same choice. (The East India Company used the same crimps to supply its ships. Young men were lured into taverns or brothels, trapped, then carried off to lock-up houses and other dens till they could be sold to Bengal ship-captains.) The selling of convicts to planters went on till the American Revolution; and there was the same high mortality among them on their ships as among the slaves. In three ships of 1740–41, the first had 153 convicts, of whom 51 died; the second had 108, of whom 37 died; the third had 50, of whom 15 died.) Further, unconvicted persons were kidnapped and transported. Early in the Restoration we meet the Spiriter of children or young persons who were sold to contractors. In 1671 an affidavit was sworn against William Thiene 'who in one year spirited away 840'. Three years earlier there were three ships in the Thames for stolen children. 'Though the parents see the children in the ships, without money they will not let them have them.' The authorities were glad enough to get poor folk cleared out of London. The expansion of the slave-trade after 1713 revived the trade in kidnapped persons. We hear of a captain trading to Jamaica who went to the Clerkenwell House of Correction, made the gaoled girls drunk, then invited them to the West Indies. There they were sold for seven or ten

years of unpaid plantation work. Large numbers of persons
were kidnapped on the coasts of Scotland and Ireland for the
planters. A famous case involving the Annesley family was
recorded in *The Memoirs of an unfortunate Young Nobleman,
returned from Thirteen Years' Slavery in America, where he had been
sent by the wicked contrivance of his cruel Uncle.*[7]

Slaves existed in England, brought back as servants by rich
planters. They often hoped to become free. Many deserted;
others, believing that baptism made them legally free, found a
sympathetic clergyman to perform the rite. In an appeal to the
Middlesex Sessions, 1696, Katherine Auger, black, petitioned
to be discharged from her master, Rich, as he was in Barbados.
She had been brought to England six years before. After she
was baptised at St Katherine's by the Tower, Rich and his wife
'tortured her and turned her out; her said master refusing to
give her a discharge, she could not be entertained in service
elsewhere'. Rich had had her arrested and shut in the Poultry
Compter. The court ordered that she be freed to serve anyone
till he returned. In 1717 John Caesar's wife petitioned the
Sessions; her husband had served Benjamin and John Wood,
printers and embossers in Whitechapel, as a slave without
wages for fourteen years. The masters had much abused John
with very hard usage, most of the time imprisoning him in
their house. Seven years before he had been baptised, yet was
held as a slave, though, 'as the petitioner is advised, slavery
is inconsistent with the laws of the realm'. She, destitute, was
likely to be a charge on the parish unless her husband was
released from confinement and enabled to provide for them
both. The court recommended the masters to reach some
reasonable arrangement as to wages; but they ignored the
recommendation and next Sessions certain JPs were ordered to
consider what wages should be allowed to Caesar.

To simplify matters masters at times entered into indentures
with slaves, so as to secure a property in their labour fully
recognised in England. Even Blackstone's declaration in 1765
which opens nobly with the words, 'The spirit of liberty is so
deeply implanted in our constitution and rooted even in our
very soil, that a slave or negro, the moment he lands in England,
falls under the protection of the law and becomes a freeman',

goes on weakly, 'though the master's right to his service may possibly still continue'. Which is interpreted to mean that, while the law protects the slave 'in the enjoyment of his person and his property, yet with respect to any right the master may have lawfully acquired in the perpetual service of John or Thomas, this will remain exactly in the same state of subjection for life'. In fact, so many slaves in Britain absconded that in 1729 retired planters petitioned for an official statement. The judgement was duly delivered 'that no slave coming into the British Isles from the West Indies became free, and that baptism had no power whatever to absolve them of their condition'.

Indeed slaves were publicly sold. 'A black boy, 12 years of age, fit to wait on a gentleman, to be disposed of at Denis's Coffee House in Finch Lane, near the Royal Exchange.' A tavern in Wapping served as an auction room for slaves; in Liverpool they were sold at the quayside. Newspapers record slave-sales into the nineteenth century. Visitors from abroad noted the descendants of black slaves scattered round the country: 'a little race of blacks and mulattoes, mischievous as monkeys and infinitely more dangerous'. But in general there seems to have been little racial prejudice. In the early decades of the eighteenth century little black boys as pages or playthings were popular with fashionable ladies or courtesans. Ignatius Sancho, born on a slave-ship, became butler to the Duke of Montagu, then a grocer and well-known London character, with his Letters (imitations of Sterne) posthumously published. In Hogarth's *Noon* a negro is shown kissing a white girl, with nobody upset. We do, however, meet the complaint: 'The lower order of women are remarkably fond of the blacks, for reasons too brutal to mention.' Dr Johnson said of his black servant Francis Barber that he carried 'the empire of Cupid further than most men.' Scandals could reach the upper classes. Soubise, favourite of the Duchess of Queensbury, upset the household and was sent off to India.[8]

Nobody, however, made any serious attempt to protest at the slave-trade. Even the Quakers were long in taking a stand. Not till mid-century was the issue faced at all, and in 1761 the London Yearly Meeting decided to disown Quakers involved in the trade. Dunton was an honourable exception to the general evasion of the facts. Already in his *Athenian Mercury* he declared: 'After a mature and serious consideration ... I cannot see how such a trade (though much used by Christians) can in any way be justified, and fairly reconciled to the Christian law.'

Defoe in *The Life of Colonel Jack* (1722) tells how his hero, a thief, is made drunk, kidnapped, and carried to Virginia. He impresses the manager and is turned from 'a poor half-naked slave' into a clerk. He considers the negroes ungrateful, brutal, and obstinate, needing a rod of iron, and justifies the whipping inflicted on them. But, oddly, he then turns round and argues that mercy has never been tried on them. He gains the master's permission to try the experiment of kindness on a negro, who is stripped and given two lashes. The punishment is then stopped and Jack says he will prevail on the great master to pardon the negro, who is won over to a steadfast gratitude. Here, as in *Robinson Crusoe* with its Friday, Defoe is assured of the white man's right to use the negroes for his own enrichment, but wants it to be done with paternalistic justice and benevolence.[9] He realises that Britain in building up her world power on the slave-trade. In a *Review* of 1713 he put the matter succinctly: 'The case is as plain as cause and consequence: Mark the climax. No African trade, no negroes, no sugars, gingers, indigoes etc; no sugars etc no islands; no islands no continent; no continent no trade.'

10
Land and Trade

At home, as we saw, there had been a steady increase in credit systems. From 1697 the inland bills of exchange had all the validity of the most formal commercial instrument, and could be negotiated and transmitted without any cumbrous legal machinery. Such bills reduced the cost of goods by reducing the cost of conveying back the money got in return; and they increased the rapidity of the circulation of capital. We get some glimpses of ordinary people using bankers to get money for personal expenses. On 21 March 1712 Swift writes: 'Ugly, nasty weather. I was in the city to-day with Mrs Walker and Mrs Percival, to get money from a banker for Mrs Wesley, who goes to Bath on Thursday.' An advertisement of August 1718 shows a young woman who gets into trouble after drawing on a banker:

> A young gentlewoman, very light-brown hair, fair complexion, middle stature, a large pit or mark of a small-pock near the corner of one of her eyes, and some few pits on her nose, about the age of seventeen years, in a scarlet camolet cloak, was about eleven o'clock before noon on Wednesday the 3rd inst., carried in a hackney coach to the house of Sir Alexander Cairnes, Bart, on College Hill, and thence carried to Mr Colebrook, a banker in Threadneedle Street, the back of the Royal Exchange, London, where she received a good sum of money, and was thence carried away in the same coach, but has not been since heard of

by the family to whom she belongs, her name being at present concealed, in hopes she or any person concerned in conveying her away will let some of her relations know she is alive; or if the said coachman who drove the said coach will give an account of what place he parted with her, or if any other stage or country coachman or other person will give an account to Mrs Parker, who keeps the coffee-house formerly called Young Man's Coffee-House, near Charing Cross, where the said gentleman may be heard of, such persons giving the said account shall be well rewarded, and have their charges paid them by the said Mrs Parker, or the said Sir Alexander Cairnes.[1]

Credit and security were also helped by marine insurance. Of the underwriters who had grown up, some had private offices, others were members of two great companies and their policies were registered in a public office. Bottomry, loans on ships' bottoms, was a much-used way of shifting or spreading out risks as well as making usurious loans and drawing in capital. The East India Company used bottomry bonds in this way. Insurance stimulated commerce by reducing the individual's risks so that he was readier to put money into commercial enterprises. Commerce became more and more something that could be clearly calculated. In such a world the State had to find new ways of raising money which finally ended its medieval bases and oriented it decisively towards the modern world. The imposition of excise dues and direct taxes, the close entanglement of the government's economies with the Bank of England and with loans, stock-dealings and the like, the advent of the national debt in 1694, all converged to link State and Trade in a new way. The continual need for funds to wage the wars provided the dynamic driving on the system to further concentrations and complexities. After 1694 the government was raising money by disposing of amenities, exchequer bills, navy bills, and other transferable securities to whoever would buy.

But the speculative side of the new money-mechanism held dangers and possibilities of disaster that were yet veiled. In the first expansion of the cash-nexus a magical power seemed to have been released, which could indefinitely make fortunes.

Hogarth in verses on his Bubble print, doubtless by himself, referred to 'Money's magic power'. In 1711 Harley set up the South Sea Company. In return for some semi-mythical commercial concessions, the Company was to relieve the government of some ten million pounds of public debts, mainly naval, which had been funded for the purpose. The trading concessions of the Treaty of Utrecht increased interest in the Company, and by 1720 its stock sold at a large premium. The situation was affected by the Mississippi Company of John Law in France, a grandiose scheme that was also soon to crash. When the Ministry entered into a shady agreement with the South Sea Company for a vast extension of its joint-stock business, fictitious stock of £574,000 was handed out as bribes to such persons as the Chancellor of the Exchequer, Craggs (Secretary of State), the king's German mistresses, and various leading MPs. In February 1720 a scheme to extend greatly the privileges of the Company was brought before Parliament. In return the Company was to take over the funded National Dept. Walpole alone repeatedly attacked the scheme, which on 7 April received royal assent. Rumours of big profits were concocted, and the stock rose. A director helped further with a lying story that Gibraltar and Port Mahon were to be exchanged for rich gold mines in Peru. A subscription was opened 'for two millions at £300 for the £100', and was heavily oversubscribed. On 30 April a second offer of 'a million at £400' was at once taken up. Thousands of persons sold property or pawned heirlooms. Change Alley, says Swift, was 'blocked with desks and clerks', and became 'a roaring Hell-porch of insane and dishonest speculators'. By late May, with £100 stock at £800, the Company made a premature dividend and circulated mad rumours of vast rises for the future. Third and fourth issues were oversubscribed. The height of the frenzy came in midsummer.

All sorts of projects were devised. In July at least 104 companies were offering stock. Money was to be made by 'a wheel in perpetual motion', 'the assurance of seamen's wages', 'insuring and increasing children's fortunes', improving malt liquors, extraction of silver from lead, importation of great jackasses from Spain, breeding of silkworms in Chelsea Park, trading in human hair. A clergyman proposed a scheme 'to discover the land of Ophir and monopolise its gold and silver'. One projector claimed to have made a marvellous invention, the nature of which was not disclosed; in one day his bag was full of gold and by night he had slipped off to the Continent. The paper value of the various stocks was estimated at five hundred million pounds, more than twice the value of all the houses and lands in Britain. The lesser swindles enraged the Great Company, and its directors took out writs of *scire facias* against some of the projectors. They thus destroyed themselves. The pricking of the minor bubbles did not clear the air, but showed all too well how baseless was the whole speculative boom.

In November came news that Law had fled from France with a huge amount of money. When Parliament reassembled in December, the South Sea Company directors were ordered to produce their accounts. The treasurer fled to the Continent with the most incriminating documents, and Craggs committed suicide. The early bribe-giving was exposed, the Chancellor of the Exchequer and the head of the government had to resign. Men who had been living riotously on their imagined wealth found themselves beggars. In Parliament Lord Molesworth proposed that the directors should be tied up in sacks and thrown in the Thames. By the end of the year the stock that had sold at 1060 per cent was seen as valueless. Many honest businesses were dragged down by the bankruptcies of their debtors.

Walpole had in fact gambled in the stock and sold out in time; but as the main critic of the Company he found his prestige greatly enhanced. He was called by general acclaim to take charge of the nation, and set about restoring public confidence. Opposing the cry for blind vengeance, he strove to rescue what he could from the wreck. To confiscate the Company's property would have produced another panic; the State itself was too deeply involved. But Walpole did confiscate most of what the directors owned, realising some £2,000,000. (Gibbon's grandfather, a director, had to hand over £50,000 out of an estate worth about £60,000.) Finally Walpole was able to pay a third of the stock's face-value to all holders, who were grateful to get anything. He had built the basis on which he was to rule the nation in a virtually one-party system for the

next twenty years, ensuring the Whigs an even longer dominance. An event which might well have been disastrous for the
Whigs as the money-men was turned to their advantage.

Since 1688 the Tory gentry had sought to assert themselves
and to curb the city-men, but the whole trend of economic
circumstances was against them, and they failed. The Whigs
had long lost all radical elements; their leaders were thoroughly
aristocratic and their alliance was with the city-magnates. There
was no longer a flow of money from the City into land, and from
land to the City. Very few landed men invested in the Bank of
England or East India Stock; and city-investors, doing well out
of such stock, were not tempted to turn to land. The Duke of
Newcastle's agent considered the fall in land-prices to come
from 'the great difference of advantage between money and
Land'. In 1707 Lord Hervey noted: 'How much better money
yields than land, which after taxes and repairs allowed never
answers above 3 per cent.' Above all the movement of money
into land was checked during the wars against Louis XIV. Not
until the end of the Spanish Succession war, when reductions
in the land and in the rate of interest were made, did the movement return. At that time the Property Qualifications Act
forced the men of money to buy estates if they wanted to enter
Parliament. Political uncertainties were largely ended when
George I acceded and the 1715 rebellion failed; and then the
land-market grew more attractive. Finally, after the crash of the
South Sea Company the confidence in paper securities broke
down and the solid asset of land was eagerly sought. The old
cleavage between the landed and the moneyed interests ceased
to be so simple and began to weaken before new mergings and
combinations.[2]

Evelyn on 11 June 1696 sets out clearly enough the attitudes
of the landed gentry at that time:

Want of current money to carry on the smallest concerns,
even for daily provisions in the markets. Guineas lowered
to twenty-two shillings, and other great sums daily transported to Holland where it yields more, with other treasure
sent to pay the armies, and nothing considerable coined of
the new and only current stamp, cause such a scarcity that

tumults are every day feared, nobody paying or receiving money; so imprudent was the late Parliament to condemn the old, though clipt and corrupted, till they had provided supplies. To this add the fraud of the bankers and goldsmiths, who, having gotten immense riches by extortion, keep up their treasure in expectation of enhancing its value. Duncombe, not long since a mean goldsmith, having made purchase of the late Duke of Buckingham's estate at near £90,000, and reputed to have near as much in cash. Banks and lotteries every day set up.

The moneyed men in Parliament might be outnumbered by the gentry, but the government was coming more and more to depend on them. The wealthy few were some ten thousand, of whom about a third owned Bank and East India stock; those were the men who formed a moneyed interest not linked with the landed interest. The financial crisis described by Evelyn, worsened by the recoinage of the currency and the problems of war-payments, led on to another crisis of two years in 1704. In 1702 Harley was told: 'You certainly ruin those that have only land to depend on, to enrich Dutch, Jews, French and other foreigners, scoundrel stock-jobbers and tally-jobbers, who have been sucking our vitals for many years.' William had been accused of diverting capital from land to government loans and thus setting out to build up a vested interest in his regime; and under Anne the Whigs were said to keep the war on to enrich themselves and their moneyed friends. The direct taxation of estates to pay for the war hit the landed gentry hard, while the men lending to the government made big profits. The Whig Junto was seen by the Tories as fighting, not for the allied security, but for their own political power and for territorial and trading privileges for Dutch and Austrians. In the 'slippery state of peace' they could not have held on; they wanted war with its manifold openings for money-manipulation and malversation; they fabricated a new form of wealth out of 'the pillage of the land'. Behind them were the bankers and stock-jobbers 'who increase their wealth and secure their power by continuing a wasting war', prostituting 'the Queen's credit for cheats and illegal gains'. Swift summed up in his *Conduct of the*

Allies: 'We have been fighting to raise the wealth and grandeur of a particular family, to enrich usurers and stock-jobbers, and to cultivate the pernicious designs of a faction by destroying the landed interest.' In 1707 Steele wrote to his mother-in-law that he was one of those voicing 'the general complaints under which everybody at present is sighing whose concerns are wholly in land'.[3]

Previously money had seemed a passive sort of thing, reflecting the power of land and status. Now it had become a strangely active force, a thing in itself, detached from the things it used once to serve. It had increased, complained St John, 'to be almost equal to the *terra firma* of our island'. It was 'a new interest ... a sort of property', a demoralising innovation, 'not known twenty years ago'. It formed a mystery, a menacing jiggery-pokery, turned against the landed gentry. Swift put the emotion they felt into concise and powerful phrases: 'Through the contrivance and cunning of stock-jobbers there hath been brought in such a complication of knavery and cozenage, such a mystery of iniquity, such an unintelligible jargon of terms to involve it in, as were never known in any other age or country of the world.' In *Robinson Crusoe* emotional and personal relationships are relatively unimportant, except when they are bound up with economic issues. Only money causes really deep feeling. The one emotional climax of the book comes when the agent in Lisbon reveals to Crusoe that he is a rich man. 'I turned pale and grew sick; and had not the old man run and fetched me a cordial, I believe the sudden surprise of joy had overset nature, and I had died upon the spot.'[4]

We can understand how the war-situation upset the Tory landowners. There had been nothing like it in previous history; the amounts of money needed were unprecedented. In struggling to raise them the government tightened the grip of the cash-nexus necessary for capitalist industrialism and at the same time laid the foundation of the modern state. Loans were raised in anticipation of revenue voted by Parliament. The Treasury borrowed £1,850,000 (at 4s in the pound) as soon as the land-tax Bill got royal assent. The government was working now, not through groups such as goldsmiths, but by direct appeals to individuals, e.g. offering annuities on loans. Lotteries were

used, and the rich corporations often drawn on for loans. Things
had been bad enough when the war went well. But the disastrous winter of 1708 brought extreme hardships on the poor,
with intensified hatred of the press gang and the army; mutiny
and desertion became a problem at home and abroad.

About 1709 the conflict reached its height. The hard-hit
gentry saw the Bank pay three dividends (amounting over the
year to sixteen per cent). There were eleven bank-directors in
Parliament, which increased the rate of interest on loans
advanced in anticipation of the Land Tax. The failure to make
peace was attributed to a deliberate insistence on terms that
France could not accept. In 1710 a mainly Tory ministry was
in power, with a resulting crisis in confidence on the part of the
moneyed men. Harley had to work hard till the spring of 1711
in stabilising finances. We see how the stock-market had become the gauge of political confidence and stability. As people
felt sure that a Stuart would refuse to recognise the National
Debt, anything that seemed like a threat to the Hanoverian
succession had a sharp effect on the market, e.g. the run on the
Bank when in 1708 the Pretender made an attempted invasion.

The nightmare that Addison described in the *Spectator* on
3 March 1711 reflected the anxieties of 1710–11. Looking in
at the Bank, he sees Publick Credit in the hall, keeping a watch-
ful and timorous eye on 'such Acts of Parliament as had been
made for the establishment of Publick Funds'. He finds later
that she could 'wither into a skeleton' in the twinkling of an
eye, then as suddenly recover health and vigour. According to
the news she changes colour. 'Behind the throne was a prodigious heap of bags of money', but the dreamer ceases to
wonder on learning that Publick Credit has the Midas-power
of converting all she pleases into gold. Then the door opens and
there enter in pairs Tyranny and Anarchy, Bigotry and
Atheism, the Genius of a Commonwealth and a Young Man
(the Pretender) who brandishes a sword at the Act of Settlement. Publick Credit faints and fades, the money-bags turn
empty (nine-tenths of them anyway had been full only of
wind). The heaps of gold become heaps of paper and bundles
of notched sticks (Treasury tallies). Then the scene vanishes.
There enters 'a second Dance of Apparitions': Liberty and

Monarchy, Religion and Moderation, the Genius of Britain. The bags at once fill up and the heaps of paper change to pyramids of guineas. The dreamer wakes with joy.

Soon after this the Tories struggled in vain to get control of the Bank. In 1711 they tried to hamstring the men of money by bringing to a head their demand that MPs must have property qualifications. An Act laid down that knights of the shire must own estates worth £600 per annum. St John, moving the commitment of the Bill, declared that he had heard of a society 'that jointed stocks to bring in members', and he drew the frightening picture of a time 'when the monied men might bid fair to keep out of the House all the landed men'. This year the government launched the South Sea Company. Another attempt to help the gentry, which failed, was Harley's Land Bank Scheme, something like a modern Building Society. The Bank was to issue loans on security of mortgages, with branches dotted round the countryside. It appealed to the backwoods squires by offering a ready source of cash and threatening the power of the Bank of England.[5]

A paper by Steele on 19 September 1711 depicts the conflict between merchant and gentry, and comes down strongly on the former's side. Sir Roger and Sir Andrew Freeport dispute at their Club. Sir Andrew trounces Sir Roger for the total lack of monetary calculation in the way he runs his estate, and analyses at some length the way in which he, as a merchant, bases everything on exact computations after having carried out careful inquiries into all relevant aspects of any deal in which he is involved. The future lies with the calculating men, who are those providing employment for the common folk. 'If it were consistent with the quality of so ancient a baronet as Sir Roger to keep an account or measure things by the most infallible way, he would prefer our parsimony to his hospitality.' The precision of quantitative analysis, characteristic of post-Galilean science (which indeed was aided by Renaissance book-keeping), has now become the ideal of the trader and industrialist, and is praised with an exalted fervour as if the essence of moral and correct behaviour lay in it.

Sir Roger is left dumbfounded before Sir Andrew's tirade, just as at this moment the landed gentry to a large extent were left unnerved and aghast before the success of the men of money. A period of violent, though confused and rudimentary, party-conflict had ended so thoroughly in the rout of one side that historians have doubted if it was party-conflict at all. But the fact was that neither side could do without the other, since both were equally based in property. The men of money needed the agricultural landlords, some of whom were as keen-sighted and forward-looking as any merchant or manufacturer, both for their produce and their system of keeping the countryfolk in order, and the landlords found out that they could not simply oppose the men of accounts as scoundrels who were ready to get money, when necessary, by Fraud and Cozenage – to use Sir Roger's terms. They too wanted a share of the booty, and new forms of alliance as well as of opposition began to appear. The merchants wanted to have country-estates, and so on. Still it was not till the reign of George III, when the Whigs had carried out their programme of commercial and imperial ex-pansion, that the Tories could stage a come-back as a party, with the result that party-conflict began again on a new level. But by that time a new factor had appeared on the scene, the popular radicalism of Wilkes, which was to lead on in the end, through various movements of reform and protest, to working-class oppositions.[6]

Our period then, for all its elements of immaturity and confusion, was the one that saw the decisive turn into the modern world, into the first stages of industrialism and a modern type of State. The man who above all had a steadfast vision of great new productive possibilities opening up was Defoe. 'New discoveries in metals, mines and minerals,' he wrote, 'new undertakings in trade, engines, manufactures, in a nation pushing and improving as we are; these things open new scenes every day, and make England especially shew a new and differing face in many places, on every occasion of surveying it'.

Notes

1. London the Monster City

1. Wrigley (2) 44 and 50; George (2) 180, 178, 169f.
2. Davis, 390, 34f; Ashton (1); Nef ii 381f. Whitehaven and Sunderland were also coalports. Wrigley (3) and (2) 59; Nef i 239; John in Carus-Wilson, *Essays in Economic History*, ii 364. Industry: George (1) 33f; Wrigley (2) 62.
3. F. J. Fisher; Wrigley (2) 55; Houghton, 165f. Processing: Fisher, 60; John (as in n. 2) 393.
4. Summarising Wrigley (2) 65–70.
5. Jessop iii 53–7; N. Lloyd.
6. Summerson, especially ch. iii.
7. Summerson, 78f. Jessop iii 61–6 (also perspective and light).
8. Summerson, 89f; *Spect.* no. 28; *Tour*, 352.
9. Dobrée, 175; Thomas, 17f. See also Newton on Bottisham, 17 Nov. 1712. Luttrell ii 206. Newton 22 March 1683 on Charles II and fire at Newmarket. Ward, 151.
10. Heywood, *Diaries* ii 270. Catholics were also blamed in the seventeenth century. Wesley: M. H. Watt, 51. Begging letter: Thomas, 19f, Trotter, appendix. Insurance: Thomas, 781; Summerson, 49f; Hill (1) 208–10. Time: Ashton (2) 99.
11. Thomas, 768; Wrigley; Hollingsworth; George (2) 26f; R. Reynolds, 72–5; Bready, 143–5; Bridenbaugh, 103f; Jessop iii 253; Hone, 53, 83, 86. Effects of inoculation and improved environment: Hartwell, 76, 88.
12. Ward, ch. vi; R. Reynolds, 72 (whipping). R. S. Roberts in Poynter (1); Poynter (2); Thomas, 788; *Notitia*, 414–16; *Tour*, 373–5.

2. Tour of London and its People

1. B. Franklin, *Autobiography*, 1905, 54f; George (2) 37; *True-Born Englishman*, ii 27–30; Thomas, 22f. Constables: George (2) 398 n. 87; Middlesex Records, Cal. Ap. 1712.

2. Van der Zee, 32, 298; Hone, 60–63, 71; Ward, 15ff. See Addison, *Tatler* no. 240. In 1704 the Common Council ordered that 580 men should watch all night, divided among the wards.
3. Cf. Hogarth's *Peregrination* and stop at Billingsgate.
4. Thomas, 23f; McInnis, 35; Ward, 121–3; Besant (1) 125; *Spect.* no. 345; Ward, 155–7.
5. George (2) 157f, 32f; North iii 172, he goes on to long emblematic analysis of Ombre (the Man).
6. Brown iii 60f; Ward, ch. xi. Ashton (3) and John Ashton, *History of Gambling in England.*
7. Margetson, 39; George (1) 35f; Timbs, etc.
8. Underhill, 23; Byrom, 52, 54, 154; George (2) 95; *Spect.* nos. 403; 49; 521; 148. Steele on Serle's, no. 49; Budgell, no. 197, also Steele, no. 145.
9. Ward, 217f; Colson, 3–6 and Ward, 208; Westerfield, 392; Martin.
10. Timbs; Molloy, 175; *Spect.* no. 9; Lady Mary, *Letters and Works*, i 476f. Concerts were coming in; T. Hickford gave them now and then from 1697 in his Great Room off the Haymarket; more regularly after 1712. In 1720s there were tavern-concerts: Young, 77f.
11. Brown iii 12ff.
12. Besant (1) 122–4; Westerfield, 341–3; W. Stout, *Autobiography*, 1851; Besant (2) 198 and (3) 126–9; Brown iii 40; George (1) ch. ii; John; T. E. Gregory; Defoe, *Compleat English Tradesman*, 1726, i 312–15.

3. The Mob

1. *Spect.* no. 336 (26 March 1712); George (2) 101.
2. Nottingham: McInnis, 85. Sacheverell: Holmes (3).
3. *Spect.* nos. 324, 347; Besant (1) 126; Trevelyan iii 203.
4. George (1) 26 and (2) 180, 118; Beattie, 70f; Plumb (4) ii 40–49; *Weekly Journal*, 12 May 1722.
5. Fielding, *Increase of Robbers*, 1751; Bready, 170; Molloy, 20–24, 177; W. Wilson i 209. Also, Howson, Hitchin, Beattie. D. Hay and E. P. Thompson for Blacks, poachers, wreckers. Hobsbawm on weaving riots.
6. Misson, 123f; Lee iii 23f; Paulson, *Life of Hograth* (1971) i 197.

4. Journalism and the New Reading Public

1. Westerfield, 366f.
2. Underhill. News: Brown iii 28; *Spect.* no. 10; Westerfield, 366.
3. *Mercurius Librarius; or a Faithful Account of all Books and Pamphlets*, 1680, twice a month, 6d paid for insertion of a book. Harley: B. M. Harl. MD 7, 544; *N. and Q.*, 2nd s. ix 418.
4. Sales: Ian Watt, 39ff.
5. Luttrell, ii 345f; Burnet (1) iv 181f, Dartmouth's note. *Guardian* no. 105; *Spect.* 294 and 430. Oaths: Stamm, 236.

6. J. Simon; M. G. Jones; Ian Watt, 41: Sylvester, 101, 170–73; Plumb (1) 31; Sutherland, 21; McInnis, 22. Also, I. Watts, *An Essay towards the Encouragement of Charity Schools*, 1728; Kennett (3); Talbott. Duck, *Poems on Several Occasions*, 1730, p. iv.
7. Guerinot; Ian Watt, 59, 63.
8. *Weekly Medley*, 26 Sept.–3 Oct.; Sutherland, 255, 236; Ian Watt, 45. Group: Sutherland, 112.
9. Bolton, 47; *Spect.* no. 135; Watt, 113, 115.
10. Watt, 48–50, 161 (marriage later).

5. Women, Fashions, Assemblies

1. Lee, Defoe, ii 115–17, 143f; iii 125–8, 323–5. Utter, 217; M. Reynolds, 318; *Notitia*, 307f. Slater on marriage in the seventeenth century.
2. Earle, 269, 244; Rowbotham, 31; Watt, 178; *Guardian*, no. 45; Defoe's *Religious Courtship*. Note independence of Hogarth's Miss Edwards. Increasing stress on funeral rites: Watt, 246.
3. Lady Mary, 10 Oct. 1752 from Brescia; Swift, 24 March 1711; *Spect.* no. 193 and 175, Steele no. 6. Parnell: *Spect.* no. 460.
4. Brown iii 122; Ward, 136. See Addison, *Spect.* 414, 455, 477, (nurseries) 5. He dislikes 'trees rising in cones, globes, and pyramids'.
5. *Spect.* nos. 232, 54. Sea-bathing is coming in; bathing machine in print of Scarborough Sands, 1735. Spas: Sydney ii, ch. 12. See Defoe's *Tour* on Tunbridge Wells, Matlock, Buxton, etc.

6. The Landed Gentry and the Labourers

1. Earle, 117f, 151; George (1) ch. i; Baxter, *Bull. J. Rylands Lib.* x, 1926, ed. F. J. Powicke; Defoe, *Plan of English Commerce*, 67; King in G. Chalmers, *Estimate of the Comparative Strength of Great Britain*, 1804, 48f; McInnis, 87; Fox Bourne, 383–5; P. Deane in Hartwell.
2. A. F. J. Brown, 23. Contrasts: Ashton (3) 17–19; Wedderburn, 6; Anon. (3) 34–5.
3. Defoe, *Review* 25 June 1708; Morant, 75f; Defoe, *Plan of English Commerce*, 268–9. Numbers in agriculture fell, first half of century: Wrigley, 57.
4. Hoon, 186, 233.
5. Hill (1) 154; Kerridge; *Econ. Hist. Rev.* lxxiv (1959) 611; C. Wilson, 141; Hill, 152. (One factor in the swelling of estates had been the illegal sale or gift of crown-lands after 1688.)
6. *Spect.* nos. 474, 326, 57, 177 (musical hounds), 122.
7. Plumb (1) 18; Margetson, 15; *Spect.* no. 167; R. A. C. Parker, *Coke of Norfolk*; G. E. Mingay, *TLS* 20 Feb. 1976.
8. Jessop iii 317f; Speck, 140f, 147.
9. *Spect.* no. 106, 122; Hill (2) 358. In general, for Plumb see *Historical Perspectives*, ed. N. McKendrick (1975), and review, *Times Lit. Supp.* by J. Lee, 22 Jan. 1976. M. Girouard, *TLS* 27 Feb. 1976.

7. Marriages and Elections

1. Habakkuk (1) and (2); Hill (2) 352; Speck, 145f.
2. Speck, 145f; Lincs RO Massingberd MSS 20/43; Temple, *Works*, 1700, i 268, cf. *Tatler* no. 199; Scott, 20ff. The new family formations emerging from the 17th century 'fulfilled a variety of vital functions, and at the same time there were fewer specialised institutions which could dupli- cate these functions or offer alternative possibilities. The arranged mar- riage offered an *entrée* into family life with expanded familial connec- tions; these families served not only as nurturing and socialising agencies but also as credit institutions, levers of political power, arbiters of educa- tional and professional advancement and marriage brokers,' Slater, 54.
3. Defoe, *Compleat English Tradesman*, 1841, i 227–40; *Compleat English Gentle- man*, 1890, 250–54. Clarissa: Hill (2) and Ian Watt.
4. Bonnell: Hamilton, 76; Jessop iii 169, 172; *Spect.* nos. 125, 57, 126; Isham, 111.
5. Defoe (2) v 142; Ellis in Holmes, 119.
6. Van der Zee, 398; Evelyn 29 Aug. 1695.
7. Plumb (1) 39, 31; Isham, 111; Brown iii 27f.
8. Speck, 136f, 146; Cartwright, 157; P. Wentworth to Lord Raby, 21 Dec. 1710; Lincs RO M.MSS 20/93 (1 April 1711).
9. Plumb (1) 11; Defoe, preface to 7th vol. of *Review*, Sept. 1712; Defoe, *Reasons against the Succession of the House of Hanover*, 1713, 2f. See Defoe, *Tour*, for the organised election battles at Coventry.

8. Projectors and Quakers

1. *Spect.* nos. 31, 25; *Tatler* no. 224. Budgell, *Spect.* no. 353, recommends Accounts and Shorthand. Anon. (3) for 1751.
2. Raistrick for full details of Quakers in industry etc; also Isabel Grubb, N. C. Hunt etc. Marriage: Hair, nos, 343, 369, 76, cf. 139.

   Note also elaborate workhouse schemes in *Of the People of England*, 1699. In 1723 an Act empowered each parish to build a workhouse for the poor, who were farmed out as workers. See Morley's *Essays* by Petty, 1894.
3. Brown iii 100f for Presbyterian meeting house in Russell Court. Ward, 2716. Hubbard, 34, 40, 48. *Spect.* no. 259.
4. *Spect.* no. 259. Clocks: Symonds. The idea of clockwork invades all spheres of thought: the universe as such a mechanism, love and the heart in Wren's letter to his beloved, etc. For banking: Raistrick and Lloyd. For role of iron, cotton, pottery in the century (industries free from vested interests), Hartwell, 39; Ashton (3); H. Hamilton, 266f; A. C. Allen, 17f; Ashton (2) 19.

   Some crucial points for the advent of industrialism (together with capital accumulation and capitalist wage-relations): supply of fodder crops encouraging mixed farming (producing meat, leather, wool, as well as cereals); rise of new industries previously confined to the home, e.g. brewing, soap-making; expansion and diversification of textile industry; growth of coal-mining, expansion of other mining, e.g. tin, copper, salt; tendency to geographical concentration, e.g. woollens in Yorkshire; increasingly complicated technology and division of labour; development of quantitative science; growth of the financial instrument (Bank, long-term mortgages etc, with fall in rate of interest); the necessary ideological rationalisations; expansion of world-trade, with colonies. In England these factors converged as nowhere else. See Hartwell for discussion.

9. *Merchants and Slaves*

1. Westerfield, 329–40; *Tour*, 500; Burke, 55; Grafton, 25, 40; Rhys, 173. Coaches: Rhys, 173. Demographic centre moves north: Ashton (3) 14, also for problems in movement; Anon. (3) 41.
2. Besant (1) 248; *Tour*, 84.
3. Defoe in *Tour*, writing soon after the Bubble, describes the Exchange as desolated. *Spect.* no. 69.
4. Hoon, 3; Westerfield, 358.
5. Law: Christian, 100–109. Adverts: Sampson, 6, 4. Post Office: Hemmeon, 159–67; Rhys, 175.
6. Jeaffreson ii 223, 62, 67–78, 101–103, 235, 249, 125. Jeaffreson has trouble with a convict, Jacob Watkins, who escaped and got back to London, appearing 'publickly amongst the watermen below the bridge. I was once in chase of him.'
7. Harris, 6; Sydney i 353, 349; George (2) 312, 142, 363, 136; Bready, 100, 106; Jeudwine, 206.
8. George (2) 137; Sydney i 352; George (2) 361.
9. Hubbard, 44. Baxter in his *Christian Dictionary* (1673) called slave-traders 'incarnate devils', but by 1697 the divines argued that the trade was all right if the slaves were well-treated: Earle, 67. Note Gildon, p. 14, for attack on Defoe's attitude.

10. *Land and Trade*

1. Molloy, 180; Westerfield, 393; Jeudwine, 89.
2. Speck, 147. There was no total cleavage. Harley launched the South Sea Company with support from rich Tories, and so on. But the generalisation holds. The Bank was Whig from the outset.
3. Cf. Evelyn, 3 Aug. on high rate of interest. Estate at Helmsley, cf. Pope '... once proud Buckingham's delight, Slides to a Scrivener or a City Knight.'
4. Speck, 136f; Holmes (1) 200; Ian Watt, 77, cf. 73. The Tories made a strenuous attempt to gain the Bank, and to offset the Whig victory Harley started the South Sea Company.
5. *Spect.* no. 428. Speck, 151f, 156f, 136. See Appleby for the sustained controversy in the 1690s (in which Locke and Barbon played a part) as to the nature of money, partly caused by the problem of the clipt (debased) silver coinage. Did money have a value in itself or was it

merely a medium of exchange? An example of the advanced viewpoint was that set out by an anonymous bank-promotor: 'Money is but a medium of commerce, a security which we part with to enjoy the like in value. And such is a bank-bill, it will obtain what we want and satisfy where we are indebted, and may be turned into money again when the possessor pleaseth, and will be the standard of trade at last.'

6.   The 17th century crisis elsewhere dragged down to a subordinate role the feudal and mercantile town-economies that had helped things forward (Spain, Italy, later the Netherlands), on account of the weak productive home base. Only in Britain was the speculative merchant capital based on a colonial trade able to provide the driving force for a fully autonomous accumulation and growth of the home-market. Otherwise the dominance of merchant capital (in trade and production) remained a redistributive mediation between producer and consumer (depending on disparity between cost-price and sale-price) as long as production was organised externally to capital and the integrated world-market (and its average or long-term price) did not exist. See J. Merrington, 93.

     The British people were better fed, clothed, housed, than their European counterparts. The home-market was 'available to cushion the more dynamic export industries against the sudden fluctuations and collapses which were the price they paid for their superior dynamism. But more than this it provided the broad foundation of a *generalised* industrial economy, 'A. J. Hobsbawm, *Industry and Empire*, 1969, 47f. See D. Parker on the role of war in all this: *Our History*, no. 53, winter 1973. The agricultural advance was an integral part of the home productive base: Kerridge and E. L. Jones. See further Christozvonov, 22f, and Hartwell for general discussion.

Bibliography

Quotations from Defoe's *Tour* can easily be located from the Index of Places there. Diaries or Swift's letters to Stella have the dates of passages given. Where no place of publication is stated, the place is London.

Aitken, J., *English Letters of the 18th Century*, 1946.
Allen, A., *Life in Britain since 1700*, 1956.
Allen, G. C., *The Industrial Development of Birmingham and the Black Country.*
Anon. (1) *The Royal Progress*, 1695; (2) *Piercing Cryes of the poor and miserable Prisoners for Debt*, 1714; (3) *Reflections on various subjects relating to Arts and Commerce*, 1752.
Appleby, J. O., *Past and Present* no. 71, 1976.
Ashton, J., (1) *The History of Gambling in England*; (2) *An History of English Lotteries.*
Ashton, T. S., (1) with J. Sykes, *The Coal Industry of the 18th Century*, 1929; (2) *The Industrial Revolution*; (3) *An Economic History of England: the 18th Century*, 1969.
Austen-Leigh, R. A., *Library* 4th s. iii 1923.

Baston, T., *Thoughts on Trade*, 1716.
Beastall, T. W., *A North Country Estate (Lumleys and Saundersons)*, 1976.
Beattie, J. M., *Past and Present* no. 62.
Besant, W., (1) *London in the Time of the Stuarts*, 1903; (2) *London in the Time of the Tudors*, 1904; (3) *London in the 18th Century*, 1902.
Blundell, N., *The Great Diurnal of Nicholas Blundell*, ed. J. J. Bagley, 1968–70.
Bolton, W. F., *A Short History of Literary English*, 1967.
Bourne, H., *Antiquitates Vulgares* (Newcastle), 1725.
Bourne, H. R. F., *English Merchants*, 1886.
Brand, B. M., *Popular Antiquities*, 1813.
Bready, J. W., *England before and after Wesley*, 1938.
Bridenbaugh, C., *Vexed and Troubled English*, 1968.
Brown, A. F. J., *Essex at Work 1700–1815* (Chelmsford), 1969.
Brown, Tom, *Works*, 8th ed., 1744.
Burke, T., *Travel in England*, 1942.

Burnet, G., *History of his Own Time*, with Notes by the Earls of Dartmouth and Hardwicke (2nd ed. Oxford), 1833; (2) *An Essay on the Memory of the Late Queen*, 1695.

Butt, J., *The Augustan Age*, 1950.

Byrom, J., *Selections from the Journals*, ed. H. Talon, 1950.

Carlson, L., *The First Magazine* (Providence), 1938.

Carr, R., *English Fox-Hunting*, 1976.

Chandaman, C. D., *The English Public Revenue 1660–88*, 1975.

Christian, E. B. V., *Solicitors*, 1925.

Christozvonov, A., *Our History* no. 63, summer 1975.

Clark, A., *Working Life of Women in the 17th Century*, 1919.

Clark, P., with P. Slack, *Crisis and Order in English Towns, 1500–1700*, 1972.

Clarkson, L. A., *Death, Disease and Famine in pre-Industrial England*, 1975.

Collins, A. S., (1) *Authorship in the Days of Johnson*, 1927; (2) *The Profession of Letters*, 1928.

Colson, P., *A Story of Christie's*, 1950.

Connely, W., *Sir Richard Steele*, 1934.

Craton, M., *Sinews of Empire*, 1925 (A Short History of British Slavery).

Cuming, E. D., in *Johnson's England*, ed. A. S. Turberville (Oxford), 1933.

Dalrymple, Sir J., *Memoirs of Great Britain and Ireland* (Edinburgh) 1771–88.

Darley, G., *Villages of Vision*, 1976.

Davis, A. P., *Isaac Watts* (New York), 1943.

Davis, R., *The Rise of the English Shipping Industry*, 1962.

Defoe, D., (1) *A Tour of Great Britain*, intro. G. D. Cole, 1927; (2) *The Review*, ed. A. W. Secord (New York), 1938.

Dickson, P. G. M., *The Financial Revolution*, 1967.

Dobrée, B., *William Penn*, 1932.

Earle, P., *The World of Defoe*, 1976.

Evelyn, J., *Memoirs*, ed. W. Bray, 1827.

Everitt, A., *Past and Present* no. 33, April 1966.

Fisher, F. J., *English Historical Review* v 1934–5.

Fitzgerald, A., *D. Defoe*, 1954.

Fox Bourne, H. R., *Life of John Locke*, 1876.

Fussell, G. E. and K. R., *The English Countryman*, 1953.

George, D., (1) *England in Transition*, 1931; (2) *London Life in the 18th Century*, 1930.

Gildon, C., *The Life and strange surprising adventures of Mr D ... Dr F ... of London Hosier*, 1719.

Gilboy, E. W., *Wages in 18th Century England* (Camb. Mass.), 1934.

Glass, D. V., (1) *Eugenics Rev.* xxxvii (4) 171–83; (2) *Population Studies*, March 1950; (3) ibid. July 1952.

Grafton, R., *Grand Concern of England explained*, 1673.

Gregory, T. E., *Economic Journal*, December 1930.

Griffiths, Hon. Mrs, *Through England on a Side Saddle* (Celia Fiennes), 1888.

Guerinot, J. V., *Pamphlet Attacks on Alexander Pope*, 1969.

Habakkuk, H. J., (1) *Trans. R. Hist. Soc.* 1950; (2) *Econ. Hist. Rev.* x.

Hagen, E., *On the Theory of Social Change*, 1962.

Hair, P., *Before the Bawdry Court*, 1972.

Halifax, Lord, *Complete Works*, ed. J. P. Kenyon, 1969.

Haller, W. and M., *Huntingdon. Lib. Q.*, v 235–72.

Hamilton, H., *The English Copper and Brass Industries to 1800*, 1926.

Hamilton, W., *The Exemplary Life of James Bonnell* (5th ed.), 1807.

Hamlyn, H. M., *Library*, 5th s. i 1946.

Harris, J., *A Century of Emancipation*, 1933.

Hartwell, R. M., ed., *The Causes of the Industrial Revolution in England*, 1967.

Hay, D., ed., *Albion's Fatal Tree*.

Haynes, J., *View of the Present State of the Clothing Trade*, 1706.

Heimans, H. E., *Het Karakter van Willem III* (Amsterdam), 1925.

Hemmeon, J. C., *The History of the British Post Office* (Cambridge), 1912.

Hill, C., (1) *Reformation to the Industrial Revolution*, 1969; (2) *Puritanism and Revolution*, 1968.

Hilman, D., *Tusser Redivivus*, 1710.

Hitchin, C., *A True Discovery of the Conduct of Receivers as Thief-Takers in and about the City of London*, 1718.

Hobsbawm, E., *Labouring Men*, 1964.

Hole, C., (1) *English Home Life*, 1949; (2) *The English Housewife in the 17th Century*, 1953; (3) *English Sports*, 1949.

Hollingsworth, T. H., *The Demography of the British Peerage*, 1964.

Holmes, G., (1) ed., *Britain after the Glorious Revolution*, 1969; (2) with W. A. Speck, *The Divided Society*, 1967; (3) *Past and Present*, Aug. 1976.

Hone, C. R., *The Life of Dr John Radcliffe*, 1950.

Hoon, E. E., *The Organisation of the English Custom System*, 1968.

Howson, G., *Thief-Taker General*, 1970.

Hubbard, G., *Quaker by Convincement*, 1974.

Hunt, N. C., *Two Early Political Associations* (Oxford), 1961.

Isham, T., *Journal*, ed. W. Rye (Norwich), 1875.

Jeaffreson, J. C., ed., *A Young Squire*, 1878.

Jessopp, A., *The Lives of the Norths*, 1900.

Jeudwine, J. W., *Religion, Conscience, Liberty, 1683–1793*, 1925.

Jones, E. L., (1) *Agriculture and the Industrial Revolution* (Oxford), 1975; (2) *Past and Present* no. 40, 1968.

Jones, M. G., *The Charity School Movement* (Cambridge), 1938.

Kennett, W., (1) *Parochial Antiquities* (Oxford), 1695; (2) *The Wisdom of Looking Backward*, 1715; (3) *The Charity of Schools for Poor Children Recommended*, 1706.

Kerridge, E., *The Agricultural Revolution*, 1967.

Knowlson, J., *Universal Language Schemes in England and France, 1600–1800* (Toronto), 1975.

Lawrence, J., (1) *A Philosophical and Practical Treatise on Houses*, 1796–8; (2) *History and Delineation of the House*, 1809.

Lee, W., *Daniel Defoe* (3 vols.) 1869.

210 BIBLIOGRAPHY

Leonard, E. M., *Early History of the English Poor Relief*, 1900.
Leonard, S. A., *The Doctrine of Correctness in English Usage*, 1929.
Lindsay, J., (1) *John Bunyan*, 1937; (2) *Hogarth*, 1977.
Lloyd, H., *The Quaker Lloyds and the Industrial Revolution*, 1975.
Lloyd, N., *A History of the English House*, 1931.
Lockyer, C., *An Account of the Trade in India*, 1711.
Longrigg, R., *History of Fox Hunting*, 1976.
Luttrell, N., *A Brief Historical Relation of State Affairs* (Oxford), 1857.

MacInnes, C. M., *The Early English Tobacco Trade*, 1926.
McKillop, A. D., *Samuel Richardson* (Chapel Hill), 1936.
Malcolmson, R. W., *Popular Recreations in English Society, 1700–1850* (Cambridge), 1973.
Mandeville, B. de, *The Fable of the Bees*, ed. F. B. Kaye (Oxford), 1924.
Margetson, S., *Leisure and Pleasure in the 18th Century*, 1970.
Marshall, D., *English People in the 18th Century*, 1956.
Martin, F., *The History of Lloyds and of Marine Insurance*, 1876.
Marx, K., *Capital* (transl. E. and C. Paul), 1930.
Mee, G., *Aristocratic Enterprises*, 1976.
Merrington, J., *New Left Rev.* no. 85.
Mingay, G. E., (1) in Warner, 60–79; (2) *English Landed Society in the 18th Century* (Oxford), 1953.
Misson, H., *Memoirs and Observations in his Travels over England*, 1719.
Mitchell and Deane, *Abstract of British Historical Statistics*.
Molloy, J. F., *Court Life below Stairs*, 1885.
Morant, P., *History of Colchester*, 1745.
Morison, S., *The English Newspaper* (Cambridge), 1932.
Morton, J., *The Natural History of Northamptonshire*, 1712.
Mullett, C. F., *The Bubonic Plague and England* (Lexington), 1956.
Murault, B. L. de, *Letters describing the Character and Customs of the English and French Natures*, 1726.

Nef, J. U., *The Rise of the British Coal Industry*, 1932.
Newton, Samuel, *Diary*, ed. J. E. Foster, 1890.

Pennington, Isaac, *Works*, 1681.
Petrie, C., *The Jacobite Movement*, 1948.
Petty, Sir W., *Essays on Mankind and Political Arithmetic*, ed. H. Morley, 1894.
Plumb, J. H., (1) *England in the 18th Century*, 1950; (2) *The Growth of Political Stability in England 1675–1724*, 1969; (3) *Men and Places*, 1961; (4) *Sir Robert Walpole*, 1960.
Powell, C. L., *English Domestic Relations 1487–1853* (New York), 1917.
Poynter, F. N. L., (1) ed., *The Evolution of Pharmacy in Britain*, 1965; (2) ed., *The Evolution of Hospitals in Britain*, 1964.

Radzinowicz, L., *A History of English Criminal Law*, 1948.
Raistrick, A., (1) *Quakers in Society and Industry*, 1950; (2) *Dynasty of Iron-Founders*, 1953.

Renard, G., and G. Weulersse, *Life and Work in Modern Europe*, 1926.

Reynolds, M., *The Learned Lady in England, 1650–1760* (Boston), 1920.

Reynolds, R., *Cleanliness and Godliness*, 1943.

Rhys, E., *Growth of Political Liberty*, 1921.

Richetti, J. J., *Defoe's Narratives* (Oxford), 1975.

Rive, A., *Economic History*, i 1926 (Tobacco).

Roberts, D., *A Quaker of the Olden Times* (J. Roberts), ed. E. T. Lawrence, 1898.

Rowbotham, S., *Women, Resistance and Revolution*, 1974.

Sampson, H., *History of Advertising*, 1874.

Saussure, C. de, *A Foreign View of England* (transl. Van Muyden), 1902.

Scarlett, J., *The Stile of Exchange*, 1682.

Schwoerer, L. F., '*No Standing Armies!*' (Baltimore), 1975.

Scott, W. R., *The Constitution and Finance of English, Scottish and Irish Joint-Stock Companies to 1720*, 1912.

Scott, W. S., *The Blue-Stocking Ladies*, 1947.

Simon, B., ed., *Education in Leicestershire* (Leicester), 1968.

Slater, M., *Past and Present*, August 1976.

Stamm, R. G., *Philolog. Q.*, July 1936.

Stanford, W. B., *Listener* (Bentley), 26 March 1959.

Stewart, D. M., *The English Abigail*, 1946.

Stone, L., *The Crisis of the Aristocracy* (Oxford, abridged), 1967.

Summerson, J., *Georgian London*, 1962.

Sutherland, J., (1) ed., *An Author to be Lett* (Los Angeles), 1960; (2) *Defoe*, 1937; (3) *Library* 4th s. xv 1934; (4) ed., Pope's *Dunciad*, 1943.

Sydney, W. C., *England and the English in the 18th Century*, 1891.

Sylvester, D. W., *Educational Documents*, 1970.

Symonds, K. W., *A History of English Clocks*, 1947.

Talbott, J., *The Christian Schoolmaster*, 1707.

Taylor, A. J., ed., *The Standard of Living in Britain in the Industrial Revolution*, 1975.

Thomas, K., *Religion and the Decline of Magic*, 1973.

Thompson, E. P., *Whigs and Hunters*, 1975.

Timbs, J., *Clubs and Club Life in London*, 1872.

Trevelyan, G. M., *England under Queen Anne*, 1934.

Trotter, E., *Seventeenth Century Life in the Country Parish*, 1919.

Underhill, J., ed., *The Athenian Oracle*, n.d.

Utter, R. P., with G. B. Needham, *Pamela's Daughter*, 1937.

Van der Zee, A. and B., *William and Mary*, 1973.

Wagner, A. R., *English Ancestry* (Oxford), 1961.

Walvin, J., *Listener*, 14 Nov. 1974.

Ward, Ned, *The London Spy*, ed. A. L. Hayward, 1927.

Ward, W. R., *The English Land Tax in the 18th Century* (Oxford), 1953.

Warner, C. K., ed., *Agrarian Conditions in Modern European History*, 1966.

Watt, Ian, (1) *The Rise of the Novel*, 1972; (2) *Studies in Bibliography* (Virginia) xii 3–20, 1959.

Watt, W. H., *The History of the Parson's Wife*, 1943.

Wedderburn, A., *Essay upon the Question, What proportion of the produce of arable land ought to be paid as rent to the landlord?* 1766.

Westerfield, R. B., *Middlemen in English Business*, 1915.

Western, J. R., *The English Militia in the 18th Century*, 1965.

Williams, G., *The Age of Agony*, 1975.

Wilson, C., *England's Apprenticeship*, 1965.

Wilson, T., *Diaries*, ed. C. L. S. Linnell, 1964.

Wilson, W., *Life and Times of Daniel Defoe*, 1830.

Wrigley, E. A., (1) *Daedalus*, spring 1968; (2) *Past and Present* no. 37, July 1967; (3) *Econ. Hist. Rev.* 2nd s. xv 1962–3.

Young, P. M., *The Concert Tradition*, 1965.

Zimmerman, E., *Defoe and the Novel* (California), 1975.

Index

1. London and Environs

Aldergate St, 61
Alsatia, 75

Bagnigge Wells, 116
Baldwin's Gardens, 68
Barbican, 67
Bartholomew Lane, 52
Bedford Row, 16
Bedlam, 35-6, 67-8, 158
Bellsize, 116
Billingsgate, 44, 45, 54
Bishopsgate St, 24
Blackheath, 159
Blackwell Hall, 173
Bow, 93
Bridewell, 34
Buckingham St, 16

Carshalton, 118
Change Alley, 192
Charing Cross, 48, 55, 59, 62, 98, 191
Charterhouse, 91
Cheapside, 59, 65
Chelsea, 7, 20, 192
Christchurch Spitalfields, 73
Clerkenwell, 54, 55
Covent Garden, 55, 61
Crane Court, 12
Cripplegate, 3, 67, 82
Croydon, 79

Deptford, 7
Drury Lane, 23, 74

East India House, 53
Epping, 124
Essex House, 16
Exchange, 62, 65-7, 178, 190

Finch Lane, 188

Fleet Bridge, 65
Fleet St, 12, 20, 46
Foundling Hospital, 27
Fullwood's Rents, 60

Goodman's Fields, 19
Gracechurch St, 44
Gravesend, 46
Gray's Inn, 16, 32, 60, 68
Greenwich, 162
Gresham College, 68
Grocers Hall, 76
Guildhall, 82

Hammersmith, 158
Hampstead, 116, 120
Haymarket, 23, 158
Hockley in the Hole, 54
Holborn, 60
Hole in the Wall, 68
Hyde Park, 75, 79, 97

Inns of Court, 19
Islington, 21, 54, 116

Kensington, 7

Lambeth, 80
Leicester Fields, 160
Limehouse, 7
Lincoln's Inn Fields, 76
Lombard St, 41, 183
Long Acre, 62
Long-lane, 67
Ludgate Hill, 32

Mall, The, 114
Marylebone, 116
Mincing Lane, 12, 16
Minories, 51, 72
Moorfields, 32

Newgate, 66, 87
Newington, 3, 5, 95
Newport Sq, 16

Old Jewry, 63
Oxford St, 83

Piccadilly, 68
Poplar, 159
Portugal St, 60
Poultry, The, 87

Ratcliff, 21
Red Lion Sq, 16
Richmond Park, 75, 117
Russell St, 55

St James's Palace, 4
St James's Park, 114–16
St Martin's Lane, 160
St Paul's, 65, 75
St Paul's Churchyard, 42, 58, 65, 71
Savoy, 75
Scotland Yard, 48
Shoe Lane, 46
Shooters Hill, 116
Shoreditch, 7
Slough, 4
Smithfield, 67
Soho, 16
Southwark, 7, 21, 23, 165
Spitalfields, 10, 77, 80
Stoke Newington, 54
Strand, 1, 16, 67

Temple, 56, 60, 75
Temple Bar, 20, 55
Thames, 1, 4, 9, 21, 93, 127, 130, 158,
    186
Threadneedle St, 190
Tilbury, 20
Tothill St, 7
Tower, 80
Trinity House, 158
Twickenham, 19
Tyburn, 80, 83–4

Villiers St, 16

Wandsworth, 108
Wapping, 21
Warwick Lane, 32
Westminster, 7, 54, 59, 73, 80, 155, 165
Westminster Abbey, 81
Westminster Bridge, 52
Westminster Hall, 70, 82
Whitechapel, 187
Whitefriars, 6
Whitehall, 24, 40, 82
Wood St, 65, 82

York House, 16

2. Other Places
Alresford, 23
Althorp, 152
American Colonies, 5, 24, 181, 186, 189
Amsterdam, 8, 121, 131
Anglesey, 126

Barbados, 187
Barnstaple, 75
Bath, 119, 138, 190
Bedford, 74
Berkshire, 79
Birmingham, 125, 126, 175
Black Country, 126
Bocking, 124, 129
Boroughbridge, 152
Bourne Bridge, 83
Braintree, 129
Bramber, 154
Brighton, 138
Bristol, 6, 10, 124, 127, 164, 175, 181
Burford, 152
Bury St Edmunds, 116

Cadiz, 47
Calais, 130
Cambridge, 74, 87, 143, 160, 175, 176
Canterbury, 122
Chatham, 47, 161
Chatsworth, 137
Chester, 182
Chippenham, 138
Cirencester, 75
Clifton, 138
Coalbrookdale, 161, 168
Colchester, 129
Coleshill, 150

Derbyshire, 126, 169
Dorset, 116
Dublin, 181
Dudley, 125
Dunkirk, 61

Edinburgh, 138, 174, 181
Eltham, 118
Epsom, 117, 120
Epworth, 25
Essex, 124, 129, 144
Exeter, 75, 112, 122, 138, 176, 182

Faversham, 4, 131
Forest of Dean, 126, 168
Frome, 75
Furness, 168

Gainsborough, 75
Glasgow, 179
Great Baddow, 144

Halifax, 25, 128, 182
Hamburg, 131, 178
Hampshire, 79, 151
Hanover, 91
Henley, 4
Hereford, 75
Houghton, 101, 137–8
Hull, 127, 178, 182
Huntingdon, 74

Ireland, 91, 107–8

Jamaica, 186

Kent, 118, 127, 131, 181
Kidderminster, 71
Kingston on Hull, 95

Lancashire, 132
Lancaster, 69
Launceston, 95
Leeds, 94, 122, 176–7, 182
Leicester, 176
Leicestershire, 136
Lincoln, 152
Lincolnshire, 25, 158
Liverpool, 127, 182, 185
Lumley, 10
Lyme, 5

Manchester, 160, 182
Melksham, 81
Melton Mowbray, 133
Middlesex, 39

Newcastle, 10, 21, 23, 127, 138
Newmarket, 82, 83, 119, 152
Norfolk, 10, 130, 137, 152
Norwich, 86, 138
Nottingham, 74, 138, 160, 176

Orkneys, 131
Oxford, 2, 35, 50, 75, 87, 152, 160, 175

Paris, 7, 8, 58
Peterson, 24
Philadelphia, 24
Plymouth, 47, 182
Portland, 20
Portsmouth, 47
Preston, 126

Queenborough, 155

Raynham, 137
Reading, 4
Rochdale, 182
Romney Marsh, 131

Saffron Walden, 164

St Albans, 88
Sheffield, 10, 126, 175
Sherborne, 75
Sherwood, 152
Shoreham, 154
Shrewsbury, 182
Shropshire, 50
Spalding, 92
Stamford, 152
Stenning, 154
Stockbridge, 151
Stourbridge, 175
Suffolk, 129, 139, 150
Sunderland, 130
Sussex, 154
Swaffham, 28

Tamworth, 35
Taunton, 182
Tiverton, 22
Tunbridge Wells, 61, 116, 117–18, 120
Tyne, 9

Utrecht, 12, 17, 185

Vigo Bay, 47

Wales, 169
Walsall, 125
Waltham, 79
Ware, 21
Warwick, 152
Weald, 168
Wednesbury, 125
Welbeck, 152
Wendover, 151
West Country, 129
West Indies, 32, 52, 181–2, 184, 186, 188
West Riding, 132
Wickham, 30
Winchester, 116
Wolverhampton, 125
Worcester, 182
Wrexham, 75

Yarmouth, 10
York, 138, 163
Yorkshire, 168

3 Persons

Adams, Mrs of Great Baddow, 144
Addison, J., 19–20, 43, 48, 51, 55–8, 63,
    71, 91, 95, 99, 100, 103, 124, 135,
    140–1, 148–9, 158–9, 170, 178–9, 197
Anne, Queen, 18–19, 25, 27–8, 40, 62–3,
    79, 109, 139, 142, 151, 156, 195
Annesley, Samuel, 3
Annesley family, 187

Arbuthnot, Dr J., 135
Arne, T., 85
Astell, Mary, 108
Atkinson, Aaron, 163
Atterbury, Francis, 100
Auger, K. (slave), 187

Baker, Thomas, 120
Barbon, N., 12–18, 26, 169, 204
Baxter, Richard, 31, 108, 123–4, 204
Bedford, Duke of, 40, 136
Behn, Aphra, 109, 159
Bellers, J., 31, 67, 164
Bentley, Richard, 38
Blyth, author of English Improver, 132
Bolingbroke, Henry St John, Viscount, 97, 100, 148, 154, 198
Bonnell, James, 146
Boothby, Squire, 133
Boyle, Robert, 89, 104, 167
Bridges, G., 131
Bromley, William, W., 139
Brooke, Lord, 152
Brown, Rev J., 111
Budgell, Eustace, 60, 78, 112
Burlington, Earl of, 18, 100
Burnet, Bishop T., 99

Caesar, J. (slave), 187
Castell, R., 85
Cat, C., 55
Cave, E., 92
Centilivre, Susanna, 109
Chamberlayne, E., 7, 107, 174, 183
Clare, Lord, 150
Coghill, Dr, 107
Collier, Jeremy, 110
Congreve, W., 55
Crosse, J. de la, 88
Curll, Edmund, 99

Danby, Earl of, 74
Darby family, 168–9
Davenant, C., 26, 122
Defoe, Daniel, 1, 3–6, 10–1, 20–1, 23–4, 27, 35, 38, 43, 57, 70–2, 81, 84, 89, 90–2, 94, 97, 101, 104, 105, 106, 116, 118–19, 121, 124, 126, 128, 137, 150–1, 154–5, 158–9, 161, 174–7, 189, 199. *Captain Singleton*, 72; *Colonel Jack*, 101, 189; *Compleat Tradesman*, 5; *Essay upon Projects*, 6, 94; *Family Instructor*, 109; *Moll Flanders*, 101; *Plan of the English Commerce*, 129; *Robinson Crusoe*, 101, 189, 196; *Tour*, 131
Dryden, J., 43, 102
Duck, Stephen, 96
Dunton, J., 86–91, 97, 105, 143, 188–9

Estcourt, Dick, 63

Evelyn, John, 24, 28–9, 92, 95, 116, 158, 194

Fielding, Henry, 81, 100
Fiennes, Celia, 119
Forrester, Miss, 135
Fox, George, 108
Franklin, Benjamin, 37–8

Garth, Dr, 55
Gaunt, John, 122
Gay, John, 52, 72, 82, 99
George I, 81–2, 117, 164, 194
Gerway, Henry, 180
Gildon, C., 101
Graham, George, 162
Granville, Mary, 111, 145–6
Gratton, J., 163
Guy, Thomas, 34–5

Halfpenny, W., 19
Halifax, Lord, 147–8
Harley, E., Second Earl of Oxford, 88
Harley, Robert, 115, 130, 192, 197
Hartley, David, 100
Harvey, Lord, 137, 139
Harvey, William, 88
Haywood, O., 25
Hogarth, W., 43–4, 51, 72, 84, 128, 158, 192
Hughes, John, 118, 171

Isham, Justinian, 149
Isham, Thomas, 25, 37

James II, 2, 3, 4, 71, 142, 152
Jeaffreson, C., 184–5, 204
Jeffreys, Judge, 2, 3, 90
Johnson, Dr S., 97, 103, 188
Jones, Inigo, 18

King, G., 39, 122–5
Kirleus, Dr T., 33
Kneller, Sir Godfrey, 55

Langley, Batty, 19
Lapthorne, R., 47, 75, 77
Law, John, 50, 92–3
Leslie, C., 90–1
Lillie, C., 47–8
Lillo, George, 109
Locke, John, 104, 128, 160, 204
Lombe, J., 161
Luttrell, 24

Mandeville, B. de, 96, 113
Manley, Mrs Mary de la Riviere, 109, 159
Marlborough, Duke of, 40; Duchess of, 137
Mary, Queen, 24, 28, 40, 93

Massingberd, Sir W., 143, 154
Mead, Dr R., 28
Millington, E., 61
Mirault, B. L. de, 84, 105, 108
Misson, H., 42, 56, 84
Monmouth, Duke of, 4, 90
Morland, S., 158
Morris, R., 19

Newcastle, Duke of, 136, 140, 150
Newton, Isaac, 26, 102, 103
Newton, S., 22, 24, 74
North, Roger, 12–15, 18, 28–9, 124, 138
Norton, C., 89
Nutley, W., 40–1

Oldmixon, J., 99
Oronoko, 109

Palladio, Andrea, 18, 136
Parnell, T., 62
Pendarvis, Mrs, see Mary Granville
Penn, William, 23–4, 67, 164
Pepys, Samuel, 28
Petty, Sir W., 122, 171–2
Phillips, Ambrose, 55
Pilkington, Laetitia, 109
Pope, A., 55, 99, 100, 101
Portsmouth, Duchess of, 24

Quare, Daniel, 162

Radcliffe, Dr, 30, 40–1, 79, 144
Redpath, G., 160
Richardson, Samuel, 97, 106, 110, 142, 146
Rochester, Earl of, 24
Rooke, Sir G., 47–8

Sacheverell, Dr, 75–7, 84, 149
Salmon, Mrs, 20, 159
Salmon, T., 109
Sancho, Ignatius, 188
Sault, R., 87
Savage, Richard, 62, 97–9
Scamozzi, 18
Settle, Elkeniah, 87
Shadwell, T., 75
Shaftesbury, Lord, 103, 105
Smith, Adam, 132
Steele, Sir Richard, 22, 40, 52, 55–6, 59, 60, 77, 91–2, 97–8, 106, 108–9, 111, 113, 119, 133–4, 145, 151, 159, 166, 196
Sterne, L., 188
Story, C., 163
Stout, W., 69
Swift, Jonathan, 4, 22–3, 29, 40, 57, 62–3, 68, 97, 99, 100, 103, 107, 110–12, 115, 131, 157, 192, 195–6

Temple, W., 38
Temple, Sir William, 104, 143
Thomson, James, 97
Tighe, Dick, 107
Toland, J., 103
Tompion, T., 162
Tonson, Jacob, 98
Townshend, Lord, 136–7
Tufness, W., 18
Tull, Jephro, 136
Tutchin, J., 4, 90–1

Vanbrugh, Sir John, 18, 136–7, 153–4
Verney, R., 101
Voltaire, 167

Walpole, Horace, 160, 186
Walpole, Sir Robert, 100–1, 130, 137–8, 155, 192–3
Ward, Ned, 32–3, 41–6, 48–9, 61, 63, 73, 101, 114–15, 166
Watts, Isaac, 97, 105
Wesley, John, 35, 83, 146, 160
Wesley, Samuel, 87
Whipping Tom, 77
William III, 4, 40, 68, 75, 139, 142, 151–2, 195
Wilson, Thomas, 30, 144
Winstanley, 158
Wiseman, Richard, 31
Wortley Montagu, Lady Mary, 29, 63, 110, 130
Wren, Sir Christopher, 16, 18, 32
Wyndham, Sir C., 23

Young, E., 97

4 Subjects

Abacus, 27
Agriculture, 10–11, 121–6, 136, 139: see also Landed Gentry
Alchemy, 159
Angliae Notitia, 7, 9, 35, 38, 107, 165: see also E. Chamberlayne
Apprentices, 8, 31, 41, 44, 86, 120
Assemblies, 116–20
Athenian Mercury, 33, 56, 87, 143, 160: see also J. Dunton

Baitings, 54, 90
Bank of England, 76, 169–70, 183, 191, 194–8, 204
Banks, 169–70, 190–1, 195
Bartholomew Fair, 67, 119
Battle of the Books, 104
Bawdiness, 109, 110, 137
Beer, 7, 38–9, 44, 62, 128
Beggar's Opera, 82
Bibles, 35, 67, 105, 123

Black Guard, 45
Blacks, 63
Booksellers, 42, 86–7, 92, 99, 100
Boroughs, 3, 151, 154
Brewing, 10, 24, 49, 106, 127
Bricks, 17, 20–1, 80
Bubble Act, 126
Button-holing, 56
Buttons, 113

Cabinet-makers, 10
Cash-nexus, 127, 139–40, 148, 154, 190–9
Catholics, 3, 80, 167
Cattle, 11, 127, 136
Chandlers, 49, 82, 127
Charity Schools, 92–6
Children at work, 128: *see also* Charity Schools
Chimney-sweeps, 65
Chinaware, 71, 119
Clocks, 10, 26, 67, 160, 161, 171–2
Clubs, 56–67, 92, 134, 198: Beef-steak, 63; Hanover, 63; Kit-Kat, 55; Mud House, 62; Schemers, 63; Scribblers, 62; Street Clubs, 63; Tory October, 62
Coaches, 174–6
Coal, 9, 10, 21, 24, 126, 127, 140, 160, 168, 172, 175
Cockfights, 90
Coffee-Houses, 55–61, 70, 79, 87, 92, 119, 157, 176: Button's, 55, 100; Child's, 60; Denis's, 188; Garraways's, 59, 62; Giles's, 58; Good's, 59; Grecian, 91; Jenny Man's, 58; Jonathan's, 60; Kent's, 57; Lloyd's, 43, 61–2; Man's 48–9; Nardo's, 55; Rainbow, 60, 61; Richard's, 57; Robinson's, 62; Serle's, 60; Squire's, 60; Tom's, 56; White's, 91; Widow's, 43; Will's, 11, 60, 62, 91; Young Man's, 191
Concerts, 201
Contraceptives, 166
Copper, 175
Crime, 81–4, 93, 96
Cromwellian period, 2, 3, 9, 18, 61, 86, 133
Customs, *see* Excise *and* Smuggling
Cutlery, 10, 126

Dampier's Voyages, 65
Deism, 103
Dictionaries, 103
Diet, 28, 123–4, 128, 154, 165, 176
Disease, 27, 36
Distilling, 49, 127
Division of Labour, 171
Drapers, 65
Drunkenness, 32, 41, 84, 137, 151, 186
Duelling, 77–8

Dutch, 8, 17, 20, 24, 25, 28, 35, 45, 61, 76, 115, 121, 131, 182, 194–5
Dyers, 24

East India Co., 131, 146, 179, 181, 186, 191, 194
Education, 3, 4, 89, 91, 92–6, 163, 164
Elections, 35, 150–6
Enclosures, 132, 136
Engines, 157–8
Estate Village, 138
Excise, 39, 183

Fairs, 37, 41, 67, 116, 119, 175–6
Farmers, 3, 58–9, 80, 122–4, 128–9, 132, 136, 152, 163
Fenmen, 133
Financiers, 31, 39: *see* Cash-Nexus *and* Banks
Fires, 22–7; fire-engines, 25–6
Fireworks, 152
Fisheries, 58
Footmen, 22, 50, 63
French, 8, 39, 40, 47, 58–9, 67, 75, 120, 129, 130, 131, 182, 195

Gambling, 45, 50–4
Gentleman's Magazine, 92
Georgian House, 17
Germans, 8
Glass, 21, 175
Glorious Revolution (1688), 1, 3, 5, 133, 147, 153
Goldsmiths, 70, 169, 195, 196
Great Fire, 12, 67, 69
Grub Street, 57, 97–100
Guns, 89, 134, 162, 163

Hangings, 83–4
Height of men, 126
Highwaymen, 51, 82–3, 93
Hospitals, 34–5, 127
House-building, 12–22
Households, 9, 122

Indentured labour, 183–5
Industrial Revolution, 1, 10, 121, 167–72, 199, 205
Inoculation, 29
Insurance companies, 25–6, 52, 173
Irish, 8, 63, 74, 114, 131
Iron, 101, 167–8, 172, 175

Jacobites, 24, 74–5, 148, 197
Jews, 66, 76, 168, 195
Jobbers, 132, 146
Journalism, 4, 6, 86–92, 96–7, 101
JPs, 127, 130, 154, 187, 203–4

Lace, 58, 130–1

Land Bank, 26, 198
Landed Gentry, 3, 9, 76, 80, 122, 125, 128, 133–4, 136, 138–9, 140, 142–7, 152–4, 190–9
Language, 102–3
Lead, 126, 169
Levant Co., 180
Levee, 111
Local Government, 3, 127, 161
Lotteries, 195, 196–7

Mansions, 136–9
Market-gardening, 10, 132
Marriage, 8, 107–8, 125–6, 134–5, 138, 142–7, 163
Mass-consumption, 12; mass-production, 16
Matchmakers, 46
Mercers, 69, 176
Merchants, 1, 5, 9, 41, 52, 66, 118, 120, 125, 127, 139, 146, 147, 173–86
Mermaids, 89
Midwives, 106
Militia, 3, 75–6, 80
Milliners, 112, 176
Mills, 11, 140, 158, 160, 168–9
Mob, 73–4
Mobility, 8, 11, 125
Mohocks, 77
Murders, 75, 93, 107
Mutiny, 75

Neighbourhoods, 59
Newspapers, 61–2, 181: see also Journalists
Non-conformists, 3, 4, 58f, 105, 165: see also Presbyterians and Quakers
Novel, 105
Numbers to houses, 19

Old Maid, 106

Parties, 147–56, 199
Pastry-cooks, 70–1
Pedlars, 18, 132, 163, 183
Physicians, 31–2
Pillory, 74
Plague, 28, 129
Poaching, 134–5
Police system, 81, 93, 130
Poor relief, 128
Population, 7, 8, 122–5, 127–8, 152
Post Office, 181–3
Presbyterians, 76, 147, 165
Price-tickets, 69
Prisons, 85, 163, 186
Prize-fights, 54–5
Projectors, 157–60

Quacks, 32–3
Quakers, 55, 67, 69, 108, 162–70, 188–9

Railways, 169
Riot Act, 79–80
Riots, 8, 73–80
Roads, 174–5, 182
Rococo, 115
Rookeries, 115
Royal Society, 102, 160, 182

Sanctuary, 6, 75
Sanitation, 21, 27, 28
Sash-windows, 17, 21–2, 70, 71
Scots, 8, 42, 160
Sheep, 136, 140
Shipping, 9–10, 191
Shops, 68–72, 120, 152, 173
Shorthand, 160
Sign-posts, 19, 20, 87
Slaves, 109, 183–9, 204
Sleds, 17
Smallpox, 28–9, 31, 85
Smuggling, 129, 175
Snuff, 47–9, 81
Soap, 10, 24, 49, 157
Society for Reformation of Manners, 93
Soldiers, 75–6, 80, 96, 111, 114, 123
Solicitors, 183
South Sea Bubble, 35, 192–4, 198
Spectator Characters: Sir Andrew Freeport, 118, 171, 198–9, and Sir Roger de Coverley, 124, 140–1, 198–9
Spelling, 111, 144
Statistics, 26, 122
Steam-engine, 10, 168–9
Stock-market, 8, 52
Street-cries, 64, 69, 84
Street-lighting, 42, 73, 81
Sugar, 10, 49, 189
Surgeons, 30–1, 87, 106, 183
Swallows, 88–9
Swearing, 90, 94

Tanning, 48, 139, 142
Taxes, 86, 122, 195
Tea, 131, 149, 157
Textiles, 9, 10, 71, 75, 80, 106, 128–9, 160–1, 174–6
Tobacco, 46–50, 69, 89, 114, 131–2
Toothache, 30
Toys, 159, 176
Tumblers, 77
Turnips, 132, 136

Vitruvius Britannicus, 18

Water Supply, 20–1
Waxworks, 20, 159

Weavers, 8, 10, 38, 77, 79, 81, 106, 124–5, 128

Witches, 25, 89

Whores, 27, 42, 44, 46, 84

Women's role: 91, 105–6, 107–11, 120, 135, 149; as prize-fighters, 54–5

Wool, 131, 170, 174–5, 178

Workhouses, 161, 164

DATE DUE